Crossroads

VIETNAM
America in the War Years

Series Editor
David L. Anderson
California State University, Monterey Bay

The Vietnam War and the tumultuous internal upheavals in America that co-incided with it marked a watershed era in U.S. history. These events profoundly challenged America's heroic self-image. During the 1950s the United States defined Southeast Asia as an area of vital strategic importance. In the 1960s this view produced a costly American military campaign that continued into the early 1970s. The Vietnam War was the nation's longest war and ended with an unprecedented U.S. failure to achieve its stated objectives. Simultaneous with this frustrating military intervention and the domestic debate that it produced were other tensions created by student activism on campuses, the black struggle for civil rights, and the women's liberation movement. The books in this series explore the complex and controversial issues of the period from the mid-1950s to the mid-1970s in brief and engaging volumes. To facilitate continued and informed debate on these contested subjects, each book examines a military, political, or diplomatic issue; the role of a key individual; or one of the domestic changes in America during the war.

Volumes Published

Melvin Small. *Antiwarriors: The Vietnam War and the Battle for America's Hearts and Minds.*

Edward K. Spann. *Democracy's Children: The Young Rebels of the 1960s and the Power of Ideals.*

Ronald B. Frankum, Jr. *Like Rolling Thunder: The Air War in Vietnam, 1964–1975*

Walter LaFeber. *The Deadly Bet: LBJ, Vietnam, and the 1968 Election.*

Mitchell K. Hall. *Crossroads: American Popular Culture and the Vietnam Generation.*

David F. Schmitz. *The Tet Offensive: Politics, War, and Public Opinion.*

Crossroads

American Popular Culture and the Vietnam Generation

MITCHELL K. HALL

ROWMAN & LITTLEFIELD PUBLISHERS, INC.
Lanham • *Boulder* • *New York* • *Toronto* • *Oxford*

ROWMAN & LITTLEFIELD PUBLISHERS, INC.

Published in the United States of America
by Rowman & Littlefield Publishers, Inc.
A wholly owned subsidiary of The Rowman & Littlefield Publishing Group, Inc.
4501 Forbes Boulevard, Suite 200, Lanham, Maryland 20706
www.rowmanlittlefield.com

PO Box 317 Oxford, OX2 9RU, UK

British Library Cataloguing in Publication Information Available

Library of Congress Cataloging-in-Publication Data

Hall, Mitchell K.
    Crossroads : American popular culture and the Vietnam generation / Mitchell K. Hall.
        p. cm. — (Vietnam—America in the war years)
    Includes bibliographical references and index.
    ISBN 0-7425-4443-5 (cloth : alk. paper) — ISBN 0-7425-4444-3 (pbk. : alk. paper)
    1. Popular culture—United States—History—20th century. 2. United States—
Social life and customs—1945–1970. 3. United States—Social life and customs—1971–
I. Title. II. Series: Vietnam—America in the war years (Unnumbered)
E169.04H344 2005
306'.0973'09045—dc22   2005008939

Printed in the United States of America

∞™ The paper used in this publication meets the minimum requirements of American
National Standard for Information Sciences—Permanence of Paper for Printed Library
Materials, ANSI/NISO Z39.48-1992.

Contents

Preface

Revolutionary changes occur sporadically in a variety of human endeavors. While we most often think of revolutions as national political upheavals like the French and Mexican revolutions, most of us have some awareness of eras such as the Industrial Revolution as well. Although the dramatic changes in U.S. popular culture from the end of World War II through the 1970s may not match the significance of these earlier examples, they nevertheless represent a fundamental transformation.

The year 1945 marked a turning point for the United States. Americans had survived over the previous fifteen years the nation's worst economic crisis and the twentieth century's most devastating war. Despite fears of what the postwar period might bring, in the following decades the country would enjoy general prosperity and substantial progress toward a more equitable society. It would also undergo the most traumatic political and social divisions since the Civil War.

The Vietnam War became the next generation's pivotal political event. The first baby boomers turned draft age just as America's military escalation demanded its first commitment of combat troops. The seeds of this war grew out of the end of World War II. America's wartime cooperation with Vietnamese nationalists fell apart as Cold War pressures pushed successive U.S. governments to support French colonialism instead. Despite American financial aid, France achieved only a stalemate in its war against the communist-led

Vietminh. With the signing of the 1954 Geneva Accords, the U.S. commitment changed. President Dwight Eisenhower took responsibility for establishing and preserving a noncommunist state in South Vietnam. The effort to achieve that goal lasted until 1975, two years after America's military withdrawal, when communist forces unified their country under a single government.

Ultimately the nation's involvement with Vietnam would filter into nearly all aspects of life. The war affected the economy, influenced college enrollments and careers, challenged citizens to reassess their values, and played a key role in the downfall of two presidential administrations. Throughout the entire era, however, politics and foreign affairs took up only a portion of national attention. Most Americans remained preoccupied with their daily lives.

In the mid-1950s a majority of people could offer an opinion on the latest movie, debate the merits of favorite athletic teams, or hum the melody of a current song, but had little or no knowledge of U.S. interests in Vietnam. A view of the Vietnam years without understanding the era's popular culture is not only incomplete but also distorted. Just as America's direct commitment to South Vietnam began, U.S. popular culture stood at the crossroads of its own dramatic changes. Motion pictures enjoyed a preeminent position, television was just emerging, spectator sports still held largely regional appeal, and popular music was poised for a shift that would hit much of the country like an earthquake.

This book traces the evolution of American culture during the Vietnam era by studying movies, television, sports, and rock and roll music. Chapter 1 explores the era before the Vietnam War, when the major forms of entertainment were tightly controlled and still dominated by the motion picture industry. The second chapter focuses on the rapid growth of popular culture, which produced both the highs of television's "golden age" of live programming and the lows of gambling, payola, and quiz show scandals. Chapter 3 highlights the 1960s, when technological advances, international influences, and social changes in race relations, living patterns, and acceptable behavior brought dramatic transitions. Chapter 4 carries the story into the early 1970s, when economic control and artistic standards had clearly progressed beyond their previously narrow range. The final chapter wraps up the 1970s and analyzes the changes in popular culture that took place during the Vietnam War.

I conclude that the transitions experienced by these key elements of American popular culture when the Vietnam generation grew and matured are revolutionary in two primary ways. First, each cultural element underwent radical change in its own structure. In motion pictures, for example, the long-dominant Hollywood studio system that integrated finance, production, distribution, and exhibition collapsed, losing much of its earlier power to independent producers and corporate conglomerates. Second, all these cultural elements were part of a larger social upheaval. The development of a postwar youth culture was essential to the success of rock and roll and created a critical audience for other forms of mass culture. Social movements involving civil rights for African Americans, antiwar activism, and expanded opportunities for women, as well as ongoing debates over corporate materialism and other personal and collective values, interacted with and mutually influenced popular culture. Expressions of popular culture provided both a measurement of and a stimulant to larger social and political changes.

Acknowledgments

Several people contributed to this project in different ways. David Anderson, now at California State University at Monterey Bay, first contacted me about writing a book for this series, and I appreciated the opportunity to research and write in areas of more recent personal interest. My initial editor, Matt Hershey, provided the right combination of professional pressure and encouragement. Both David and Matt offered constructive suggestions that resulted in significant improvements to the book's quality. The team of editors at Rowman & Littlefield has been excellent. Associate editor Laura Gottlieb took over from Matt and helped bring this project to a successful conclusion. Editorial assistant Andrew Boney, production editor Erin McKindley, and copy editor Bevin McLaughlin made everything work at the end.

My immediate family contributed much to my personal history of popular culture. As usual my wife, Ann, encouraged my work, read the manuscript to offer a nonhistorian's perspective, and helped select the pictures. Together we have built a great music collection and watched a lot of screens. Her love and support have been constant reminders of how good life can be. Both my mother and late father, Alice and Dale Hall, were musically gifted and watched my ball games with seemingly inexhaustible interest. The older of my two brothers, Marshall Hall, is a talented singer/musician, and my younger brother, Matthew Hall, is a guitar player and voracious reader of history. My extended family has grown quite a bit in recent years, and this wonderful collection of in-laws, nieces, nephews, and others has done as much as anyone to expose me to new music, dance, films, literature, and games. Each of them means something special.

My interest in popular culture is applied as well as scholarly. It has been some time since I used my modest talents to run track, sing, or play guitar, but my softball career has now stretched over thirty years. For the past four years I have also coached girls' basketball in the Beal City Public Schools. This has been a very satisfying experience, and I especially appreciate the talent and character of all my players on the Aggies' seventh- and eighth-grade teams.

It is quite rewarding to apply my interests as a professional historian to these fascinating questions of modern popular culture. Writing this book has been an extension of the research I began in preparing an undergraduate course on the history of rock and roll and a seminar on American popular culture. It also serves as a prelude to developing a new course on the 1960s. I hope that readers will find the material to be as absorbing as I have.

1

Popular Culture
before Vietnam

World War II and the decade that followed launched modern American society. Some people believed the era offered an opportunity to exert global influence in the "American Century." For others it promised the possibilities of a more rewarding personal life denied or postponed because of fifteen years of depression or war. Time would validate much of that optimism, but not all.

The global perspective often dominated public interaction during the Cold War. Many citizens were intrigued and concerned by the collapse of old colonial empires, the emergence of new communist societies, and war in Korea. At the same time most people spent their lives thinking about and participating in other activities. The ordinary events of mass society included various forms of popular culture, the artistic and entertainment experiences of everyday people.

Popular culture in the postwar United States underwent a revolutionary transformation. Members of the Vietnam generation—those who experienced the nation's growing involvement in Southeast Asia from roughly the 1954 Geneva Accords to the unification of Vietnam in 1975—lived through the most profound of these changes. Before 1955, however, the country's future direction was not readily apparent, and the status quo seemed resilient.

The movies towered over the entertainment industry in the 1940s and early 1950s. The major production studios offered a regular dose of optimism and fantasy but also reflected some of the era's anxieties. Although Hollywood

largely maintained its allure during this period, cultural, social, and legal challenges eroded its leading position. Television made its first significant appearance in the postwar years, although it remained limited in both programming
and availability until the mid-1950s. Its potential as a major force in entertainment was obvious, but it would soon reveal an ability to shape as well as
reflect the society around it. While baseball reigned as the nation's national
pastime, other professional sports leagues were still searching for mass public
appeal. College football and boxing were among other popular diversions.
Athletics remained primarily a local and regional interest, but some of the nation's foremost social issues were already intimately linked to sports. Rock and
roll music evolved rather than emerged newly born at a specific time. For
most of the postwar decade, its characteristic sounds appeared in various
rhythm and blues (R&B) or country songs, while record sales and radio airwaves highlighted popular music's greater appeal.

These entertainment industries were all tightly controlled. Popular music
was dominated by a half-dozen recording companies and the movies by five
major studios. The country's main professional sports leagues fielded teams
almost exclusively in the Northeast and Midwest, and only Major League
Baseball had more than a dozen franchises in 1954. Television programming
in 1955 came from only three national networks. For the most part these circumstances would not survive the decade, and for the movies the foundation
was already eroding.

MOVIE CULTURE

As the United States emerged from the tumultuous experience of World War
II, motion pictures dominated American popular culture. The war had, in
fact, enhanced the movies' position through wartime travel restrictions due to
gasoline rationing, the declining quality of professional sports as many athletes entered wartime service, and limits on record sales because of lacquer
conservation. In 1946 the film industry enjoyed its highest attendance and
greatest profit ever, grossing $1.7 billion. Movie theaters attracted ninety mil-
lion people each week, accounting for 90 percent of the nation's entertainment spending. The average patron went to the movies three times a month.[1]

Five major studios—Paramount, Warner Brothers, Metro-Goldwyn-Mayer,
RKO, and Twentieth Century-Fox—exercised overwhelming dominance of the
industry and were run by studio heads who wielded near-dictatorial power. Un-

der the "studio system," these five companies controlled actors' careers with long-term contracts but offered them consistent work and built some of them into star personalities. Numerous smaller companies challenged the majors, but independents had difficulty competing with these studios' financial resources.

Many wartime and postwar American films reflected the social, political, and cultural anxieties of the 1940s and 1950s. Some focused on the dark side of human nature and used various techniques to underscore that darkness. Minimal lighting, shadowy backgrounds, close-ups and dramatic camera angles, flashbacks, voice-over narration, and psychological investigations characterize these pessimistic and bleak thrillers. French critics called the style "film noir" (black film). European émigrés directed many of the best of these. Billy Wilder's *Double Indemnity* (1944), Otto Preminger's *Laura* (1944), Fritz Lang's *Scarlet Street* (1945), Alfred Hitchcock's *Notorious* (1946), Orson Welles's *The Stranger* (1946), Abraham Polonsky's *Force of Evil* (1948), Rudolph Mate's *D.O.A.* (1949), and Carol Reed's *The Third Man* (1949) are early and outstanding examples of this style. The people in these films often appear as alienated and lonely, sometimes so paralyzed by fear that they lose their moral strength. These weaknesses allow no heroes. Characters in the films exude oppressive pessimism, corruption, cynicism, purposelessness, and distrust. Social chaos and moral uncertainty prevail.

Hollywood's entertainment dominance, however, rested largely on presenting a more idealized version of life. Some of the era's best films fall into this category. *It's a Wonderful Life* (1946) examines the tension between pursuing material wealth and the satisfaction of service to community. Lead character George Bailey wants to leave his hometown for larger dreams but feels trapped by circumstances to stay, performing mundane but necessary tasks for common people. Disillusioned by his fate and contemplating suicide over a lost bank deposit, he encounters an angel who reveals the positive results to society from his life. George's hope is restored by his friends' generous aid in his time of need. The romantic comedy *Roman Holiday* (1953) stars Audrey Hepburn as a traveling princess who escapes her confining duties and supervision one evening in Rome. She ends up being rescued from a medicine-induced daze by a newspaperman, played by Gregory Peck. They spend the next day enjoying the city and eventually fall in love before she returns to her royal obligations. Even in more realistic films such as *The Best Years of Our Lives* (1946) and *Marty* (1955), conflicts often end with a positive outcome.

This generally inoffensive viewpoint derived in part from the major studios' acceptance of self-imposed restrictions on content as a means of avoiding external regulation. Civic concerns, especially among some church leaders, about Hollywood scandals and the movies' potential to undermine the nation's moral standards led to public pressure that studio heads feared would lead to government-imposed guidelines. Instead they adopted in 1930 the Motion Picture Association of America's (MPAA) production code, which described in great detail what was acceptable and what was inappropriate for inclusion in the movies. Written by a Roman Catholic priest and laymen and presided over by former Republican postmaster general Will Hays, the code prohibited profane language and obscenity, as well as themes related to interracial romance or sexual diseases, and demanded vigilance in dealing with religious faith, crimes, drinking, illegal drugs, and dancing. Continued complaints, and the Catholic Church's formation of the League of Decency, led the MPAA to create a Production Code Administration (PCA) to monitor scripts and completed pictures before granting its seal of approval. The studios agreed not to distribute or exhibit in their theaters a film without a PCA seal. This narrowed range of acceptable behavior ruled Hollywood film production almost undisturbed for more than twenty years.

Cold War politics imposed its own restraints. The most visible and highly publicized target of the House Committee on Un-American Activities (HUAC) was the motion picture industry. Hoping to expose, and perhaps eliminate, communists working in Hollywood, HUAC opened its public hearings on October 20, 1947. During two weeks of testimony, a series of anticommunist witnesses that included Jack Warner, Louis Mayer, Walt Disney, Gary Cooper, and Ronald Reagan cooperated with the committee, hoping to sacrifice a few leftists in order to maintain the industry's power and reputation. The "unfriendly" witnesses who followed them refused to answer questions about their political affiliations, and these "Hollywood Ten" were jailed for contempt of Congress and blacklisted by Hollywood producers to avoid further government attacks. The Hollywood Ten sacrificed years of employment in their chosen careers. Some of the biggest stars in motion pictures initially defended the civil rights of the accused, but their enthusiasm waned because of the victims' confrontational tactics and made little impact. Another round of hearings in the early 1950s brought more publicity, bitter feelings, and eventually the blacklisting of nearly two hundred people. Films embracing liberal values found few outlets in such a repressive climate. The issues involved in the anticommunism of the early Cold War eventually played on cinema screens for theater audiences. Hollywood produced an excess of cheaply made movies, such as 1952's *My Son John*, that explicitly recognized and condemned a communist threat to the United States. Often, however, the studios couched this message within a science fiction story, in which, as Nora Sayre observes, "the doom-laced scripts yielded metaphors for the larger malignancies of the Cold War."[2] Movies like *Invaders From Mars* (1953) and *Invasion of the Body Snatchers* (1956) feature aliens that infiltrate society by controlling the minds of humans. Many of these films portray intellectuals and scientists as foolish idealists who, fortunately for society's sake, give way to military forces that save civilization by destroying the enemy. Suspecting that the public was inclined toward hysteria, authorities tended to value secrecy rather than education. Not all films in this genre admired the perceived human inclination to react violently to creatures and events they did not understand. In *The Day the Earth Stood Still* (1951) a space traveler warns humans to live peacefully or face destruction. Concern over the effects of atomic radiation and uncontrolled scientific experimentation ran throughout numerous films that featured enormous insects that threatened humanity. As Sayre further notes, "The future—once an exhilarating concept—grew more ominous: there was no longer any assurance that one had any place in it, that continuity could be counted on."[3]

Two of the best films of the 1950s offer differing political viewpoints. *High Noon* (1952) is a western starring Gary Cooper as Will Kane, the marshal of Hadleyville about to marry and retire to ranching. On his Sunday wedding day three men ride into town and wait for the noon train to bring Frank Miller, recently freed from prison and seeking revenge on Kane. With an inevitable gunfight at high noon, Kane appeals to the community for support and finds only excuses. His deputy, angry at not being chosen to replace Kane, refuses to help; the hotel clerk sees Miller's return as good for business; the church congregation debates the problem but concludes that killings will keep business investment away and urges Kane to leave town. His fiancée, Amy, is a pacifist so opposed to killing she is ready to leave Will unless he follows their advice. The lone volunteer changes his mind after finding there will be no

Gary Cooper and Grace Kelly in High Noon *(Library of Congress)*

help. Abandoned by the community he has served, except for Amy's last-minute change of heart, Kane stands alone and outguns the Miller gang. In the wake of his victory, townspeople rush into the street with praise, but he throws his badge into the dirt and leaves Hadleyville. The film's creators clearly offer a parable of the nation's suffocating anticommunism. They portray social consensus as worried about an efficient process rather than the more complex issues of moral and ethical values. Only the lonely nonconformist appears heroic in *High Noon*, but even he is unable to change society. Kane feels betrayed both by the centralized authority that pardoned a killer and by the ordinary townspeople who abandoned him in a crisis. The Miller gang represents the McCarthyite tactics of HUAC, and the uncourageous townspeople take the role of HUAC witnesses who cooperated by giving up the names of innocent people.

On the Waterfront (1954) is an apologetic for cooperating with the committee. The film was directed by Elia Kazan, who had testified before HUAC, renounced his earlier leftist views, and given up the names of former friends and colleagues as communists. The film's plot presents a corrupt waterfront union mob against an honorable crime commission and its supportive citizens. In the face of unbroken silence from longshoremen, police are unable to dig out corruption and violence on the docks. Finally, persuaded by a priest and a young woman to tell what he knows to the commission, Terry Malloy, played by Marlon Brando, testifies to the committee and suffers a savage beating from the mob in return. This film presents informing, then, as both a rational and moral imperative.

Even beyond the politics, postwar changes shook the confidence and exalted position of the movies. Hollywood's benevolent tyrants faced serious challenges within their own industry. Behind-the-scenes workers conducted strikes, some of them violent, in 1945 and 1946. Though successful, in the bitter political climate of the 1940s, the strikes divided conservatives from liberals and leftists. Not surprisingly, conservatives blamed much of the turmoil on communists.

The studio system suffered an irreparable blow in 1948 when the Supreme Court ruled in United States v. Paramount Pictures, Inc., et al. that a monopoly existed in the motion picture industry. The following year the courts ordered the studios to sell their theaters, an unwelcome task they achieved by 1954. With movie production and distribution now separated from exhibition, theater owners could negotiate only for those films they wanted rather than having to take every film produced by the parent company. The studios' inability to maintain this block booking, which had insured a steady market for films regardless of their quality, meant declining revenues.

From its high point in 1946, Hollywood suffered a postwar decline. The number of films released fell from 425 in that year to fewer than 300 in 1954. During the same period, weekly attendance dropped from 90 million to 46 million. Nearly one out of every four movie theaters closed.[4]

Larger social changes affected the film industry. Early twentieth-century movie theaters existed primarily in urban areas and attracted a distinctly working-class clientele. The postwar move of so many Americans to suburbs took much of the audience away from the urban movie palaces. The baby boom diverted parents' attention and money to concerns of child rearing, and higher ticket prices limited the attendance of lower-income people. Affluent Americans enjoyed more entertainment choices after the war and spent relatively less at the movies. Film historian Robert Sklar cites survey data revealing that, of the 70 percent of the nation's theaters able to make a profit, fewer than half made money on ticket sales alone.[5] A variety of reasons existed, then, for the decline of the motion picture industry after the war. Most of the blame, however, fell on a more visible culprit.

TELEVISION

The concept of television was not new in 1955. A rudimentary form of television transmission existed prior to World War II, but new technological advances virtually stopped until the war's conclusion. Peacetime brought the beginning of TV's advance into national life. Manufacturers increased their production of television receivers, while four networks—CBS, NBC, ABC, and DuMont—created more programming in the late 1940s and early 1950s. The Federal Communications Commission (FCC) froze the number of television licenses in 1948 while it investigated transmission interference problems and extended the freeze when the Korean War broke out. Only 108 stations broadcast during this period, with those scattered across the country but clustered around most major cities. Even with the limited number of licensed stations, people continued to buy TV sets. The number of televisions in American homes rose tenfold to thirty-two million in the first half of the decade. The freeze kept the leading networks, CBS and NBC, in an advantageous position and dissuaded at least three corporations from launching networks of their own.

Television programs through the early 1950s still played to a limited, predominantly urban audience, but some of the medium's pioneers created memorable shows. The networks initially broadcast programs performed live in New York City. Among the most popular were variety shows such as *Texaco Star Theater*, hosted by Milton Berle; Ed Sullivan's *Toast of the Town*; and *Your Show of Shows*, starring Sid Caesar and Imogene Coca. Berle became TV's first big star, and he eventually earned the title of "Mr. Television." His vaudeville background translated well to the small screen, and his comic routines often featured Berle dressed in outrageous costumes. *Your Show of Shows* ran from 1950 to 1954. Although comedy was the program's core, it also featured singers of opera and Broadway musicals, ballet and other dancing, and jazz musicians. Lead writers Mel Tolkin and Lucille Kallen had support from future notables including Woody Allen, Mel Brooks, Larry Gelbart, and Neil Simon. The performances were broadcast from a New York theater, and the performers played to the sizeable audience rather than to TV cameras. "It was up to the cameraman to find us," noted Coca. The show's style made it distinct from most early TV programming, called "radio with pictures" by one writer.[6] The description was literally true in many cases, as several early TV shows were based on top radio programs. In addition to providing entertainment, television offered information. John Cameron Swayze hosted an evening news summary, *The Camel News Caravan*, and became a celebrity.

Despite the creative and economic opportunities, television entertainment programming placed incredible demands on performers and writers. Routines developed over many years and utilized repeatedly for different audiences on road tours had a short broadcast life. Comedian Danny Thomas lamented, "You . . . work years building routines, do them once on TV, and they're finished."[7] Writers quickly realized that television possessed an insatiable appetite for new material, and providing quality scripts for every show was nearly impossible.

Television quickly became a tool in managing children. A program that could entertain young children often provided welcome relief for a mother preparing dinner or parents needing some temporary distance or silence from their offspring. Early television's major contribution in this area was *Howdy Doody*. The title character was a wooden puppet that interacted with a human, Buffalo Bob, and a clown named Clarabell who communicated with a bicycle horn. The live show took place in a studio in front of an audience of children called the "peanut gallery." Begun in 1947 on NBC, *Howdy Doody* offered occasional lessons in proper behavior, nonstop fun, and blatant commercialism. When retailers discovered the value of connecting products to the show, sponsors had "Buffalo" Bob Smith instruct kids to tell their parents what brands and items to buy. "We were real hucksters. . . . You might say we were real whores," Smith later confessed.[8] Other early examples of successful children's programs were the puppet variety show *Kukla, Fran and Ollie*, and the low-budget science fiction space adventure *Captain Video and His Video Rangers*.

Television's impact soon became obvious. In cities with TV stations, movie attendance dropped 20 to 40 percent, and audiences for sporting events and radio programs also declined. Library book circulation decreased, and restaurants experienced a dip in business during the broadcast of popular television shows. TV made it more convenient for suburbanites to avoid urban movie theaters and dramatically cut into magazine circulation. Television was starting to affect home life and schoolwork. Most any business with a television could draw a crowd. Appliance stores turned them on as a way of generating sales. Neighborhood bars used televised sports, which constituted over half of TV airtime in 1947, to attract customers.

Of all the new shows that appeared in the first half of the decade, the most popular was clearly *I Love Lucy*. The third-rated show in its first year (1951–1952), *I Love Lucy* ranked number one in four of the next five seasons. The show starred the husband and wife team of Lucille Ball and Desi Arnaz. Ball played a charmingly peculiar wife to Cuban nightclub bandleader Arnaz, who spent much of his time trying to curb Lucy's ill-advised efforts to join him in a show business career. Set in a middle-class Manhattan neighborhood, the show also built on their relationship with best friends and landlords, Fred and Ethel Mertz. Lucille Ball's mastery of visual humor and the excellent cast and writing were at the center of the show's success. Filmed in front of a live audience, *I Love Lucy* set the standard for later TV series. Its high quality has kept it in syndication ever since. With the show still on top, Ball and Arnaz ended it in 1957 because of the heavy workload.

Live drama became one of television's greatest successes, and critics often refer to the period when it thrived as "the golden age of television." *Kraft Television Theatre* appeared in 1947, the first of several TV dramas to emerge, such as *Studio One* and *Ford Television Theater*. The physical limits and intimacy of live TV enhanced psychological themes and exposed audiences to a "real-time" tempo nearly gone from often heavily edited films. The continuous demand for material provided great opportunities for talented writers, attracting many outstanding scripts and drawing good ratings. Among the best programs were *Marty* and *Twelve Angry Men*. Written by Paddy Chayefsky and starring Rod Steiger and Nancy Marchand, *Marty* appeared in May 1953 on the *Philco Television Playhouse*. The story deals with a plain-looking man in his midthirties who has nearly given up on finding a mate after years of rejection. At a dance he meets a similarly unremarkable woman, and they

Lucille Ball (Library of Congress)

recognize their common experiences while enjoying each other's company. Against the objections of his mother and friends, who fear losing him, Marty decides to pursue the relationship. Reginald Rose wrote *Twelve Angry Men*, which appeared on *Studio One* in September 1954. Rose's plot examines the deliberations of an all-white and all-male jury in a murder case. The jurors' biases and personalities influence their view of the young, poor Puerto Rican defendant. Slowly the lone dissenter from a guilty verdict leads a review of the case and persuades the others individually or in small groups to change their vote. The show won Emmy Awards—first presented in 1949—for writing, directing, and acting.

Live performances also contained risks. Disappearing props, flickering lights, and collapsing sets posed difficult creative obstacles for both casts and crews. Situations often led to humorous results. In the middle of a long speech while dressed in a swimsuit, Eva Marie Saint noticed frantic waves from offstage, "until finally I looked down and saw that my bathing suit had slid down below my bosoms. There I was on live television, with my bare bosoms showing. So I just sort of slid under the table and fixed it and continued talking." Paul Newman recalled a scene in which a corpse was lying on a road: "As the actors in the foreground were delivering their lines, with the camera still on him, the corpse got up, brushed himself off, then walked offstage."[9]

Network television's early days offered programming of considerable diversity. As one of the foundations of postwar American life, organized religion provided a surprisingly successful topic. Against the predictions of some TV executives, one religious program became a prime-time hit for the DuMont network. *Life Is Worth Living* featured Fulton Sheen, a Roman Catholic bishop, who provided a weekly connection between everyday life and Christian morality. Sheen was a natural in front of the camera and became a national celebrity. He even won the 1952 Emmy Award as television's most outstanding personality, beating out Lucille Ball and Edward R. Murrow, among others. With the exception of a short summary each week, Sheen's remarks were unrehearsed. Baptist minister Billy Graham also appeared weekly, in *The Hour of Decision*, for a few years in the early 1950s. In the wake of economic depression and global war, religious faith provided many Americans with an ethical standard and meaning for life.

The new medium's growing popularity was beyond dispute, but not everyone was impressed with television's commercial offerings. Boston University president Daniel Marsh told his 1950 graduating class, "If the television craze continues with the present level of programs, we are destined to have a nation of morons."[10] That perception strongly aided advocates of reserving channels for educational purposes. The Joint Committee for Educational Television overcame earlier FCC objections to this idea by submitting data that showed "the sheer vacuity of television's content and its depiction of violence." The study moved the FCC in April 1952 to set aside 242 television channels for noncommercial use. Public television would not really develop until the 1960s, suffering a lack of resources, the absence of strong direction, and inferior channel assignments, two-thirds of which were on UHF and unavailable to most set owners.[11]

Concern over programming content would attract ongoing public scrutiny. Among the debates about the social impact of television was the question of violence. The rise of television in the early 1950s coincided with increased concerns about juvenile delinquency. One early investigation came when the House Committee on Interstate and Foreign Commerce charged its FCC Subcommittee with examining how much "immoral and otherwise offensive matter, or . . . improper emphasis on crime, violence, and corruption" existed in radio and TV programs. House members were especially concerned with the impact of programming on young people and possible communist infiltration. One historian defined the subcommittee's hearings during the latter months of 1952 as "congenial." The committee, chaired by Oren Harris (D-AR), did not "pass any conclusive judgment" or recommend legislation to address the appearance of crime and violence on TV.[12]

As these events reveal, despite its promising beginning, TV faced serious ordeals. The political atmosphere that threatened motion pictures also made an impact on the small screen. As Erik Barnouw observes, during the new Red scare television "would learn caution, and cowardice."[13] Throughout the paranoid years of 1948 to 1952, the newsletter *Counterattack* and a report entitled *Red Channels*, both produced by three former FBI agents, targeted "communists" working in the movies and television, gaining an influence far beyond what their evidence supported. The appearance of one's name in these publications could seriously curtail or end a performer's career. Ed Sullivan, host of TV's *Toast of the Town*, typified television's surrender to Red-baiting pressure; he used *Counterattack*'s specious claims to clear politically "questionable" performers that he wanted to appear on his show. Under threat of product boycotts, program sponsors sometimes dropped their support of shows using listed actors, and the networks themselves created executive positions to screen potential "subversives." The blacklist extended beyond actors to include the story lines of TV episodes.

Senator Joseph McCarthy's hovering anticommunist presence over television did not go totally uncontested. Among the rare challengers was the show *See It Now*, developed by Edward R. Murrow and Fred Friendly in 1951. *See It Now* covered issues in greater depth than allowed by the networks' fifteen-minute daily news programs. Beginning in late 1953, Murrow occasionally highlighted key issues or personalities that clearly countered the political views of the national security state. The show's October 20, 1953, broadcast, "The Case against Milo Radulovich," addressed the air force's discharge of Radulovich as a security risk. The broadcast exposed the discharge as based solely on charges made by unidentified accusers that Radulovich's father and sister had participated in unspecified "questionable" activities. Perhaps swayed by this public exposure, the air force later reversed its decision.

A March 9, 1954, *See It Now* broadcast, "A Report on Senator Joseph R. McCarthy," took on the senator himself. Murrow largely allowed McCarthy's own filmed actions to speak against him, and his concluding observations warned Americans to be on guard to defend their democracy at home as well as abroad. Criticisms such as these won Murrow praise in some quarters but also attracted conservative attacks. A month after *See It Now*'s report on McCarthy, CBS allowed the senator thirty minutes to respond, but he predictably used the time to challenge Murrow's loyalty. Only then did President Dwight Eisenhower publicly challenge McCarthy by siding with Murrow. McCarthy's own use of televised hearings against the U.S. Army in April 1954, known as the "Army-McCarthy hearings," and their exposure of his disreputable tactics played an influential role in his ultimate political demise. The coverage of McCarthy marked TV news as a significant influence with a special ability to convey information that the print media and radio lacked.

Murrow's *See It Now* was television's first news program that could compete with newspapers and radio in providing detailed analysis or immediacy to news stories. A one-hour special in December 1952, "Christmas in Korea," brought the Korean War into the homes of Americans. For the most part, however, early TV news was too visually oriented and too brief to offer much more than superficial coverage.

Even as television accepted the restrictions imposed by the country's political climate, its postwar success ultimately depended on its ability to reach a
truly national audience. With competing networks providing full prime-time
programming schedules by 1948 and the FCC's granting of additional broadcast licenses starting in 1952, television achieved the status of a national mass
medium by mid-decade. Consumers responded enthusiastically. Only a million TV sets had been sold by 1949, but by the middle of the 1950s over half
of all American homes had them. Television's appeal drew listeners away from
the radio, and commercial sponsors followed the audience.

The programs that these viewers watched said much about the larger society. Race relations on television reflected the unsatisfactory conditions that
were just then stimulating the modern civil rights movement. African Americans faced segregation and discrimination in housing and education, and
black performers only occasionally turned up on network television. Their
primary opportunities came from guest appearances on variety shows, where
singers and musicians like Louis Armstrong, Ella Fitzgerald, Harry Belafonte,
and Lena Horne performed for appreciative audiences. Situation comedies
and other continuing series built around black characters were rare. Those
that did appear were often carryovers from radio or built around negative
racial stereotypes.

The most popular early show focusing on African Americans was *Amos 'n'
Andy*. The characters of hardworking family man Amos Jones and the lazy,
dim-witted Andrew Brown were created and played on radio by two whites,
Freeman Gosden and Charles Correll. A third character, the Kingfish, was a
slick hustler. The move to television required black actors, with Alvin Chil-
dress as Amos, Spencer Williams Jr. as Andy, and Tim Moore as the Kingfish.
A key aspect of the comedy was an exaggerated and often ungrammatical
black dialect. The show spent two years in Nielsen's top twenty-five in the
1951–1953 seasons but generated some controversy. *Amos 'n' Andy* was the
rare show that provided a well-paid outlet for black actors and included realistic and positive relationships and characters. The heart of the show, however,
continued to be the negative stereotypes that reinforced racist attitudes about
black Americans.

Characters on other shows also portrayed blacks in stereotypical fashion.
Beulah featured an overweight, jovial African American maid who was most
concerned with the happiness of her white employers. *The Jack Benny Show*, a

long-running program that peaked in the mid-1950s as the nation's fifth-highest-rated show, included Benny's black, deferential on-screen servant, Rochester. These and other characters sometimes exhibited intelligence and independence, but the National Association for the Advancement of Colored People (NAACP), among other organizations, criticized *Amos 'n' Andy* and *Beulah* for depicting blacks "in a stereotyped and derogatory manner."[14]

Other TV offerings from the early 1950s included former radio shows dealing with white working-class ethnics. *The Goldbergs, Mama,* and *Life with Luigi* dealt with Jews, Norwegians, and Italians respectively. While these programs shared with African American programs certain stereotypical presentations of American subgroups, historian Mary Ann Watson points out a key difference: the goals and stereotypes of black characters were generally negative, while the goals and stereotypes of white ethnics were generally positive. Within a few years, however, ethnic differences would disappear on television, as nearly all shows presented white, middle-class, suburban, homogenous families.[15]

Television's portrayal of women in the postwar years also mirrored prevailing attitudes. The wartime opportunities that enabled women to enter previously closed occupations and develop economic independence often disappeared with the return of male veterans. Although some women fought to maintain their new positions, the general expectation was that they would return to providing a good home life for their husbands and children. TV programs almost always portrayed homemakers in positive ways while depicting women with careers as unfulfilled. Unlike men, women evidently could not have both. Married women on TV who worked outside the home often found their careers were either too difficult or unrewarding. Husbands who were smart let them "get it out of their systems" before returning to their "natural" role. This theme occurred in a variety of comedies, such as *I Love Lucy, I Married Joan,* and *The Honeymooners.* The threat to male pride as sole breadwinner was often at the heart of family disputes over the appropriateness of wives working outside the home. Even unmarried women on TV rarely received encouragement to pursue a career.

While television content certainly reinforced rather than challenged existing social attitudes, its mere existence and growing pervasiveness created fundamental social change. Watson argues, "More than any other aspect of American life, the history of television reveals the story of the reorientation of culture and the shift in American values that occurred after World War II."[16]

As television's popularity increased, its impact on motion pictures was significant and obvious to the movie moguls, who watched with anxiety.

HOLLYWOOD REACTS

Faced with new competition and declining attendance, Hollywood countered with technological innovations not available on television. Most of these proved to be short-term fads rather than real improvements for film viewers. The Cinerama process, which used three cameras side by side to provide a wider-angle view, produced its first feature film in 1952, *This Is Cinerama*. Distracting lines on the screen and the expense of renovating theaters with the curved screen required for viewing, however, limited its availability to a handful of cities. Twentieth Century-Fox introduced an improved wide-screen process in 1953, which it called "CinemaScope," using a single wide-angle lens camera. Its screen projection was two and one-half times wider than it was high and left some images slightly distorted. Directors felt the broad scope sacrificed some of their ability to portray close personal relationships, but audiences particularly liked the huge vistas of movie spectacles. *The Robe* was Fox's first CinemaScope release, and several films followed close behind. The other major studios utilized this or similar wide-screen techniques. The early CinemaScope films returned record income for Twentieth Century-Fox, and overall ticket sales increased in 1953 for the first time since 1946. Despite criticism from many artists associated with this new trend, it made a significant impact on the industry. According to camera operator Leon Shamroy, "CinemaScope may have ruined the art of motion pictures for a decade. It also saved the industry."[17]

In 1952 the independent film *Bwana Devil* introduced 3-D, which required audience members to wear special glasses to achieve the effect of three-dimensional figures. Some of the major studios followed with their own 3-D films, but the public soon got over the technique's novelty. The increased use of Technicolor in motion pictures highlighted television's inability to broadcast other than in black and white. When the motion picture industry returned to its decline later in the decade, additional novelties—such as Smell-O-Vision, which combined odors released from theater seats that matched the visual scenes—failed to generate more than mild amusement.

Another way of meeting the new medium's challenge was to cooperate with television. Small studios and independent film producers were the first to see this possibility. Filmed rather than live TV series appeared briefly in 1948, but they made a greater impact during the first half of the 1950s. William Boyd, who had starred as Hopalong Cassidy in over sixty movies, edited his old films into shorter segments for television and filmed over fifty additional episodes, which first appeared in 1949. Ziv Television Programs produced and syndicated *The Cisco Kid* from 1950 to 1956, as well as other shorter-lived programs. Hal Roach Studios contributed successful shows as well, most notably the comedy *My Little Margie.*

The early movies and filmed series that appeared on TV generally suffered from low budgets and offered inferior quality. Most provided action-adventure fare, since, according to filmmaker Frederick Ziv, the public wanted "escapist entertainment," and the beer sponsors "were not interested in that small segment that wanted opera, ballet or symphony." Low budgets meant "we had to produce these things cheap. . . . And cheap is the word. Not inexpensive, but cheap."[18] That sentiment also confronted those seeking television career guidance at the turn of the decade. One book, published in 1950, comments, "Most of the feature films presently shown on television seem to have been scraped from the cutting room floor or dragged unwilling from the musty cinema tombs. They range in quality from mediocre to extremely bad. They have, however, the unquestionable attraction of being cheap."[19] Despite quality problems, film represented about 60 percent of independent station programming.[20]

Clearly television's arrival had significant implications for the motion picture industry. For another element of American popular culture, its effects would soon be clear as well.

SPORTS IN AMERICA

Sports participation and spectating has a long history in American life. More than a few observers, however, note a significant change in the role of sports after World War II. Prior to the war, athletic pursuits fit within a person's larger leisure activities, and sports paid little enough that for most professionals they served as a seasonal occupation. While some fans no doubt supported their teams with great devotion, attitudes toward athletics did not approach the near obsession frequently found in later decades. As professional sports in particular expanded in the 1950s, 1960s, and 1970s, people attached increasing significance to winning and losing. Under some circumstances athletic victory or defeat was viewed as a sign of a city's, or nation's, worth and vitality. As more money poured into sports franchises, competition became less of a game and more of a serious event. Americans gave sports what historian Randy Roberts describes as an "unwholesome degree of attention."[21]

Sports of the postwar era in the United States still recognized a distinction between professional and amateur athletics. The concept of amateurism derived from the English upper class, whose members wanted to conduct their games separate from the common folk. This elitism was part of the American experience as well, although perhaps not quite to the same degree. Americans also shared the English principles of not accepting money for play and competing according to a notion of sportsmanship that embraced gentility and prohibited the use of unfair competitive advantages. While many major spectator sports had moved to professionalism, sports formerly associated with elite private clubs like track and field, tennis, and golf, as well as the Olympic Games, continued to maintain fairly rigid amateur standards.

The amateur ideal and a relatively limited view of sports remained strong in the early 1950s. It would, however, be rare shortly thereafter for an athlete such as Englishman Roger Bannister to give up sport at his peak. This world record holder in the mile run received virtually nothing for athletic endeavors as he trained for a career in medicine. "Now that I am taking up a hospital appointment," said Bannister, "I shall have to give up international athletics."[22] Bill Russell, one of America's most revered basketball players, recalled of his enrollment at the University of San Francisco, "Basketball was play; college was serious. . . . I thought of college ball . . . as an extracurricular activity." Playing ball for a living was not initially an enticing career either, as he noted: "Pro basketball was not a visible profession, not something kids thought about much."[23]

At the end of World War II professional sports hardly represented a national obsession. If professional baseball claimed the status of the national pastime, in 1954 its teams were limited to the Midwest and Northeast. Its westernmost franchise stood in St. Louis, and Washington, D.C., fielded the team closest to the states of the old South. The National Football League (NFL) was far less prominent than baseball, its franchises less stable and its player salaries lower. The NFL also lacked a southern franchise, although it absorbed the Baltimore, Cleveland, and San Francisco franchises from the rival All-American Football Conference in 1950. The National Basketball Association resulted from a 1950 merger of two smaller leagues with similar geographic limitations and several teams in smaller cities like Fort Wayne, Indiana.

Professional leagues spread geographically for a variety of reasons. Franchises followed the population, especially into the Sun Belt, leaving older cities for larger and newer ones. Jet aircraft also allowed easier travel to more distant markets than before. Football was the first professional sport to locate on the West Coast, in 1946. Baseball franchises relocated in the 1950s—the Boston Braves to Milwaukee, St. Louis Browns to Baltimore, Philadelphia Athletics to Kansas City, Brooklyn Dodgers to Los Angeles, and New York Giants to San Francisco—before adding expansion franchises in the 1960s. Team owners used cities' desire for the prestige of a franchise and the belief that professional teams stimulated the local economy to win economic concessions—tax breaks, public financing of stadiums—that often fed private gain at public expense. Later owners would use the threat of relocation to demand even newer and more profitable stadium deals. Many new stadiums were built in suburbs near major highways for easy access and avoided the congestion and dilapidated conditions of many inner cities. Critics complained about misplaced priorities but rarely stopped newly proposed stadiums.

Among college sports, football enjoyed the greatest popularity, with the country's top teams playing to sold-out stadiums. The Rose Bowl and a handful of other sites hosted intersectional powers each New Year's Day, while the Associated Press was the most prominent of several organizations that selected all-American teams and national champions. Questions about recruiting, academic standards, and competition, which had been around almost since the beginning of intercollegiate athletics, generally remained submerged under the enthusiasm of fans and alumni. Basketball on most college campuses attracted far less attention. Although the National Collegiate Athletic Association (NCAA) conducted an annual tournament at the end of the season, until the mid-1950s the sport's most prestigious event was the National Invitational Tournament held in New York City. In the decade after the war, Notre Dame, Oklahoma, and Army dominated college football, while Kentucky, LaSalle, and Oklahoma A&M were among basketball's leading powers.

Sports and television often proved mutually beneficial. Because early TV was better able to capture activity in small areas that did not require excessive camera movement, the enclosed "rings" of boxing and wrestling made them an ideal match for television coverage. Professional wrestling in the postwar years was more entertainment than legitimate sport. It employed obvious good-versus-evil matches utilizing political or ethnic "enemies" against virtuous "American" wrestlers. Overtly theatrical and choreographed rather than competitive, wrestling drew an enthusiastic audience. By the end of the decade, however, the novelty had worn off and wrestling had largely faded from TV screens, not to emerge again until reborn in the 1980s for cable television. A pioneer of this theatrical wrestling style, which he adopted in 1943, was George Wagner, better known as "Gorgeous George."

Wrestling faced a brief challenge from the roller derby. Another entertainment sport, roller derby's exposure on TV gave it an audience that nearly rivaled that of wrestling at the turn of the decade. A combination of roller-skating and brute force, roller derby featured separate teams of female and male participants. By 1951, however, public interest waned and the sport returned to its previous obscurity.

Boxing was TV's most prolific sport, with almost nightly prime-time network coverage as well as local offerings. In the early 1950s NBC's *Gillette Cavalcade of Sports* and CBS's *Pabst Blue Ribbon Bouts* made boxing the highest-rated sport on television. The camera was able to cover the small boxing ring, and the regular stops between rounds provided natural breaks for commercial advertisements. Eventually the proliferation of televised boxing satiated the audience's desire, and the sport's popularity declined. More significant was TV's ability to transform the sport. For fans watching on TV rather than in fight clubs, the subtleties of boxing were less entertaining than a looping knockout punch. Television officials, by favoring big punchers and boxers untarnished by numerous defeats, undermined the system of gradual skill development in local clubs and severely decreased the admission-paying audience of subchampionship bouts. Ironically, TV coverage of local fights created more betting interest, which encouraged criminal infiltration into boxing promotion. Congressional investigations in the late 1950s publicized the strong links between the sport and organized crime, further diminishing boxing's popularity. NBC canceled its Friday night fight coverage in 1961. Television was thus responsible for both energizing and weakening boxing in the post–World War II era.

Television's interest in Major League Baseball did not come without problems. In particular it threatened the vitality of the minor leagues. With TV offering free major league games to home viewers, the number of minor leagues fell from fifty-nine in 1949 to thirty-eight in 1953, and attendance dropped from forty-two million to twenty-one million in the same time period. By 1969 the number was down to ten million, and only twenty leagues survived in 1970. Efforts to block broadcasts of major league games in minor league cities collapsed under Justice Department warnings, although in 1953 federal courts did permit TV blackouts in major league cities to protect live gate revenues. Major league attendance also declined as television viewing increased in the early 1950s and stations carried numerous home games. The big leagues would not match their average attendance of the 1948–1952 era until 1978. Each team negotiated its own television contracts, and the desire for larger TV markets and their potential income was a key factor in franchise moves during the 1950s and beyond. Television revenue was becoming more important than live paid attendance.

Televised sports were still developing in the first decade following World War II. Technological improvements were needed to truly convey the action and excitement of a baseball game, for example, but local bars learned to attract larger crowds by adding TVs tuned to sporting events. Among advertisers, Gillette Razor Company reaped significant financial rewards from its sponsorship of baseball's World Series and boxing matches from Madison Square Garden. Though not apparent at the time, television's interest in sports would eventually have considerable impact on how they developed in the United States. Sports would not be exempt from changes imposed by other social events: "The civil rights movement, the Cold War, suburbanization, the consumer culture, the baby boom, the new leisure, and the electronic miracle of television transformed the form and function of American sport."[24]

Television changed sports, but sports also stimulated social change. Sports played a significant part in ending legalized racial segregation in the United States. Sprinter Jesse Owens and boxer Joe Louis probably enjoyed more widespread popularity than any other African American athletes prior to the 1950s. Their highly publicized roles in defeating athletes from Nazi Germany—Owens in the 1936 Berlin Olympic Games and Louis in two bouts against Max Schmeling—made them ideological standard-bearers for many but forced some Americans to face the realities of racial discrimination at home. Their political moderation and personal humility also helped make both athletes more acceptable to many white Americans.

In many ways the changes occurring in sports anticipated the achievements of the civil rights movement propelled by the dual tactics of legal challenges and direct action. Before the Supreme Court's *Brown v. Topeka Board of Education* ruling in 1954 and the Montgomery bus boycott in 1955, the country's leading professional sports leagues had already accepted racial integration. The number of professional black athletes was small at first but became much larger during the 1960s. The National Football League's Los Angeles Rams and the All-American Football Conference's Cleveland Browns each signed two African American players in 1946. The Rochester Royals of the National Basketball League integrated in 1946, and the National Basketball Association followed in 1950, with the Boston Celtics, New York Knickerbockers, and Washington Capitols adding black players to their rosters. In baseball, Jackie Robinson's promotion to the National League's Brooklyn Dodgers in 1947 did as much to change the face of modern sports as anything. The American League's Cleveland Indians called up Larry Doby that same summer. Baseball's other teams gradually added black players to their major league rosters, with the Boston Red Sox being the last in 1959. In individual sports, Althea Gibson became, in 1950, the first black athlete to compete in the U.S. Tennis Championship, a tournament she won in 1957 and 1958.

These advances did not come easily or without some costs. When the Brooklyn Dodgers' Branch Rickey proposed racial integration of the major leagues in 1946, team owners voted against his proposal fifteen to one.[25] As increasing numbers of the finest black players signed with the major leagues, the Negro Leagues suffered a rapid decline. The Negro National League closed in 1948, and the Negro American League, down to four teams, ended in 1960.

If some professional sports seemed slightly more progressive than society in general, in other areas sports merely followed American racial segregation. In the South, African Americans were restricted to playing for historically black colleges, even after previously all-white schools began admitting black students. Universities in the North and on the West Coast, however, recruited some black players in the 1950s. Golf and tennis remained almost exclusively white throughout the decade.

U.S. participation in international sporting events often held similarly deep social significance. Nowhere was this more apparent than at the Olympic Games, organized by the International Olympic Committee and presided over as president from 1952 to 1974 by Avery Brundage of the United States. The rising costs of putting on the Olympics encouraged escalating commercialization of the games. Perhaps more importantly they became increasingly politicized. The modern Olympic Games have never been above political influence, and since athletes participate as members of national teams, international issues are impossible to ignore. The Cold War and the postwar independence movements of former colonies were motives for using this international forum to achieve publicity.

Beginning with the Soviet Union's participation in the Olympics in 1952, the United States–Soviet Union rivalry was the most visible political use of the games, each side trying to use athletic victories as symbolic of its national and ideological superiority. As U.S. decathlon champion Bob Mathias recalled, "There were many more pressures on the American athletes because of the Russians than in 1948. They were in a sense the real enemy. . . . It wasn't like beating some friendly country like Australia."[26]

The postwar economic boom and resulting explosion of suburbs indicated an expanding middle-class affluence that meant more leisure time and money to spend on sports activities. All types of sporting events enjoyed increased attendance. Americans not only watched, but increasingly filled, golf courses, tennis courts, bowling alleys, and softball fields. School sports programs flourished alongside private organizations like Little League baseball, which enrolled over one million players. The future looked bright, but dark clouds loomed ahead.

SPORT SCANDALS

Debates about the merits of athletic competition in developing positive values and character in young people are nothing new. From the inception of intercollegiate sports in the nineteenth century, supporters have emphasized the benefits of competition, learning teamwork, and developing a sense of good sportsmanship. They have often made a sharp distinction between the rather grimy and distasteful atmosphere surrounding professional sports and the more wholesome amateur sports played in colleges and universities by student athletes. While these differences did exist for most sports in the early 1950s, major spectator sports were already attracting the attention of people that would blur the distinction.

College sports became truly national in the postwar period. With rare exceptions, people had primarily enjoyed following their local colleges or alma maters, and intersectional games were far less common than they became later. Fans and school officials increasingly wanted to see their teams ranked in national polls conducted by sportswriters and coaches. The belief that winning sports teams brought valuable publicity and increased financial contributions only strengthened the drive for stronger athletic programs. With universities raising sports programs' operating funds primarily through ticket sales, winning teams were necessary to generate adequate revenue. This increased emphasis on winning led quickly to recruiting for athletic ability. Recruiting those athletes often came with significant institutional cost: unethical arrangements between coaches and athletes, academic cheating, exploitation of players, and often a loss of control by university authorities.

The climax of postwar problems in collegiate sports came early in 1951 at the hands of gambling interests. Although gamblers had occasionally induced players to deliberately lose games, athletes' competitive nature served as an inhibiting effect. The creation in the early 1940s of the point spread, however, meant that players could still win their games while benefiting from gamblers' money. Basketball was most susceptible to gamblers' pressure, since one or two players could much more easily influence the outcome of a game than they could in football or baseball, for example. "Fixing" college basketball games began as early as 1945. Rumors circulated in 1950 that players from New York City area powers like Long Island University (LIU) and City College of New York (CCNY) were manipulating games, a practice known as "point shaving," for gambling interests. That year's national champion, CCNY, had seven of its players found guilty of shaving points, and some players who fell below the school's minimum admission standards had been admitted to the university with forged transcripts.

The scandal broke in February 1951. Prompted by reports of a bribe, New York district attorney Frank Hogan investigated and had over thirty players from local universities arrested, including LIU player of the year Sherman White. The scandal also implicated renowned coaches like LIU's Clair Bee, who later admitted, "I was so absorbed in the victory grail that I lost sight of the educational purposes of athletics."[27] Long Island University, with one of the nation's most successful basketball teams, dropped its entire sports program. Though many observers initially blamed this corruptive influence on "the East" or "the city," by the summer months the investigation implicated players from Midwestern schools, including Toledo, Bradley, and Kentucky. Several of the country's best players were included among the guilty. The National Basketball Association banned several of them for life. The college game suffered a crippling blow, and the scandal irreparably harmed the leading athletic status of several New York City schools.

A second shock to America's belief in the integrity and value of college sports came in August that same year. The U.S. Military Academy at West Point dismissed ninety cadets, half of them football players, for cheating on exams. Coming in the middle of the Korean War, evidence that some of America's future military leaders had violated the school's honor code was especially hard to take. President Harry Truman ordered an investigation of the sports programs at both West Point and the Naval Academy at Annapolis. As shocking as the scandals were to many, no significant national reforms followed them, and the special treatment of college athletes and the corruption of the system continued.

The scandals did, however, help transform the oversight of college athletics. To regulate recruiting and competition, the colleges relied on the NCAA, which had organized in 1905. Prior to World War II the NCAA dealt primarily with rules for affiliated sports and running championship events. Members ignored many recruiting and financial guidelines, and the organization wielded little power. In the years that followed things began to change. When individual schools began negotiating television agreements, live attendance fell significantly. The collective response in 1951, which arranged to limit televised college football games, diverted additional authority to the NCAA. The fixing and cheating scandals and ineffective self-policing led NCAA members to vote in 1952 to allow scholarships based solely on athletic ability and gave the organization rather than the colleges the power to penalize schools that violated NCAA rules. That same year Walter Byers became the organization's first full-time executive director. The NCAA added an enforcement division in 1958.

Although it was not readily apparent at the time, the public would eventually overlook the blemishes of athletic competition. By mid-decade the conditions were right for an explosion of popularity that would establish for sports an exalted place in American society. Also virtually unforeseen was another dramatic cultural shift.

POPULAR MUSIC

In the 1940s and early 1950s, America's most popular music was adult oriented. Successful styles included jazz-influenced pop by Frank Sinatra, Tony Bennett, and Sarah Vaughan; vocal harmonies from the Andrews Sisters and the McGuire Sisters; ballads by crooners such as Bing Crosby and Perry Como; the country-influenced music of Tennessee Ernie Ford; and the work of other stars such as Nat "King" Cole and Dinah Shore. Broadway show tunes and novelty songs also frequently became hit recordings. Nearly all successful people associated with the music business—from vocalists, songwriters, and instrumentalists to owners, producers, and technicians—were adults creating and marketing music for a mature public. The largest recording companies and the major radio networks targeted the broadest possible audience to enhance their profits. The result was a mainstream music that appealed primarily, though not exclusively, to middle-class whites. Pop lyrics were generally innocuous, frequently dealt with romantic themes, and, until the 1950s, constituted the music most often heard by the first baby boomers.

The pop music charts, dominated by their own conformity of predictable, controlled adult fare, offered no direct link to teenage lives. More than other forms of popular culture, the emergence of rock and roll music relied on the development of a distinct youth culture in the postwar years. Increasingly raised in safe, financially secure communities, middle-class adolescents often had extensive leisure time and their own disposable income. In the 1950s this meant that young people identified themselves as separate from other generations and became the subjects of distinct marketing strategies. At the same time these adolescents were often burdened by a pervasive political and social conformity created largely by the Cold War and sought a modest form of resistance to a vaguely defined uneasiness. That resistance came from the fusion of diverse musical styles, especially those from marginalized segments of the American population, which ultimately emerged as rock and roll. Don Hibbard and Carol Kaleialoha believe that "rock 'n' roll provided its predominantly middle-class audience with a vent for its discontent, a form of excitement, and a sense of group identity, while it pursued its socially prescribed goals."[28]

The structure of the recording industry was another critical factor in the rise of the new music. By the early 1950s income from records had surpassed sheet music sales. In the years before rock and roll's rise, six major recording companies dominated popular music: Columbia, RCA-Victor, and Decca in New York; Capitol and MGM in Hollywood; and Mercury out of Chicago. These businesses categorized their artists and marketed their records to different audiences. When wartime restrictions on record manufacturing persuaded the major companies to curtail their interest in R&B music, independent record labels emerged and served as a catalyst for rock and roll's development.

Music rooted in African American communities contributed most to the new sound. The insistent rhythms and mournful tales of the blues traveled from their cradle in the rural Mississippi River delta during the internal migration of blacks in the first half of the twentieth century. By the end of World War II, African Americans had created several northern and western urban communities that produced a form of blues more electrified instrumentally and more lyrically hopeful than rural delta blues. Chicago area artists such as Muddy Waters and Howlin' Wolf helped shape this evolving musical style. The vocal emotionalism of gospel music and the saxophone and upbeat feel of jump band jazz mixed with urban blues to create rhythm and blues, the foundation of rock and roll music. Lyrics emphasized life's gritty side but also the allure of romance and strong hints of sexuality. In combining these lyrics with a strong rhythmic backbeat, rhythm and blues attracted a growing audience.

The music of rural southern whites also contributed important ingredients to rock and roll. Country and western music offered a variety of sounds in the prerock era. Western swing played by Bob Wills and His Texas Playboys coexisted with Bill Monroe's bluegrass music, but Hank Williams's honky-tonk sound epitomized postwar country music until his death in 1953. Although country music typically featured a distinctive southern vocal twang and emphasized the fiddle and steel guitar, it shared some melodies with blues music. Together these two styles offered listeners lyrics of loss and despair almost completely absent from mainstream pop music.

Industry leaders presumed that both country and western music and rhythm and blues interested only specific, limited audiences—rural southerners for country and African Americans for R&B. Through the early 1950s record sales generally reinforced the view that both styles lacked the mass appeal of popular music. Country and R&B music remained marginalized, and companies marketed these styles to narrower audiences than mainstream music. Until 1949 *Billboard* magazine referred to these marginal styles as "hill-billy" and "race" music respectively.

Radio became a critical medium for the development of rock and roll. The number of radio stations in America doubled from 1945 to 1950, but the broadcast networks shifted significant resources to television, draining most of the variety and comedy shows from radio starting in the late 1940s. The problem grew worse when the FCC ended its freeze on licensing TV stations in 1952, creating a potential crisis for radio programmers. Left with large amounts of airtime to fill, and with live music more expensive, radio stations increasingly turned to recorded music. With hundreds of disc jockeys (DJs) allowed to make their own selections, the nation heard an eclectic variety of music. Inevitably this occurrence eroded existing social lines and exposed white teenagers to the heavier rhythms and earthier lyrics of black R&B singers. DJs who identified the trend of whites buying records of black artists, and who played those songs with personal flair on their stations, became leaders in spreading the style of rock and roll. These included Cleveland's Alan Freed, who started his show, "Moondog House," in 1951. Freed popularized the term "rock and roll" for the emerging musical style and organized local R&B concerts for interracial audiences. When he took a job at New York's WINS in 1954, Freed turned it into the city's top radio station. Other broadcasters, hurting from the competition of television, noted the phenomenon and programmed more R&B music. Both the recording industry and citizens concerned about rock and roll's "corrosive" influence on American youth waited to see if it would have staying power.

In growing numbers during the early 1950s, white teenagers tuned in radio stations playing black music to hear the exciting rhythms and more suggestive lyrics of R&B. They also paid money to bring those records into their homes, making independent companies like Chess in Chicago, Atlantic in New York, Imperial in Los Angeles, and King in Cincinnati unexpected beneficiaries.

To recapture their lost market, major companies often had their own pop artists record cover versions of R&B hits. These covers, new renditions of previously recorded songs, usually polished the musical edges and diluted the lyrical content to broaden its appeal. This practice stirred controversy both then and later, with critics arguing that recording executives were "refusing to accord independent labels and their African-American artists the success that they deserved."[29] The implication was that covers were racially based. Without discounting the existence of racism in the music business, it seems more likely that covers were driven by a search for profits. White pop singers certainly covered black R&B artists, but they also covered white country and pop records. Black singers, too, covered other artists, both black and white. One song, "Autumn Leaves," appeared on *Billboard*'s pop charts performed by six different artists in 1955. The practical result of this, however, was that numerous artists, particularly black R&B singers, lost airplay and sales to competing versions of their songs. At the same time covers expanded the market for rhythm and blues and helped open the pop market to black singers and musicians. Songwriters or copyright holders made money regardless of whose version sold.

Musical styles blurred further with crossover records. A crossover was a record directed at a particular market that also appealed to additional audiences, such as an R&B song bought by young whites. In the early 1950s minor pop hits occasionally came from unexpected directions, such as the Dominoes' "Sixty Minute Man" and Hank Williams's "Jambalaya." One version of "Crying in the Chapel," recorded in 1953 by a black vocal group called the Orioles, became the first major R&B crossover, climbing to number eleven on *Billboard*'s pop charts. Other songs followed, especially crossovers from R&B to pop, and both the vocal groups and record buyers became younger. The newer songs reflected this, replacing adult perspectives, obvious sexual references, and rougher sounds with more melodic tunes and more innocent lyrics. This evolution toward music with a younger attitude that retained a rhythmic beat resulted in rock and roll.

Trying to identify the first rock and roll record is a virtually impossible task. R&B songs like Jackie Brenston's "Rocket 88" (1951), crossovers like the Crows' "Gee" (1953), and the western swing–influenced "Crazy Man Crazy" (1953) by Bill Haley and His Comets are among those often mentioned. Haley's "Rock around the Clock," however, is easily identifiable as the first rock and roll record to reach the number one position on *Billboard*'s pop chart, in July 1955. That year effectively marks the beginning of the rock era.

Several business innovations helped smooth the way for the popularity of rock and roll music. The introduction of the Top 40 programming format in 1951 was a key development for radio that influenced how songs received airplay. This concept is credited to Todd Storz of Omaha station KOWH, who noticed that people listening to records on jukeboxes played the same songs repeatedly. Noting that the jukebox had forty record slots, he started programming the top forty songs in his market for repeated airtime. When KOWH's audience share rose from less than 5 percent to over 45 percent, the format quickly spread. While broadcasters typically offered listeners a variety of music, Storz's idea narrowed what the public heard. It also shifted control of programming decisions out of the hands of disc jockeys. Stations would play what people wanted to hear, based on sheet music and record sales and jukebox plays. What the public apparently wanted differed from what many music industry leaders and social critics wanted. As music writer James Miller comments,

> Top 40 became a crucial conduit for giving people what they wanted to hear—particularly when what they wanted to hear was not what the guardians of cultural taste supposed that they should hear. . . . The systematic repetition of popular recordings on radio stations reinforced the popular taste, marked in any era, for essentially repetitive musical forms.

At the same time, Miller notes, the new format linked popular music with "one of the most insidious trends in postwar American society, the deployment of market research to create a placid emporium in which consumers are given the dubious satisfaction of never finding, or fulfilling, a fresh or disturbing desire."[30]

The record business was also changing. Until the late 1940s the standard record was a rigid and fragile shellac disk played at 78 revolutions per minute (r.p.m.). The development of vinyl records with microgroove technology soon made those obsolete. Columbia and RCA introduced competing products: Columbia a 12-inch disk that turned at 33 1/3 r.p.m., and RCA a 7-inch record played at 45 r.p.m. By 1951 each company was producing both formats, and jukeboxes capable of playing the 45s appeared that same year. The 12-inch long-playing record allowed a half hour of uninterrupted music. The 45, however, had space for complete songs on each side, was less expensive, and became the standard means of selling popular songs to a teenage audience.

New technology contributed significantly to musical changes. Although the piano, saxophone, drums, and other instruments played key roles in the development of rock and roll at various times, the style's defining instrument became the electric guitar. As early as the mid-1920s guitar players gained volume by amplifying their vibrating guitar strings electronically, inserting pickups just under the strings of their hollow acoustic guitars. After World War II, however, several inventors created electric guitars with solid wooden bodies since the amplifier rather than the body created the sound and sustained the sound longer. Guitar bodies could, then, be any shape. Among the most important innovators were Les Paul, Paul Bigsby, and Leo Fender. The Gibson Company produced a Les Paul model in 1952, and Fender, who produced his first solid body guitar in 1948, released his most famous model, the Stratocaster, in 1953. By the late 1950s, rock guitarists, led by Buddy Holly, moved increasingly to the solid body electrics.

By 1955 all the pieces were in place. New technology had dramatically altered the entertainment business. The resulting vacuum in radio programming meant unprecedented demand for recorded music, and independent record labels helped fill the need. Changes in postwar race relations accelerated because the airwaves easily avoided existing barriers for listeners interested in new sounds. Social taboos could be quickly, if only temporarily, avoided with the turn of a radio dial. The changes, however, both musically and socially, would not come without a strong challenge.

In the mid-1950s these major elements of popular culture functioned within centralized industries and under various social and economic limitations. All forms of popular culture also operated within certain ideological restrictions imposed by the Cold War. The anticommunist hysteria effectively limited subject matter in scripts and either forced people out of the arts or drove them underground. The communist demon could effectively be attached to virtually any unpopular issue or event to undermine its success. Reactionaries classified both rock and rollers and civil rights activists as "Reds," a common derogatory term for communists. To avoid any possible taint, Cincinnati's baseball team even changed its name in the early 1950s from "Reds" to "Redlegs," keeping the new name until the decade ended. Despite the repressive climate, the nation moved forward.

If America's culture revolution was not under way in all respects, at least the groundwork had been laid by mid-decade. The movie industry's dominance was already under attack, and the studio system was in retreat. Television was still more potential than realization, but its promise and impact were clearly evident. Musical evolution had moved to the brink of rock and roll's birth, with teenagers impatiently waiting. Sport survived scandal, as it had be-

fore and would again, and was poised to move from popular diversion to national passion.

The impending revolution in popular culture would initially be more in
form than content. Television, for example, did not challenge existing attitudes in its programming, but its emerging place as the center of home and
family entertainment would dramatically alter the country's leisure time activities. Both professional and college sports were ready to become national
preoccupations, and colleges were moving toward a concentrated authority in
the NCAA. The movie and record industries were headed in the opposite direction, with control slipping away from a handful of powerful companies in
both cases. That the fates of all of these enterprises would be closely connected
in the years that followed was apparent from their convergence in the golden
age of the 1950s.

NOTES

1. Ronald Davis, *Celluloid Mirrors: Hollywood and American Society since 1945*
(Fort Worth, TX: Harcourt Brace, 1997), 2; Robert Sklar, *Movie-Made America: A
Cultural History of American Movies*, rev. ed. (New York: Vintage, 1994), 270.

2. Nora Sayre, *Running Time: Films of the Cold War* (New York: Dial, 1982), 204.

3. Sayre, *Running Time*, 204.

4. Charles Champlin, *The Movies Grow Up: 1940–1980* (Chicago: Swallow/Athens:
Ohio University Press, 1981), 63–64.

5. Sklar, *Movie-Made America*, 274.

6. Davis, *Celluloid Mirrors*, 178.

7. Danny Thomas, quoted in Harry Castleman and Walter J. Podrazik, *Watching
TV: Four Decades of American Television* (New York: McGraw-Hill, 1982), 68.

8. Bob Smith, quoted in Mary Ann Watson, *Defining Visions: Television and the
American Experience since 1945* (Fort Worth, TX: Harcourt Brace, 1998), 14.

9. Eva Marie Saint and Paul Newman, quoted in Shaun Considine, *Mad As Hell:
The Life and Work of Paddy Chayefsky* (New York: Random House, 1994), 63.

10. Daniel Marsh, quoted in Castleman and Podrazik, *Watching TV*, 46.

11. James Day, *The Vanishing Vision: The Inside Story of Public Television* (Berkeley:
University of California Press, 1995), 20–22. Broadcast bands were divided into VHF

and UHF spectrums. The first stations broadcast on the more desirable VHF frequencies, and most early television sets could not receive UHF frequencies.

12. Willard D. Rowland Jr., *The Politics of TV Violence: Policy Uses of Communication Research* (Beverly Hills, CA: Sage, 1983), 99–100.

13. Erik Barnouw, *Tube of Plenty: The Evolution of American Television*, 2nd rev. ed. (New York: Oxford University Press, 1990), 112.

14. Melvin Patrick Ely, *The Adventures of Amos 'n' Andy: A Social History of an American Phenomenon* (New York: Free Press, 1991), 7.

15. Watson, *Defining Visions*, 30.

16. Watson, *Defining Visions*, 2.

17. Leon Shamroy, quoted in Davis, *Celluloid Mirrors*, 18.

18. Frederick Ziv, quoted in Morleen Getz Rouse, "A History of the F. W. Ziv Radio and Television Syndication Companies: 1930–1960" (Ph.D. diss., University of Michigan, 1976), 120, 124.

19. William I. Kaufman and Robert S. Colodzin, *Your Career in Television* (New York: Merlin, 1950), 43–44.

20. William Boddy, *Fifties Television: The Industry and Its Critics* (Urbana: University of Illinois Press, 1990), 73.

21. Randy Roberts, *Winning Is the Only Thing: Sports in America since 1945* (Baltimore: Johns Hopkins University Press, 1989), x.

22. Roger Bannister, quoted in Gerald Holland, "1954 and its Sportsman: Roger Bannister," *Sports Illustrated*, January 3, 1955, 7.

23. Bill Russell, quoted in Bill Russell and Taylor Branch, *Second Wind: The Memoirs of an Opinionated Man* (New York: Random House, 1979), 78, 79.

24. Richard O. Davies, *America's Obsession: Sports and Society since 1945* (Fort Worth, TX: Harcourt Brace, 1994), 33.

25. Mark Ribowsky, *A Complete History of the Negro Leagues, 1884–1955* (New York: Birch Lane, 1995), 289.

26. Bob Mathias, quoted in Richard Espy, *The Politics of the Olympic Games* (Berkeley: University of California Press, 1979), 38.

27. Clair Bee, quoted in Davies, *America's Obsession*, 24.

28. Don J. Hibbard and Carol Kaleialoha, *The Role of Rock* (Englewood Cliffs, NJ: Prentice Hall, 1983), 13.

29. David P. Szatmary, *Rockin' in Time: A Social History of Rock-and-Roll*, 3rd. ed. (Upper Saddle River, NJ: Prentice Hall, 1996), 28.

30. James Miller, *Flowers in the Dustbin: The Rise of Rock and Roll, 1947–1977* (New York: Fireside, 1999), 56.

2

Golden Age and Blacklist: 1955 to 1960

People could feel the tremors of change in the mid-1950s. Life seemed to hold more possibilities than before as social, cultural, and physical barriers cracked or crumbled. Nine years after the previous world record performance, on May 6, 1954, Roger Bannister became the first person to run a mile in under four minutes. In July that same year Sun Records released Elvis Presley's first record, "That's All Right." At the end of the year ABC televised the first episode of a series on Davy Crockett, launching a national craze over the nineteenth-century frontiersman. In 1955 James Dean appeared in the film *Rebel without a Cause*, leaving a symbol of tortured but threatening youth. Each of these events in their own way signified a new era.

The latter half of the 1950s was a time of tremendous growth in some forms of popular culture. Television in particular reached previously unknown heights, challenging the preeminence of motion pictures during what some call its "golden age." The movies also did well, producing some of cinema's best-known titles and utilizing new technologies. Rock and roll music appeared for the first time, with several of its earliest artists providing vital influences that would be followed by succeeding generations of musicians. Some of sports' brightest stars shone in the 1950s. Baseball's Mickey Mantle, Willie Mays, and Duke Snider roamed the outfield; basketball had its new generation of agile giants in Wilt Chamberlain and Bill Russell; and pro football broke into the national consciousness with a sudden-death championship game.

At the same time, the features that made these activities popular, and profitable, made them targets for unethical influences. By the end of the decade scandals tarnished several forms of popular culture. Gambling would once again impose itself on sports; music suffered from bribery and other vices, both real and imagined; while even television staggered under commercial influences and the humiliation of public deception. Hollywood avoided major scandal even as it continued to operate under the cloud of the blacklist. Domestic and foreign influences, however, eroded long accepted standards of appropriate content for public viewing. As in so many other areas of American society, the arrival of the 1960s promised dramatic change in popular culture.

TELEVISION'S GOLDEN AGE

Television rose quickly to claim a significant role in American society. In its first decade it would fascinate the nation and influence the development of most other forms of popular culture. At its best, television programming elicited praise for its brilliant writing and treatment of socially relevant issues. With these achievements, however, came growing pains. Run primarily for financial gain, the networks and their affiliates increasingly made decisions for commercial rather than artistic reasons. In generally upholding the social status quo, they also maintained limited opportunities for minority populations. At its worst, TV faced charges of encouraging violence and suffered an embarrassing exposure of public deception.

While television was capable of high-quality entertainment, it operated in a more restrictive creative environment than motion pictures. In addition to the suffocating political cloud of McCarthyism, which curtailed any real challenge to the status quo, advertising agencies and commercial sponsors wanted to avoid any program content that might offend American consumers. The prevailing social conservatism meant producing family-oriented shows that were generally cheerful and adhered to middle-class ethics, and certainly did nothing to question existing authorities. One critic of of this reality was playwright Paddy Chayefsky, who called television "democracy at its ugliest."[1]

Anthology series remained among the more critically acclaimed TV programs in the mid- to late 1950s. Live performances continued to the end of the decade on *Goodyear Television Playhouse, The U.S. Steel Hour,* and the highly respected *Playhouse 90.* Filmed anthologies such as *Fireside Theatre* and *General Electric Theatre* retained high ratings even longer than live presentations.

Some of the plays originally written for television, like *Marty* and *Twelve Angry Men*, later became acclaimed motion pictures as well. When art clashed with commerce, however, it suffered.

By mid-decade ad agencies and sponsors had gained greater control of script content. Advertisers believed complex scripts and a focus on ordinary life undercut the simple solutions and social climbing promoted by consumer products. They also felt troubled by controversial social and political issues that some performances raised. Their influence was pervasive. Tobacco companies insisted that smoking on TV shows should be limited to admirable characters and not associated with criminals. A sponsoring gas company deleted the word "gas" from a drama on World War II war crimes, "making it sound as though six million Jews perished in —— chambers."[2] One of television's most respected writers, Rod Serling, complained that shows suffered from this pressure. "In some cases, you can't even use the word 'American,'" he revealed. "It might be the name of a rival tobacco firm."[3] An associate producer moaned, "TV has more sacred cows than India."[4] Intrusions such as these pushed directors, writers, and actors away from TV to work under less restrictive conditions. The anthology series fell into decline.

The fading status and popularity of TV anthologies emphasized a significant shift in the industry. Although television production began in New York, by the mid-1950s Hollywood became TV's primary production center, as shows moved increasingly from live broadcasts to prerecorded film. The larger studios followed the trail blazed by smaller independents. Walt Disney's relationship with ABC produced a rare hit for that network with *Disneyland* from 1954 to 1958. With this crack in Hollywood's resistance to television, Columbia Pictures established a TV subsidiary, Screen Gems, which turned out winners like *Father Knows Best*. Warner Brothers, having earlier resisted TV's growing encroachment, became the first major studio to move into television production, in 1955. Its first successful show was a one-hour western for ABC entitled *Cheyenne* that starred Clint Walker as virtuous cowboy Cheyenne Bodie. The studio limited costs by utilizing stock footage from its library of western motion pictures and built a frontier town on its lot, shooting very little of the show on location. Even so, each episode, usually shot in five days, was budgeted at fifty thousand dollars. Jack Warner recognized that producing telefilms would permit his company to maintain the studio system of exclusive contracts with actors and other key talent, and the constant productivity allowed the studio to maintain a full production and administrative staff even during lulls in moviemaking.

Two other major movie studios, Twentieth Century-Fox and Metro-Goldwyn-Mayer, moved into TV production the same year as Warner Brothers, even as they reduced their output of theatrical films. Columbia/Screen Gems, United Artists (which bought out Ziv), and Revue Productions, a subsidiary of the MCA talent agency, also entered TV production. MCA produced *Tales of Wells Fargo*, *Wagon Train*, and *M Squad* for NBC in 1957. CBS drew from diverse sources to get *I Love Lucy*, *December Bride* (both from Desilu), *Schlitz Playhouse* (MCA), and *Perry Mason* (Twentieth Century-Fox). By 1955, with television accessible to over half the nation, Hollywood studios produced most of TV's prime-time programming, holding the dominant position in expertise and equipment in filmmaking.

The only major studio not producing telefilms, RKO, made its own momentous decision in 1955. General Teleradio bought RKO's film catalog and studio for $25 million. Desilu ended up with the studio, and distributors offered 740 RKO movies to TV stations. Other studios followed close behind. In 1956 Warner Brothers received $21 million and Twentieth Century-Fox $30 million for their feature films, and the following year Paramount took $50 million, while Screen Gems distributed Columbia and some Universal films. All of these deals were for films made prior to 1948 and, since they did not require residual payments, provided the studios with a wave of cash. The distributors paying these huge sums proved to have made a profitable investment, as TV stations across the country cut staff, closed their studios, and shifted to running feature films for large blocks of their programming. WOR-TV in New York, for example, went from nightly live drama in 1954 to none two years later. Its schedule was 88 percent film.

Hollywood had about one hundred telefilms in production by late 1957. Most went to local stations through the networks, but popular syndicated programs included *Sea Hunt* and *Highway Patrol*. The new trend in TV series was action shows in which good triumphed over evil. Crime dramas such as *Dragnet*, *M Squad*, and *Perry Mason* joined international conspiracy shows such as *Captain Midnight*, *I Led Three Lives*, and *A Man Called X*—and even animal shows such as *Lassie* and *Fury*—in portraying a simple but satisfying resolution. Heroes rarely had internal conflicts; in the middle of the Cold War that might have been suspect. As Erik Barnouw concisely puts it, "Problems came from the evil of other people, and were solved . . . by confining or killing them."[5]

By far the most common setting for these morality plays was the old West. Numerous television westerns appeared prior to the mid-1950s, but the likes of *The Lone Ranger, Hopalong Cassidy, The Adventures of Rin Tin Tin, The Roy Rogers Show,* and *The Gene Autry Show* offered simplistic morality tales and action-oriented stories that appealed primarily to children. The arrival of *Gunsmoke* led a stampede of adult-styled westerns that dominated the ratings from the 1957–1958 season through the 1961–1962 season. During these years 46 percent of television's top ten shows, and at least the top three programs in four of those years, were westerns. These adult westerns differed from previous shows by emphasizing drama and character development. The list of popular series in the 1950s, in addition to *Gunsmoke,* is a long one: *Have Gun Will Travel, The Life and Legend of Wyatt Earp, Wagon Train, Tales of Wells Fargo, The Rifleman, Cheyenne, Maverick, Wanted: Dead or Alive, Sugarfoot,* and the anthology series *Dick Powell's Zane Grey Theater.* All of these rated in the top twenty-five for at least two years, and many other shows had large followings as well.

The industry's entertainment and economic concerns were intimately connected from the beginning. Television proved to be a perfect vehicle for promoting products. Manufacturers found that advertising through TV could bring dramatic results. The Hazel Bishop Company, for example, increased its annual sales of lipstick from fifty thousand dollars to $4.5 million in two years after its ads first appeared in 1950. Utilizing planned obsolescence—that products should quickly become unusable or outdated—advertisers pushed Americans to increasing levels of spending and encouraged the desire for more products. This desire for "things," materialism, was greatly enhanced by the power of television. Stars pitched a variety of products, from constantly changing styles of cars to competing brands of cigarettes. Advertisers hoped to associate their products, usually those that could be quickly consumed and replaced, with a psychological benefit, like higher status or sex appeal. In the case of cigarettes, the success of advertising was only too apparent. Death from lung cancer soared in the 1950s as various tobacco companies sponsored some of television's leading shows. Critics of American materialism raised key issues and stimulated national debate but in the long run failed to significantly alter the consumer society.

Significant shifts in television programming took place in the 1950s. Among the most important came when NBC president Sylvester "Pat" Weaver, a former advertising executive, introduced the "magazine concept" to the network. Instead of having sponsors and ad agencies create shows for network use, the network would produce programs and allow advertisers to buy commercial time inserted into the programs. The motivation behind the switch was to give the network greater control of programming. All the networks chafed under the sponsor-controlled system. As Weaver indicated,

> The programming just had no direction. Programs landed next to each other by mere chance, with each agency building its show in a way that was aimed at nothing more than keeping its client happy. There was no planned relationship of one program to another or to the competition, and no particular attempt to create a listening pattern for the people at home.[6]

In this effort the television networks welcomed Hollywood's influence. The movie studios resisted advertising agency control—Warner Brothers refused initially to allow script reviews, for example—without requiring networks to assume the production costs. The percentage of single-sponsor programs fell from 75 percent in 1955 to 40 percent by the end of the decade and declined steadily thereafter.

Weaver also revised sponsor contracts, which allowed NBC to reserve occasional times to run special programs, which he called "spectaculars," without having to reimburse the sponsors' or ad agencies' costs. An example of these spectaculars was a broadcast of the Broadway play *Peter Pan* in March 1955 after the end of its theater run. An estimated sixty-five million people watched. To one scholar, this indicated "the age of television had arrived."[7]

Even as the networks were acquiring greater control of television programming, new challenges to their dominance were awakening. Cable television, originally known as "community antenna television," differs from broadcast TV by communicating through wire cables rather than over airwaves. The first cable systems began in the late 1940s in Pennsylvania and Oregon. Subscribers paid to be connected by cable to a community antenna system and also paid a monthly charge for programming. Cable television primarily benefited remote areas without local stations or with poor reception, but it supplemented minimal programming in some regions and solved reception problems in others. By the mid-1950s the number of cable systems rivaled that of broadcast stations. Noncommercial television also received a boost with the founding in Ann Arbor, Michigan, of the National Educational Television and Radio Center (NET) in 1954. By 1958 NET had dropped its involvement with radio and moved its headquarters to New York. By the following year it was providing eight hours of programming each week to over thirty stations nationwide.

Television content continued to attract national attention. A significant inquiry came from the Senate Subcommittee to Investigate Juvenile Delinquency, chaired during the Eighty-third Congress by Robert Hendrickson (R-NJ) and later by Estes Kefauver (D-TN), when Democrats took control of the Senate after the 1954 elections. Initially concerned with the rise of youth crime rates, Kefauver's committee looked into possible links between juvenile crime and aggressive behavior on television. The hearings themselves were more confrontational than those of the 1952 Harris committee. In April 1955 Kefauver utilized social science studies to give an impression of a linkage between TV violence and juvenile delinquency. The committee's August 1955 final report recognized that no "comprehensive, conclusive study" proved the relationship, but the subcommittee believed "television crime programs are . . . much more injurious to children and young people than motion pictures, radio, or comic books." It concluded that some children could be susceptible to criminal examples provided by television. Another concern noted by the Kefauver committee was that continued exposure to criminal violence could desensitize Americans to its impact. The hearings failed to show a conclusive link between television and violence, but the public widely believed that one existed. Although the committee recommended that the FCC consider program content during license renewals, no formal action followed the hearings.[8] In the end not much came of the debate.

The flood of television buying soon pushed the issue away, and TV violence actually increased. This was especially true in 1950s westerns. The addition of *The Untouchables* in 1959 set a new standard for TV violence. The show, set in 1930s Chicago and built around federal treasury agent Eliot Ness, contained almost weekly scenes of gun battles and bullet-riddled bodies. By the 1960s studies suggested that exposure to televised violence increased the chances of aggressive behavior later in life. The networks, self-servingly, argued the opposite.

Race was another significant social issue that spread to the small screen. In the mid-1950s black celebrities still found their opportunities on television far more limited than those for whites. The celebrated African American singer and pianist Nat "King" Cole was a popular guest on numerous variety shows, and NBC agreed to air *The Nat King Cole Show*, which first appeared in November 1956. The network covered the program's costs since initially it had no corporate sponsor. Advertisers feared that supporting a program with a black entertainer in charge could cost them business among white conservatives or doubted that black stars could sell their products. Cole's status on the show as a social equal to whites was apparently too much of a change for a society still wrestling with racial equality. Sponsors did step forward sporadically, but the network usually carried the show financially. Despite low ratings and sponsorship problems, NBC lengthened the show from fifteen to thirty minutes in the summer of 1957. An impressive list of performers and better ratings still failed to attract a consistent national sponsor, although some companies bought airtime in specific cities. When financial considerations persuaded the network to shift the show to a less attractive time, Cole refused the change and the show ended. He commended the network's efforts to make the show work but blamed advertisers for its failure, commenting, "Madison Avenue is afraid of the dark."[9]

Other groups fared just as badly. American Indians appeared frequently in western series, but stories rarely provided an American Indian perspective. Shows often portrayed Native Americans as violent enemies of U.S. expansion. Asians almost never showed up on television. Eastern Europeans were likely to be spies undermining America in the Cold War. The problem was not that identifiably ethnic or racial minority TV characters were portrayed in comical or stereotypical ways. Television ultimately makes fools of every class, ethnicity, sex, and race. The problem for so long was that minorities either did not appear or appeared only as negative stereotypes. A broader context existed only for white Americans, and many white-only shows portrayed an inaccurate vision of American life.

Television remained a staunch defender of the conservative status quo when it came to romantic love. Its portrayals of romance with virtually no depiction of sexuality made it unrealistically chaste. The 1950s ushered in greater public discussion of sex through the publication of Alfred Kinsey's academic investigations, *Sexual Behavior in the Human Male* (1948) and *Sexual Behavior in the Human Female* (1953), and the more hedonistic monthly magazine *Playboy* (1953). Movies, though still quite restrained by later standards, also addressed themes of human sexuality and offered occasional glimpses of amorous behavior. Rock and roll music, which rose in popularity in the second half of the 1950s, similarly offered audiences the suggestion of sexuality, especially in the live shows of performers like Elvis Presley and Little Richard. Television, on the other hand, remained asexual. In one famous incident, Ed Sullivan ordered his cameramen to show Presley, whose stage gyrations had earned him the nickname "Elvis the Pelvis," only from the waist up. TV shows upheld conservative religious attitudes toward sex outside of marriage, and on television even married couples slept in separate beds.

Similarly, until the 1970s and beyond, television portrayed American families as they existed in the immediate post–World War II years: a married mother and father raising their biological children. Exceptions were rare. The shift in the composition of American families starting in the Vietnam War era sparked a national debate, which often incorporated families depicted on television shows.

Television programming in the 1950s generally reinforced the American work ethic. People who worked hard would most certainly enjoy an improved standard of living, while those who looked for an easy way out would usually find their plans ending in failure. *The Life of Riley, Leave It To Beaver*, and *Father Knows Best* represented the standard TV treatment of the work ethic. Life presented occasional breaks from hard work. New children's programming offered the wise *Captain Kangaroo*, the variety of *The Mickey Mouse Club*, and the adventure of *Sergeant Preston of the Yukon*.

One particular program format drew especially strong criticism from some quarters during the 1950s. A handful of shows, such as *Strike It Rich* and *Queen for a Day*, used human misfortune as a form of entertainment. On *Strike It Rich* contestants described their need for such things as medical procedures, housing repairs, or work-related equipment and won money for answering questions. A key part of the show occurred when viewers phoned in offers to help meet the contestants' needs. Most of the calls, however, were prearranged with companies that received on-air mentions. Observers debated whether the program celebrated American kindness or exploited personal suffering for profit. *Queen for a Day* had four women describe their misfortune, then the studio audience selected the most deserving by their applause. The winner received various prizes donated by companies for their promotional value, but the other contestants were quickly forgotten.

Elvis Presley (Library of Congress)

Television news coverage faced difficult competition with the more lucrative entertainment shows. NBC, CBS, and ABC each established their own news teams, with small film crews in key U.S. and European cities supplemented by field correspondents. Until the early 1960s the networks offered fifteen-minute early evening shows hosted by an anchorman who connected a series of short film clips. As television historian Erik Barnouw indicates, however, this approach had serious drawbacks. The number of news personnel was far too small to cover all newsworthy items, and many of the events chosen for coverage were staged for the cameras. The medium's need for visuals and its reliance on planned activities meant that the creators of those events, such as press conferences or speeches, had great influence in framing public perceptions. Events not captured on film rarely became "news." More significantly, TV limited what people perceived as news. "The notion that a picture was worth a thousand words meant, in practice, that footage of Atlantic City beauty winners, shot at some expense, was considered more valuable than a thousand words from Eric Sevareid on the mounting tensions in Southeast Asia," claims Barnouw. "Analysis . . . was being shunted aside as non-visual."[10]

Television's connection to the political world was never a comfortable one. President Eisenhower opened his press conferences to film crews in 1955, but TV's reliance on these managed events allowed the administration to frame and interpret issues without independent analysis. The executive branch also successfully persuaded CBS to stop using reports from U.S. reporters in China. Challenges to the government's manipulation were rare. At the same time, politicians were reluctant to invade prime-time television for fear of antagonizing a public hungry for entertainment. During the 1956 presidential campaign both Republicans and Democrats featured five-minute ads tacked onto the end of twenty-five-minute shows to avoid having to cancel the programs and incur the public's displeasure. Adlai Stevenson referred to this selling of the candidates as "the ultimate indignity to the democratic process."[11] Stevenson could not have known at the time, but television would soon face an even greater humiliation.

Quiz shows rivaled telefilms as entertainment in the second half of the 1950s. Programs featuring contestants and prizes were not new, but the June 1955 debut of *The $64,000 Question* made possible a much larger cash award. Ordinary people could win cash by correctly answering a series of questions in a specific category, and winning players returned each week to escalating sums of prize money. A glass isolation booth and a trust officer added to the solemnity and integrity of the contest questions. Put together by an independent producer and sponsored by Revlon, the show became a huge success. Within five weeks it had become the nation's top-rated show, and Revlon sales exploded. *Time* magazine feared the new program would "set back by at least a season, if not by years, TV's already enfeebled yearning to leaven commercialism with culture."[12] Not surprisingly, the show's success soon generated imitations, among them *The Big Surprise, The $64,000 Challenge,* and *Twenty-One.* Some contestants took away winnings in excess of one hundred thousand dollars.

What the public did not know was that producers of these shows were manipulating the outcome. Their maneuvers included selecting contestants with greater audience appeal, testing candidates to find their strengths and weaknesses (and writing questions accordingly), asking rehearsal questions very similar to the ones asked on air, and asking favored contestants questions they could answer while posing more difficult ones to unpopular contestants. Revlon officials often tried to influence which contestants would succeed or fail on *The $64,000 Question.*

Eventually rumors surfaced that some of the quiz shows were fixed. On rare occasions an offended contestant revealed a practice question had been repeated on the air, but the press was undisturbed. As *Look* magazine assured the public, "no TV quiz shows are fixed in the sense of being dishonest."[13] Herbert Stempel posed a more serious threat to the system, however. Hoping to revive the failing show *Twenty-One* in 1956, one of its producers made a deal with the bright but poor and nondescript Army veteran attending New York's City College. Stempel received answers in advance and made tens of thousands of dollars. What he provided the show was a caricatured, lower-class, disheveled "brain," who was coached in his dress, appearance, and mannerisms to generate maximum drama. The partnership worked fine until the producer decided to replace Stempel as champion with Charles Van Doren, a handsome English instructor at Columbia. The unseating of Stempel was carefully staged, but he resented losing the public acclaim. Van Doren's nearly four-month reign as champion won him national notoriety, even as he became increasingly uncomfortable in his role. He even appeared on the cover of *Time* magazine, which labeled him "a new kind of TV idol—of all things, an egghead . . . whom many a grateful parent regards as TV's own health-restoring antidote to Presley."[14] Van Doren made well over one hundred thousand dollars before producers scripted his defeat to Vivienne Nearing in March 1957.

Envious to the point of obsession, Stempel made numerous accusations that his defeat was arranged. Observers generally dismissed his comments as unsupported tirades. In May 1958, however, everything changed when a standby contestant for the show *Dotto* lifted a sheet of answers provided ahead of time to the program's winner. When the contestant contacted the show's sponsor, Colgate-Palmolive, in August, the network and company canceled *Dotto* immediately. New York district attorney Frank Hogan decided to investigate, and days later New York newspapers finally reported Stempel's accusations about *Twenty-One*.

Hogan convened a grand jury to examine the growing charges. Van Doren, who had been given a lucrative deal with NBC's *Today* show, denied Stempel's accusations. Other game show contestants also denied corruption to the New York grand jury in January 1959, and the story quieted until summer when the jury made its report. Some witnesses revealed that Revlon had dictated which contestants would win or lose. When the judge surprisingly impounded the evidence, Hogan objected, and Congress's House Special Subcommittee on Legislative Oversight held public hearings as part of its own investigation of quiz shows that fall. The hearings revealed the extent of fraudulent collaboration and the widespread perjured testimony given to the New York grand jury. Van Doren, disconsolate and filled with remorse almost from the time of his appearance on *Twenty-One*, appeared under a subpoena on November 2. "I would give almost anything I have to reverse the course of my life in the last three years," he confessed during his testimony.[15] Although the scandal was larger than Van Doren and *Twenty-One*, as the contestant who reaped the highest rewards for his deception, he became the focal point of public disillusionment. Van Doren was fired from his jobs at Columbia University and NBC, and columnists attacked both him and the system.

The quiz show scandals stimulated a significant debate about recent social changes and prodded Americans to examine their values. Political scientist Hans Morgenthau claimed Van Doren's actions grew out of "a world which condones the betrayal of truth for the sake of wealth and power."[16] John Steinbeck wrote: "If I wanted to destroy a nation I would give it too much and I would have it on its knees, miserable, greedy, and sick . . . on all levels, American society is rigged. . . . I am troubled by the cynical immorality of my country. It cannot survive on this basis."[17] Years later, journalist David Halberstam pondered the impact of the scandal, emphasizing television's "addictive power" and its ability to create a "pseudo-intimacy . . . that would have profound ramifications, as television increasingly became the prime instrument of politics." More importantly, Halberstam concluded, the scandal demonstrated that "television *cast* everything it touched: politics, news shows, and sitcoms. The demands of entertainment and theater were at least as powerful as substance."[18] The quiz show scandals at the end of the decade revealed that materialism drove the networks beyond the ethical boundaries observed by many Americans.

Despite this major stumble, in the 1950s television had quickly established its enormous potential. Its expansion gave greater exposure to rock and roll, provided broader access to sporting events, and threatened the motion picture industry. The movie moguls looked for ways to maintain their supremacy.

CRACKING THE CODE

Hollywood's studio system continued its decline throughout the 1950s. In the postwar years a number of European nations restricted U.S. film company profits, in part to protect their own film industries but also to aid their economic recovery. This limitation of key overseas markets, combined with Hollywood's domestic problems, caused the studios to look for ways to cut costs. These included drastically reducing the number of artistic and technical personnel under contract. To weaken the competition of television, many of the remaining contracts prevented actors from appearing on TV, which eliminated potential income. Leading film stars recognized that certain advantages existed in contracting for individual films and taking a percentage of a film's profits rather than a salary. Directors also sought greater control of the creative process by moving increasingly toward producing films independent of studio authority. Through World War II two-thirds of all U.S. movies came out of the major studios. By the end of the 1950s, however, there were an estimated 165 independent Hollywood producers responsible for two-thirds of the nation's feature films.[19] The major studios, plus Columbia, United Artists, and Universal, continued to distribute most of the independent films and often contributed significantly to their funding as well. The percentage of independent productions released by Hollywood's eight leading studios rose from 20 percent in 1949 to 57 percent in 1957.[20]

The *Paramount* decision meant the end of block booking, increased marketing costs, and greater uncertainty about an individual film's success. Banks that provided funding, wanting to reduce their risk, insisted on big-name stars and proven formulas, which further eroded the studios' control while limiting the movies' creativity. This change produced greater leverage for the most popular actors and gave their agents significantly more input on a film project. The most prominent agencies started developing their own projects, bringing together actors, writers, and directors, and asking the studios and banks to accept the entire package. Once again, this trend further undercut the studio heads' power over the industry.

Hollywood films had long avoided certain controversial topics, but shifting social standards in the 1950s stretched the areas of acceptability. Although some of America's early films contained occasional glimpses of nudity, the Production Code Administration (PCA) had effectively eliminated it. Since 1934 the PCA had screened Hollywood studio films in response to a threatened boycott led by Roman Catholics over standards of decency. Criminal and immoral behavior on film had to be reformed or punished, and the code banned altogether a variety of activities—"homosexuality . . . interracial sex, abortion, incest, drugs"—and nearly all language that might offend the sensibilities of middle-class and religiously devout patrons.[21] As Americans became acquainted with new film styles from other nations, and as foreign films received increased praise and circulation in the United States during the postwar years, occasional cracks in these standards appeared.

From the mid-1940s to the early 1950s Italian neo-realists dealt candidly with the bleak circumstances of the war and postwar years. Films like Roberto Rossellini's *Open City* (1945) and Vittorio De Sica's *The Bicycle Thief* (1948) focused on the individual struggles of ordinary people against larger social forces. Directors generally shot these movies on location rather than in studios, often featured nonprofessional actors, and operated on slim budgets. The neo-realists' collective effect provided an alternative to the fantasy-based movies prevalent in Hollywood and shattered the view that justice always prevails. As they "broke with romantic film conventions of the past," they "signaled the start of a revolution of rising expectations . . . for the movies and what they might say or show about real life."[22]

At the end of the 1950s a number of French filmmakers crafted a film style known as "new wave." With a creative independence rarely allowed to their

American counterparts, French directors produced inexpensive films that often departed from a traditional narrative form. Utilizing techniques like jump cuts (which move immediately from one scene to another without a transition), slow or accelerated motion, freeze frames, maximum close-ups, shaky handheld cameras, unusual narration or musical accompaniment, and alternating humor and violence, these films broke out of typical time and space restraints. Film editor John Victor-Smith observed, "When the French New Wave decided that people no longer had to walk in and out of doors, this was an important change."[23] Early examples of French new wave include François Truffaut's *The 400 Blows* and Alain Resnais' *Hiroshima Mon Amour,* both from 1959, and Jean-Luc Godard's *Breathless* (1960).

Italian films of the same era shared a reaction to traditional narrative and a focus on emotional isolation. Their themes were more psychological and their outlooks more optimistic than those of the neo-realists, but they were less likely than the French to use intrusive editing techniques. Movies like Federico Fellini's *La Dolce Vita* and Michaelangelo Antonioni's *L'avventura* in 1960 led a growing stream of motion pictures into the United States. Filmmakers from other countries also impressed American audiences in the 1950s, especially Sweden's Ingmar Bergman and Japan's Akira Kurosawa.

Foreign films competed against Hollywood with increasing success for major festival awards and for access to theaters around the world. European motion pictures in particular dealt seriously with adult issues, often focusing on a psychological dilemma rather than a story, refusing to adopt "Hollywood's two most frequent forms of closure—the killing of a bad guy or the marriage of John and Jane."[24] Film historians Gerald Mast and Bruce Kawin observe that Italians emphasized "the close, careful observation of ordinary human beings in their social contexts," while the French created "a new content through style." Together these two movements "revolutionized the values and aesthetics of the motion picture."[25]

Several factors contributed to the loosening of restrictions on film content at this time. The ability of groups such as the American Legion and the predominantly Catholic Legion of Decency to effectively threaten a boycott of films antagonizing their values was waning. Joseph Breen retired as head of the PCA in 1954, and his successor accepted a wider range of human activity as suitable for theater audiences. Hollywood's first real challenge to the code came in 1953. Otto Preminger's *The Moon Is Blue* contained candid sexual language and did not explicitly condemn nonmarital sex as an immoral act. United Artists distributed the film without code approval and still made money. Other films released without the PCA's seal of approval, including *The Man with the Golden Arm* (1956), were also profitable, and the industry's self-imposed restrictions slowly began to unwind. At the end of 1956 the PCA revised its guidelines to permit previously unacceptable subjects: abortion, illegal drugs, kidnapping, and prostitution. Beginning with *Baby Doll* (1956), the PCA approved American films that increasingly dealt with sexual themes. With declining audiences, producers knew that sex and violence would sell.

European films of the 1950s were often more daring than American cinema. As a way of finding a profitable niche, some theater owners, usually in a large city or a university town, showed foreign films on a regular basis. Targeting younger and more sophisticated patrons, about five hundred of these "art houses" existed by the early 1960s. The growth in film festivals also brought a growing number of imported movies into the United States. Sweden's *One Summer of Happiness* and France's *Lady Chatterley's Lover* appeared in the first half of the decade, contributing to greater variety in themes and language. The 1956 French film *And God Created Woman* was among the first imported movies to attract major public attention and revenue, with young Brigitte Bardot playing a sexually independent free spirit. With art houses and film festivals enhancing the popularity of foreign films, European attitudes toward sexuality became more visible and challenged America's production code.

While these trends are significant, the most popular and celebrated films of the era deal with more traditional themes. *The Bridge on the River Kwai* (1957) is a World War II story in which British prisoners of war under Japanese control are forced to build a bridge in Burma. Much of the film's drama comes from the battle of wills between the Japanese camp commander and the senior British officer. The Englishman ironically takes great pride in completing a project that aids his enemy, but an escaped American prisoner returns to blow up the bridge. The 1959 comedy *Some Like It Hot* utilizes sexually suggestive writing in its story of two unemployed male musicians who dress as women to find work in a female band. Alfred Hitchcock's *North by Northwest* (1959) is a spy thriller, in which a man victimized by a case of mistaken identity ends up being pursued onto the face of Mount Rushmore. Hitchcock also directed *Vertigo* (1958), which combines a psychological study with a suspenseful romance. Actor Charlton Heston starred in two Biblical epics, *The*

Ten Commandments in 1956 and *Ben-Hur* in 1959. *Ben-Hur* was the most expensive (fifteen million dollars) and most honored (eleven Oscars) film to that date. The story follows Judah Ben-Hur, a Jewish prince enslaved by a childhood friend who returns to Judea as a Roman officer. After saving the life of a Roman military commander, Ben-Hur regains his status and freedom and wins revenge on his betrayer in a dramatic chariot race.

Several other films in the late 1950s received critical acclaim. *Paths of Glory* (1957) is director Stanley Kubrick's comment on the perversity of war. Set within France during World War I, the film portrays the French command staff as distant, incompetent, and unconcerned with the human costs of war. Kirk Douglas stars as Colonel Dax, who questions the sanity of his orders but carries out a bloody and unsuccessful attack against a fortified enemy position. To save his career, the commanding general charges three randomly selected soldiers with cowardice. Dax defends the three at trial, but the men are executed according to plan. John Ford's *The Searchers* (1956) features John Wayne as Ethan Edwards in a classic western. Out to avenge the murders of his family and rescue his niece, Debbie, from Chief Scar's Comanche band, Ethan turns against his niece upon learning that she has married Scar. Prevented from killing Debbie by his friend, Ethan eventually returns her home, but his fear of race mixing made a provocative statement at a time of increased civil rights agitation in the United States. Elia Kazan's *A Face in the Crowd* (1957) follows charismatic vagrant Lonesome Rhodes from his rural home to national celebrity on radio and television. Promoted to media stardom by reporter Marcia Jeffries, Rhodes's egomania turns him into a dangerous political threat that is blocked only when Jeffries reveals his deception on TV. This was an early warning about the impact of mass media on politics. Other period films that have grown in reputation since their unexceptional debuts include Orson Welles's 1958 crime thriller *Touch of Evil* and Alexander Mackendrick's *Sweet Smell of Success* (1957), about the sordid aspects of the New York tabloids.

Even with successes like these, the motion picture industry experienced ongoing financial problems. Like many other forms of popular culture, American films in the 1950s looked for an answer by connecting with the emerging youth culture. This subculture grew out of reduced adult supervision during World War II, the baby boom, increased affluence, and changes in youth spending habits and economic power. Nearly three-fourths of all moviegoers early in the decade were under thirty years old, and a substantial number were teenagers. Teens, particularly in the suburbs, often had enough money and independence to build an identity separate from the adults in their lives. Businesses soon learned that profits awaited those that could develop products that appealed to adolescent desires and trends. Hollywood found a formula by mid-decade.

Several films dealt with youthful anxieties, generational rebellion, and juvenile delinquency. These reflected the growing mid-decade concern with teen culture and crime, which were the subject of numerous books and a congressional investigation. *The Wild One, The Blackboard Jungle,* and *Rebel without a Cause* from 1954 to 1955 featured ominous youthful rebels whose attitudes, dress styles, and language reinforced adult fears for their children. The classic youthful screen rebel was twenty-four-year-old James Dean, who starred in 1955's *Rebel without a Cause.* He plays Jim Stark, the center of a trio of middle-class delinquents whose problems stem from inadequate parenting. Dean's death in an automobile accident only four weeks prior to the film's release rendered him permanently young.

In *Blackboard Jungle* (1955), Glenn Ford plays high school English teacher Rick Dadier, who confronts student thugs in an economically deprived setting. He is one of several teachers assaulted by students, but rather than turning them over to the police, Dadier attempts to persuade the young people to pressure one another to change their behavior. He divides them by singling out Miller, played by Sidney Poitier, encouraging him toward cooperation and a successful adulthood. Ultimately succeeding, Dadier saves the majority by expelling two students who are beyond redemption. The film's violence and stark portrayal of American education drew substantial criticism. Because this was the first major film with a rock and roll sound track, the public sometimes linked the new music with youth crime. As author Jim Miller describes it, "The cultural essence of the music . . . would be all about disorder, aggression, and sex: a fantasy of human nature, running wild to a savage beat."[26]

The generational clashes in these films are personal confrontations rather than statements against society. The majority of the adolescents, even the delinquents, are depicted as basically good but lacking nurturing love, support, and strong role models. Change, especially in *Blackboard Jungle,* comes from individuals rather than institutional or collective actions.

Blackboard Jungle represents the first important connection between rock and roll music and motion pictures. The music of Bill Haley and His Comets highlights the film's sound track and propelled "Rock around the Clock" to the top of *Billboard*'s pop chart. Haley and the Comets starred in two of the numerous rock and roll films that appeared soon afterward. *Rock around the Clock* and *Don't Knock the Rock*, both released in 1956, feature moderate generational conflict over the new music, with parents ultimately accepting the innocence and value of their children's musical preferences. *Rock around the Clock* showed the power of the teenage market, becoming "the first hugely successful film marketed to teenagers to the pointed exclusion of their elders."[27]

With proof that teens could support a film by themselves, studios turned out more youth-oriented movies. Many of these maintained themes of generational conflict and featured rock and roll artists. *Jailhouse Rock* (1957) stars Elvis Presley, whose character was considerably more sensuous and threatening than Bill Haley. It was the third of several popular films starring Presley. In 1956, *The Girl Can't Help It* provided on-screen performances by Little Richard, Fats Domino, and Gene Vincent. It revolves around the story of a criminal who tries to turn his girlfriend into a rock star; this plot, though basically satirical, reinforced the negative views of rock and roll's critics. Alan Freed, a well-known disc jockey and popularizer of the term "rock and roll," starred in several related films, usually as a generational mediator dealing with conflicting musical tastes and teen behavior. In addition to *Rock around the Clock*, Freed appeared in *Rock, Rock, Rock!* (1956), *Don't Knock the Rock* (1956), *Mister Rock and Roll* (1957), and *Go, Johnny, Go!* (1959). Among the musical artists most likely to show up on-screen were Haley, Fats Domino, Little Richard, Chuck Berry, Frankie Lymon and the Teenagers, the Platters, the Moonglows, Eddie Cochran, and Gene Vincent. Within a few short months at the end of 1956 and in early 1957 a wave of rock and roll teen pictures debuted, including, along with those listed above, *Shake, Rattle, and Rock!* (1956), *Love Me Tender* (1956), and *Rock, Pretty Baby* (1957).

Smaller independent companies joined the major studios in avidly pursuing the teenage market. After *Blackboard Jungle* and *Rebel without a Cause* showed the popularity of films about rebellious youth, many independents marketed specifically for a younger audience. Drag racing, drug use, and violence were recurring topics. American International Pictures was especially successful in profiting from teen-oriented movies, distributing films made by independent producers like Roger Corman. American International believed it would maximize its chances for turning a profit by targeting nineteen-year-old males.[28] The teen audience also supported the bulk of the decade's horror movies. British imports like *The Curse of Frankenstein* (1956) helped popularize youth-oriented horror films. Among the most notable of the decade's independent films of this genre are *The Fly* (1958), *Attack of the 50 Foot Woman* (1958), *Tarantula* (1955), *The Mole People* (1956), *The Amazing Colossal Man* (1957), *Attack of the Crab Monsters* (1958), *The Incredible Shrinking Man* (1957), *The Blob* (1958), *The Mummy* (1959), *The Tingler* (1959), and *I Was a Teenage Werewolf* (1957).

In contrast to the juvenile delinquent films, several movies by major studios and independents alike focused on innocent adolescent fun. Twentieth Century-Fox put singer Pat Boone in *Bernardine* and *April Love*, both in 1957, and used Fabian in *Hound Dog Man* (1959) and Tommy Sands in *Sing, Boy, Sing* (1958). Debbie Reynolds starred in *Tammy and the Bachelor* (1957) for Universal, which also put Sandra Dee and John Saxon in *The Restless Years* (1958). Columbia released *Because They're Young* (1960) and *Gidget* (1959), while *Where the Boys Are* was MGM's entry (1960).

Teens saw many of these films at drive-in theaters, which had open-air screens that people watched from their cars. Drive-ins first appeared in 1933, but not until after World War II did the idea really take off. For much of the 1950s, drive-in theaters provided a suburban and rural alternative to older downtown venues. In 1958 the number of outdoor screens reached forty-seven hundred, which accounted for nearly one-third of the nation's movie theaters, one-third of theater attendance, and one-fourth of all film rentals. The drawbacks of drive-ins—inferior sound and picture quality, the discomfort of sitting in a car, competing outdoor and traffic noise, and occasional bad weather—eventually eroded much of their adult audience. What remained was a younger crowd, either young parents who could avoid baby-sitting expenses or teens who used the distance from their parents and the semiprivacy afforded by cars to conduct physical encounters. The outdoor theaters increasingly relied on cheaply produced films by small independent studios with a youthful appeal.

Throughout the late 1950s the motion picture industry experienced considerable change. Foreign and domestic influences produced content that occasionally challenged prevailing social standards. The importance of independent producers increased, and the search for profits brought more films targeted at younger audiences. The movies continued to enjoy a national spotlight, a status that sports was just beginning to reach.

SPORT'S NEW ERA

If baseball could claim to be the national pastime before World War II, other professional sports reached national prominence only in the late 1950s. Until then they had largely been regional interests. Sports went through a transformation similar to that of other businesses during the twentieth century. As Randy Roberts notes, "Industrialization and the rise of mass culture transformed professional sports by forcing national perspectives on what had essentially been local affairs."[29] Local teams still commanded community loyalty, but as the decades passed more people were interested in the larger sporting picture. Measuring local teams against others and current players against those of the past demanded rationalization and professionalization and led to organized leagues in place of barnstorming teams.

The modern structure of the major professional sports leagues was not in place until the 1950s. Baseball's National and American Leagues had been operating cooperatively since 1903. The National Football League (NFL) began in 1920 but gained stability only in 1936. It absorbed three teams from the rival All-American Conference in 1949. The National Hockey League (NHL) organized in 1917, withstood competing leagues until 1926, and emerged from World War II with only six teams. The National Basketball Association (NBA) formed with the merger of two existing leagues in 1949. These leagues provided order to their respective sports with balanced schedules and uniform rules. As Roberts observes, "Professional sports functioned in a national marketplace, appealed to a nationwide clientele, and played to the expectations of a mass culture. Modern economic forces had rationalized competition."[30]

Televised sports progressed unevenly during the 1950s but ultimately had a significant impact. With television sets in so many American homes by mid-decade, sports team owners initially feared TV would draw customers from their games. Major League Baseball attendance did, in fact, drop by nearly one-third from 1948 to 1953, although its teams were making a combined twelve million dollars from selling rights to television by the end of the decade. College football suffered a significant decline as well, as more games appeared on home screens. The NFL, with a rule prohibiting TV coverage of home games, actually increased the league's attendance throughout the

1950s. Television coverage of sports in the 1950s was usually limited by technology and, unable to provide much more than "snowy" distant shots, usually failed to communicate the feel of live attendance. "Not until the 1960s did the technology develop to the point where the camera could transmit the excitement and flow of the action," notes historian Richard Davies. "The introduction of color, instant replay, deployment of multiple cameras, close-up pictures, hand-carried minicams, 'rifle' microphones to pick up on-field sounds, and better picture definition eventually opened up new vistas for sports telecasting."[31]

Football was more easily covered than baseball. The larger ball could be seen more clearly, and the action of a given play generally occurred within a smaller area. The key event that made pro football's national reputation was the NFL's 1958 championship game between the Baltimore Colts and the New York Giants. When Baltimore tied the game with a field goal with just seven seconds remaining, the contest went into sudden-death overtime, in which the first team to score would win. As thirty million people watched on television, quarterback Johnny Unitas led the Colts down the field for a touchdown, winning a thriller, 23–17.

The most popular sports featured repeat champions in the late 1950s. The Colts added another NFL crown in 1959, while on the collegiate level the University of Oklahoma won two national football titles, in 1955 and 1956. In basketball the University of San Francisco captured consecutive championships in those same years behind the play of Bill Russell. In the pro game the Boston Celtics began a run in 1957 of eleven titles in thirteen years. Bob Cousy's flashy but accurate passing and Russell's defensive shot-blocking prowess helped redefine the guard and center positions in the NBA. A third all-pro, Bill Sharman, made the Celtics almost unbeatable in the playoffs. Baseball's New York Yankees and the Brooklyn/Los Angeles Dodgers each took two World Series titles. In hockey, the Montreal Canadiens, led by Jean Beliveau, won every Stanley Cup from 1956 to 1960.

Not all players win championships, but some stand out individually. The NBA's outstanding players included Bob Pettit of St. Louis and Dolph Schayes of Syracuse, who passed George Mikan as the pro game's career scoring leader. The college game starred San Francisco's Russell, Wilt Chamberlain of Kansas, Elgin Baylor of Seattle, Cincinnati's Oscar Robertson, and West Virginia's Jerry West. The 1957 championship game matching North Carolina and

Kansas was among the decade's most thrilling. Carolina used a swarming zone defense to limit Kansas's Chamberlain and, even with leading scorer Lennie Rosenbluth fouled out, beat the Jayhawks in triple overtime and ended their season undefeated. In professional football, Baltimore's Unitas, Cleveland's Jim Brown, New York's Frank Gifford, San Francisco's Y. A. Tittle, and Philadelphia's Norm Van Brocklin were among those named player of the year by the major news wire services between 1955 and 1960. Baseball's Mickey Mantle of the New York Yankees and Ernie Banks of the Chicago Cubs each won two MVP awards. Mantle won the American League's Triple Crown in 1956, leading the league in batting average, home runs, and runs batted in. That same year the Yankees' Don Larsen pitched the only perfect game in World Series history against the Brooklyn Dodgers. In the NHL, Detroit's Gordie Howe won the most valuable player award three times between 1956 and 1960. Horse racing attracted more fans than any other sport in the mid-1950s, following the likes of Nashua, Bold Ruler, and Round Table.

The most important international athletic competition took place despite political concerns. The 1956 Summer Olympics in Melbourne, Australia, followed a major crisis over the Suez Canal and the Soviet Union's invasion of Hungary. A handful of countries boycotted the games for reasons related to those matters. In the competition itself, the United States trailed only the Soviet Union in total medals. Sprinter Bobby Morrow won three gold medals in track, and Pat McCormick took gold in both women's diving events. During that year's Winter Olympics in Cortina, Italy, the only U.S. gold medals went to individual figure skating champions Tenley Albright and Hayes Jenkins.

Behind the games, money helped shape the future of American athletics. The major sports leagues functioned essentially as economic monopolies. Major League Baseball operated with an antitrust exemption granted by the Supreme Court in 1922. The 1969 merger of the NFL and American Football League would also take place under a congressional antitrust exemption. Other devices reduced competition for player services and kept salaries low. The reserve clause first appeared in baseball contracts and was later widely used by the NHL. This gave individual teams exclusive rights to deal with a player for his entire career. By preventing players from negotiating with other teams without their permission, teams eliminated competition for the players' services. Football and basketball teams more often used the option clause in their player contracts. This gave teams exclusive rights to a player for one year after the contract expired. Both leagues, however, generally required new teams signing players to compensate the players' original teams, either in money or players, thereby undercutting an athlete's ability to negotiate. Player drafts also supported the sport monopolies. Designed in part to provide competitive balance, the annual drafts gave the worst teams the first chance to choose the best amateur players. They also gave the drafting teams exclusive rights to negotiate with those players. All the major sports used player drafts by 1953 except baseball, which followed in 1965. Although some professional athletes made large salaries, many had to take other jobs in their off-season to support themselves.

Cold War anxieties exacerbated antilabor attitudes and made organizing professional athletes against major sports monopolies almost impossible throughout the 1950s. Branch Rickey, who was responsible for the racial integration of the National League, even argued that opponents of baseball's antitrust exemption and reserve clause had "avowed Communist tendencies."[32] The threat of organizing in 1946 brought some financial improvement to baseball, but players ultimately rejected a union the following year.

The NFL argued in 1957 for a congressional antitrust exemption similar to that of Major League Baseball. Although Congress refused that request, it later offered valuable support. In 1961 the NFL signed a television contract with CBS, giving the network rights to all league games, with the league pooling TV income equally among all the teams rather than each team keeping money from its own market. This was similar to the deal the new AFL had signed the previous year with ABC. A federal judge ruled the agreement was an antitrust violation. Under pressure from professional sports leagues, however, Congress passed the Sports Broadcasting Act in 1961, which allowed leagues to sell national broadcast rights collectively. More than other professional sports organizations, the NFL worked cooperatively to build success for the entire league. This pooling agreement allowed teams in smaller cities to have the money to compete athletically and survive financially.

Players found ownership's solidarity difficult to counter. Although the NFL Player's Association formed in 1956 around issues of insurance and pensions, not until 1968 was it able to reach a collective bargaining agreement. Hockey players organized the NHL Player's Association in 1957 to get a share of the league's TV contract money. In return for a pension fund, the players dropped their antitrust suit against the league, but the union was quiet thereafter.

Professional basketball was not a stable enterprise in the 1950s, and owners did not share home gate receipts with visiting teams. The league's weak financial status and the racial diversity of the players worked against an effective union, though the National Basketball Players Association formed in 1961. The Major League Baseball Players Association organized in 1953, but it won only minimal financial gains and left intact the owners' restrictions on the players' ability to bargain.

Despite the lack of effective player organization, professional athletes in major sports improved their financial status during the 1950s. Their median income rose over 130 percent, nearly double that of other American workers. Income from television was the major reason for the increase. Owners made minor adjustments to provide for their athletes, but players generally accepted the restrictions that limited their negotiating ability. Things would change in the 1960s.

Women's athletic opportunities trailed far behind those for men in the 1950s. The view that most athletic endeavors were masculine precluded encouraging females from developing their sporting skills. Greater participation came with reassurances that female athletes could still be feminine. The Cold War provided the government with additional motivation to advocate athletics for women. Hoping to use the Olympic Games as a means of showcasing national achievement, in 1958 the United States Olympic Committee (USOC) formed the Women's Advisory Board to recommend measures to improve the performance of America's female Olympic athletes. A 1960 donation of a half-million dollars allowed the USOC to establish training institutes for women. These concentrated on elite track and field athletes.

African American athletes made gradual progress in achieving sporting success and social acceptance during the decade. Althea Gibson won two of tennis's most prestigious tournaments in 1957, Wimbledon and the U.S. Open. The NBA took a major step toward national popularity when Bill Russell in 1956 and Wilt Chamberlain in 1957 joined the league. The six-foot-ten-inch Russell and the seven-foot-one-inch Chamberlain engaged in one of the game's fiercest rivalries over the next several years. Although racial integration took place in professional sports during the 1950s, opportunities for black athletes remained limited. The fact that many of the nation's best golf courses and tennis facilities were owned by private clubs that frequently excluded racial and religious minorities put those sports beyond the reach of those

Bill Russell (6) and Wilt Chamberlain (13) (Library of Congress)

groups. Many team sports, basketball in particular, observed an unwritten rule to limit the number of blacks on each team.

College sports followed the professionals' evolution into big business. Unlike universities almost everywhere else in the world, American postsecondary institutions are a major source of sports activity. College athletic departments often operated under different expectations and rules than academic departments, usually enjoyed less stringent oversight by university administrators, and attracted special interest and considerations from alumni, government officials, and business interests, all of which invited corrupt practices. In order to produce the revenue necessary for an athletic department's operations, coaches needed to win, and to win they needed talented athletes.

The demands on athletes, especially in the major income-producing sports of football and men's basketball, sometimes isolated them from typical campus experiences. Many were also recruited solely for their athletic abilities, could not meet their university's educational standards, and had no hope of doing successful academic work. In order to maintain amateur status, college athletes received scholarships that paid their tuition, fees, and other college expenses, but not cash. Often, however, the desire for talent led some individuals to offer illegal and unethical inducements to athletes. Outstanding city players like New York's Connie Hawkins attended college at places like the University of Iowa because "they seemed like nice people, and they offered me the most money."[33] In schools with major sports programs, athletics often took priority over academics. Time demands on college athletes increased as more games were added to schedules and postseason tournaments proliferated and included more teams.

The increased attention on college sports continued to make them a lucrative target for gambling interests. Ten years after its 1951 scandal, college basketball once again suffered through a major public embarrassment. By the late 1950s rumors stimulated a second major investigation by New York district attorney Frank Hogan's office. In March 1961 the scandal broke with the arrest of two fixers. Just like in 1951, the investigation exposed only the tip of the problem, but authorities charged thirty-seven players from twenty-two colleges with point shaving. This affected schools from New York—including Ivy League Columbia—to Philadelphia and into the South. Hawkins was among those players who did not take money to shave points but whose associations with gamblers nevertheless resulted in their being banned from playing in the

NBA. Iowa also unceremoniously dropped him as a student. The gamblers, headed by former NBA player Jack Molinas, were convicted of fixing games between 1956 and 1961. By then public scandal had less shock value than in 1951, with recent investigations into TV quiz show fixing and payola to rock and roll disc jockeys.

RISE OF ROCK AND ROLL

As disruptive as other cultural changes were, perhaps none rivaled the social impact of rock and roll in the 1950s. The music's influence extended beyond stylistic change into the realm of much broader cultural transformation. Rock and roll touched on social fears that stretched from youth concerns to racial tensions and sexuality, with these three often grouped together. In their rebellion against adult authority, "teenagers felt empowered by rock 'n' roll to listen, dance, and scream in their own space."[34] Most obviously, however, rock and roll represented a dramatic shift in musical style away from the existing mainstream popular music.

The records that young people bought reflected a variety of artistic styles. Rock and roll's earliest stars included Fats Domino, who played boogie-woogie piano and sang a series of slower R&B melodies with a country-influenced vocal style. He enjoyed a series of R&B hits before crossing over to the pop charts in 1955 with "Ain't That a Shame" and reached number two with "Blueberry Hill" the following year. Fats was neither an innovator nor a charismatic performer, but this polite, smiling, soft-spoken man had a talent for songwriting, and his twenty-one Top 40 hits in the 1950s made him one of the decade's most consistently successful artists.

Chuck Berry is the epitome of early rock and roll. He was the style's first influential electric guitar player, whose blazing song introductions and solos set a standard copied by nearly everyone. Berry was also a clever lyricist who, even at age twenty-eight—when he first hit the pop chart, in 1955—had a gift for writing songs about school, cars, and young romance that connected with teenagers. His stage performances, highlighted by his famous "duckwalk," revealed a great showman. His vocal style blended blues with country. His Chicago recording company, Chess Records, gave New York DJ Alan Freed cowriting credits to Berry's first release, "Maybellene," to give the record extensive airplay, which helped it rise to number five. A string of nine Top 40 hits, including "Johnny B. Goode," followed during the 1950s.

"Little Richard" Penniman was rock's original wild man. Richard was a Georgia native evicted by his parents at age thirteen, and his early efforts at recording blues went nowhere. His 1955 recording for Specialty Records of a cleaned-up version of a lascivious tune called "Tutti Frutti" became a break-through hit, however, giving Richard his successful sound. His uninhibited style featured frantic, pounding piano playing; shouted lyrics with whooping falsetto; a high pompadour hairstyle; and facial makeup. For the next two years Little Richard rocked with the best of them, but his outrageous manner threatened suburban parents.

Elvis Presley was more influential in spreading the new music than any other performer. The Mississippi-born Presley moved to Memphis at age thir-teen, and he eventually attracted the attention of Sam Phillips, owner of Sun Records. Phillips had recorded African American blues singers like Howlin' Wolf and B. B. King before they moved on to Chicago in the early 1950s. Elvis's earliest recordings in 1954 blended musical styles, blurring boundaries with songs that contained country-flavored energy and a big beat. The sound became known as "rockabilly." With youthful good looks, an expressive voice, and exuberant live shows that often stimulated teenage girls to rush the stage, Presley developed a loyal following touring the South, became a regular on the popular "Louisiana Hayride" radio program, and scored some regional hit records. His last Sun records in 1955 reached the top ten on *Billboard*'s coun-try charts.

Presley's appeal, however, went far beyond the traditional country audi-ence. When Sam Phillips sold Presley's contract to RCA Victor in 1955, Elvis carried rock and roll to a massive audience. His post-Sun recordings were more polished and mainstream, losing much of their rockabilly feel while re-taining the energy and charisma. His first RCA release, "Heartbreak Hotel" (1956) placed in the top five of the pop, R&B, and country charts, and "Don't Be Cruel" (1956) became the first of three Presley records to hit number one on all three lists. He dominated the record charts in the second half of the decade, with more hits than any other artist regardless of musical style. He also starred in over thirty movies during his career.

As a white artist, Presley was a more acceptable conveyor of a sound that had its critics, but even race did not deflect everything. His uninhibited movements on stage persuaded many adults that he and his music were not appropriate for their children. One observer recalls that Presley's appearance on television could turn preteens "shell-shocked straight into puberty overnight."[35] Both he and his music would be widely attacked as part of the larger assault on rock and roll.

Elvis's first recordings helped to define the rockabilly style, and Sun Records remained its most important home. The country influence was greater in this style than in the music of black artists like Little Richard and Chuck Berry. Rockabilly was performed primarily by whites, and featured twangy guitars and a stand-up bass that, when played by snapping the strings in a "slap-back" style, provided the rhythm instead of drums. This high-energy music also incorporated uninhibited vocals and the use of echo for both vocals and instruments. Bill Haley's 1953 to 1956 records mark the emergence of rockabilly, but Presley's more unrefined sound attracted even greater attention.

Louisiana-born Jerry Lee Lewis was the rockabilly version of Little Richard. His assaults on the piano were even more aggressive than Richard's, and his vocals and lyrics were only slightly tamer. In 1957 and 1958 three of his records hit the top ten on *Billboard*'s country, R&B, and pop charts. Lewis's ego and outrageous style were vividly displayed on a spring 1958 rock and roll tour organized by Alan Freed. Angered that Chuck Berry was being allowed to close the show, Lewis whipped the crowd into a frenzy during his set and broke into "Great Balls of Fire." In the middle of the song he drenched the piano with gasoline and set it on fire, finished playing, and walked offstage to tell Berry, "Follow that."[36]

Tight country-styled vocal harmony paired with rock and roll rhythm characterized the Everly Brothers. Their songs projected a naively youthful view of love. Most of their hits were ballads, but even their faster songs had a smoother sound than most rockabilly. They recorded twelve Top 40 records in the 1950s, and their harmonies influenced numerous artists who followed.

Buddy Holly's legacy was far greater than his three top-ten records would indicate. The instrumental lineup of Holly's band, the Crickets—two guitars, bass, and drums—became the standard for rock and roll bands. Other singers covered this talented songwriter's music and tried to mimic his trademark vocal "hiccups." The Lubbock, Texas, native used the studio creatively, using multitracking and other recording methods effectively. Several of his best songs, such as "That'll Be the Day," were rockabilly, but his records ranged from country twang to orchestral violins.

As rock and roll continued to evolve, the original rockabilly sound lost its commercial appeal. Many of its practitioners moved toward a smoother pop sound or toward country music, and by 1958 it had almost disappeared from the charts. The music of Carl Perkins—whose "Blue Suede Shoes" became a rock and roll standard—Billy Lee Riley, Gene Vincent, Eddie Cochran, Johnny Burnette, and others still stands as some of the wildest and most exciting music of the rock era.

Most early styles of rock and roll originated from southern musical styles, but in the late 1950s northern cities produced melodic vocal groups singing what was then referred to as either rock and roll or rhythm and blues but was later called "doo-wop." The term came from the frequent use of nonsense syllables sung by background singers. Doo-wop derived from street corner singing, and most records in this style used few supporting instruments or none at all. Both the soft, slow ballads and the up-tempo melodies featured lyrics of idealized adolescent love, often sung by teenagers themselves. The faster songs retained the rock and roll rhythm and added the emotional vocal flourishes of gospel singing. The youthfulness of the singers, sweetness of the lyrics, and the anonymity of the often unpolished and similar sounds of the groups reduced public resistance to African American artists, who were the most successful purveyors of this style. In addition to black groups like Frankie Lymon and the Teenagers, however, white groups such as Dion and the Belmonts and racially integrated groups like the Dell-Vikings recorded highly successful songs. Three groups, the Platters, the Coasters, and the Drifters, achieved the most consistent success with this style, with the Platters sending four songs to number one on the pop charts, the first time with "The Great Pretender." The Coasters sang a number of clever songs written and produced by Jerry Lieber and Mike Stoller, one of rock and roll's greatest hit-making teams. Songs like "Yakety Yak" told humorous stories of generational conflict, often featuring spoken bass lines and rousing saxophone solos.

For the increasingly youthful record buyers, the juvenile artists and innocent lyrics of most doo-wop music were especially appealing. Other styles of rock and roll would target younger teens as well. Whoever they listened to, adolescents in the 1950s found personal connections in rock and roll music. "I don't know how we could have made it," remembered Ellen Sander, ". . . without our trusty companions: transistor radios tuned to the rock and roll in the air and a stack of 45s, as intimate as a diary."[37] Adult listeners would have to look harder but could still find more mature and sexually oriented records, even after public disapproval reversed that trend. Rock and roll would continue this dual approach to love, offering both innocence and sexual desire in the following decades.

Regional differences in music further eroded in the face of the nationally televised *American Bandstand*, hosted by Dick Clark and originating from Philadelphia. The show began as one of several local TV dance music shows, but when it became a national network program in August 1957 it helped define a common musical, dance, and clothing style among teenagers. Clark featured numerous performers whose youthful good looks, nonthreatening image, and pop-oriented records made rock and roll tamer and more uniform. Sometimes chosen more for their physical attractiveness and clean image than their musical abilities, these singers were known collectively as "teen idols."

The increased presence of rock and roll music had noticeably influenced the record business by the late 1950s. Record sales in the first five years of the rock and roll era almost tripled, reaching over six hundred million dollars by 1959. Much of that money went to independent labels, as the six major companies' share of the top ten dropped from 80 percent in 1955 to one-third at decade's end. According to music scholar Charlie Gillette, about 43 percent of the top-ten hits during the later 1950s were rock and roll songs. Racial barriers eroded as white artists crossed over into the R&B charts and blacks appeared on the pop charts. In 1957 recordings by black artists constituted 31 percent of *Billboard*'s top-ten pop hits, while recordings by whites accounted for 52 percent of 1958's R&B hits. Women, however, found the new style less beneficial. The share of top singles by female artists fell from one-third in 1954 to only 8 percent in 1958.[38] Portable transistor radios and car radios, both available in the early 1950s, gave the new sound and its young listeners a great deal of mobility. The affluence of a rapidly growing teenage population in the later 1950s made teens a welcome target for consumer products of all types.

For a variety of reasons rock and roll music faced serious opposition. The fact that rock's rhythmic beat came from predominantly African American musical styles made it a target of white racists. One leader of the White Citizens Councils of Alabama claimed, "The basic, heavy-beat music of Negroes . . . appeals to the base in man, brings out animalism and vulgarity."[39] Whites in both North and South were concerned with the implications of racially integrated social events like concerts. Undeniably rock and roll encouraged racial integration and increased mainstream recognition and economic opportunity for blacks. One writer points out a more fundamental transformation, claiming, "The eruption of rock 'n' roll entailed a profound shift in cultural values on the part of mainstream youth, a shift away from Euro-American sensibilities and toward African-American ones."[40]

Other adults, regardless of race, disapproved of the music's sexuality. Author Vance Packard warned that rock and roll stimulated "the animal instinct in modern teenagers," while one New York journalist found Elvis Presley's stage movements "suggestive and vulgar, tinged with the kind of animalism that should be confined to dives and bordellos."[41] Martin Luther King Jr. believed rock and roll "often plunges men's minds into degrading and immoral depths."[42] Critics created the term "leerics" to describe the often thinly disguised sexual innuendo.[43] The allure, and the anxiety, of the music's physical impact were real. Writer Jeff Greenfield credits rock and roll with causing "the first tremors along the Generational Fault." As the initial step toward a counterculture, "rock and roll was elemental, savage, dripping with sex; it was just as our parents feared."[44]

If social concerns drove much of this criticism, business interests accounted for other assaults on rock and roll. Having lost a significant share of the record market, the major labels struck back in a variety of ways. Initially they had their own singers record cover versions of potential hits, almost invariably sweetening the melody, eliminating possibly offensive lyrics, and polishing the vocals to appeal to a pop audience. Pop music executives and performers, suffering because of the public's changing musical tastes in the late 1950s, also attacked rock and roll. Frank Sinatra linked the music to youth crime, calling rock and roll "the martial music of every sideburned delinquent on the face of the earth."[45] Columbia Records executive Mitch Miller claimed that "much of the juvenile stuff pumped over the airwaves these days hardly qualifies as music," while Nat King Cole complained, "It doesn't take talent to get to the top today; it takes connections."[46]

When the National Academy of Recording Arts and Sciences presented the first Grammy Awards in May 1959, the music industry establishment failed to recognize the contributions of rock and roll. *Variety* called the nominations "a demonstrative brushoff to the prevailing trend in the pop field . . . rock 'n' roll."[47]

For all of these reasons and more, rock and roll became an issue of confrontation. Historian Glenn Altschuler believes that the music "deepened the divide between the generations" and "kept many Americans in the 1950s off balance, on guard, and uncertain about their families and the future of their country."[48] Black adults as well as white worried about the new music's ability to "release economic and emotional inhibitions and undermine the authority of the family, the church, and the state."[49] Those who believed rock and roll was connected with immorality and violence tried to eliminate the music. Theater owners occasionally ran the movie *Blackboard Jungle* without the opening and closing sound track, and some communities prohibited rock and roll concerts.

Adults often defended rock and roll even while attempting to polish its rough edges. The trend in R&B music after 1954 was toward a smoother vocal style and less offensive lyrics to attract younger record buyers less interested in adult sexuality. The profusion of teen-oriented rock and roll movies in the 1950s was designed to overcome the music's negative stereotypes, depicting rock and roll as misunderstood and harmless. The emphasis on "teen idols" by major companies, aided by the publicity of Dick Clark and others, was part of the effort to make rock and roll appear safe to adults even as it appealed almost exclusively to teenagers and preteens. The success of sanitized rock and roll was evident in the enormous popularity of artists such as Pat Boone.

Critics lamenting the nation's growing embrace of rock and roll usually blamed either the public's bad taste or disc jockeys who imposed inferior music on their listeners. Even with the spread of the Top 40 format, DJs did most of the record selection for radio shows throughout the decade and became a target of rock and roll's opponents. The volume of new releases, between 50 and 250 each week at the end of the decade, meant the competition for airplay was intense, and paying disc jockeys to promote their records was common practice for recording labels and record distributors. Financial inducements to musical performers or radio programmers, known as "payola," had been common in the music business for decades and, while being ethically questionable, were not illegal. Despite payola's long history, in the second half of the 1950s critics frequently blamed the practice on independent labels' efforts to have rock and roll records played, implying that the "inferior" music would never get played without bribery. In actuality, DJs had to play songs their audiences wanted to hear to keep their ratings.

Contributing significantly to this growing debate was a struggle between competing publishing agencies. Most established pop music writers were affiliated with the American Society of Composers, Authors and Publishers (ASCAP), which collected their royalties. A newer publishing agency, Broadcast Music Incorporated (BMI), developed in reaction to an ASCAP strike in 1941 and represented many younger songwriters, including rock and roll composers. During the 1950s ASCAP completely lost its dominance of the record charts to BMI because of changing musical tastes. The older pop-oriented AS-CAP tried to pressure radio stations to stop playing BMI songs, and when that proved unsuccessful it argued that rock and roll's popularity derived from monopolistic practices or payola.

Television's quiz show scandals gave rock and roll's critics a new opportunity for attack. Amid accusations and rumors, government bodies opened investigations of the practice of payola as part of their "concern" over teenagers being exposed to "bad" music. Two probes began in November 1959, one by New York district attorney Frank Hogan and the other by the House of Representatives' Special Subcommittee on Legislative Oversight, the same body that had launched the quiz show probe. What began as a broader investigation quickly narrowed to the politically safe targets of rock and roll music, small independent labels, and disc jockeys. A *Life* magazine article that month carried the popular fantasy that payola was a recent phenomenon started by small labels pushing bad music. Jack Gould of the *New York Times*, however, noted that disc jockeys represented a small target when it came to national corruption and that the payola attacks came from "many of the country's foremost composers . . . who have been dismayed to witness the dominance of rock 'n' roll on the nation's airwaves."[50] *Billboard* saw "frustrated music men—out of step with current song and recording trends" who "blame their plight on rock and roll and construe that rock and roll is an outgrowth of payola. The cancer of payola cannot be pinned on rock and roll."[51]

Even though payola was not a federal crime, and not a crime in most states, under FCC threats of losing their licenses several radio stations fired DJs they believed had taken payola. Whether they defined payola as direct cash payments or financial interests in music-related businesses that might be a conflict of interest, stations fought to clear themselves of suspicion and insulate themselves from government recrimination. Although leading DJs in several major cities either demanded or accepted gifts from record companies and distributors, the most visible subjects of the investigations were Alan Freed and Dick Clark. Clark represented a more acceptable brand of rock and roll. He had financial ties with several music publishers and record labels, as well as distribution and production companies, a talent agency, and a record-pressing plant. Forced to choose between his broadcasting career and his music investments, Clark sold his interests and kept his job at ABC. The network believed the temptation of pushing a record produced by one of his companies, or featuring a song owned by another, represented a blatant conflict of interest. Clark persuaded his employer and the congressional investigators that he had not accepted money to play specific records.

Alan Freed did not fare as well. He also denied taking money up front to promote songs but admitted to accepting gifts from grateful companies whose records and artists he had played. Freed was not an establishment man. He was more closely identified with black culture and a rebellious attitude. In late November Freed lost his radio job at WABC for refusing to sign a statement that he had never taken money to promote records, and also his job at WNEW-TV, despite signing a similar statement for them. Freed had accepted undeserved credit, and royalties, as cowriter of several hit songs, a reasonably common practice to ensure airplay. Stations tried to prevent payola by requiring their DJs to divest themselves of related investments, as Clark had done, or took measures to curtail or monitor the records they played. *Variety* magazine noted that radio stations, under government pressure, were making a switch to more "melodic" and "pro caliber" music.[52]

The Federal Trade Commission (FTC) also investigated payola accusations. In early December it charged three record companies and six distributors with deceiving the public and restricting competition through payola and ordered them to cease and desist, under penalty of federal lawsuits. The FTC, however, had no jurisdiction over DJs. The FTC's investigation continued during 1960, and by August of that year it had charged over one hundred companies with payola. Hogan's investigation in New York resulted in charges of commercial bribery against eight station workers, five of them DJs, some of whom received small fines and suspended jail sentences, but made no charges against the companies making the payments.

The payola scandal was clearly directed toward eroding or ending rock and roll's increasing share of the popular music market. Rock and roll's critics believed that ending payola would mean rock's demise. In the middle of the investigations, in fact, some stations dropped their rock and roll format or played fewer rock and roll records. *Down Beat* spoke for several music magazines in January 1960 when it proclaimed: "Rock and roll at last is identified with the rotten practice that helped create it and feed it sustenance—payola. Today bad music squats in the dock, accused."[53] The House subcommittee apparently agreed. As its hearings continued in 1960, Representative John Moss (D-CA) claimed, "I don't know of any time in our history when we had comparably bad, uniformly bad music."[54] Committee member Peter Mack Jr. (D-IL) asked one witness, "Don't you think that somebody's going to have to do something—the Governments or the networks—if we are to stop the trash that comes over the airwaves?"[55] Testimony revealed the existence of payola, hardly a surprise, with the subcommittee eventually claiming to have uncovered payola given to over two hundred DJs in forty-two cities. Oren Harris, chair of the House subcommittee, commented on the cultural implications of his investigation: "The extent to which questionable business practices in the popular music and broadcast industries result in the suppression of genuine talent and in foisting upon the public remunerative but mediocre music, has large implications for the cultural future of America."[56] Harris, however, seemed to be protecting Dick Clark, delaying Clark's testimony and attempting to suppress any evidence that involved him. Despite Clark's image, his association with rock and roll brought some criticism, but, by and large, as author Kerry Segrave notes, "If rock couldn't be killed, better to have it controlled and run by the likes of Clark than by the likes of Freed."[57]

The Harris report in the summer of 1960 preceded proposed House legislation designed to limit payola, which some subcommittee members criticized as too weak. The Senate weakened the legislation even further. The final bill did not make payola a federal crime. It merely required DJs to publicly announce their receipt of financial considerations for playing certain records. The whole enterprise was a pathetic political and cultural attack resulting in an impotent law. Lawmakers, satisfied that they had scored political points and saved America, moved on while payola continued to flourish underground.

By the end of the 1950s the initial burst of rock and roll music was nearly over. Many of the biggest and most creative early stars were in decline for various reasons. Little Richard gave up rock and roll for the ministry in late 1957. That same year twenty-two-year-old Jerry Lee Lewis married his thirteen-year-old third cousin—his third wife—and suffered public disapproval that crippled his career. Elvis Presley was drafted into the army from 1958 to 1960. Buddy Holly died in a February 1959 plane crash that also took the lives of Ritchie Valens and J. P. "Big Bopper" Richardson. Later that year the government indicted—and later imprisoned—Chuck Berry on questionable charges of violating the Mann Act, which banned the transportation of women across state lines for immoral purposes. Although rock and roll music entered the new decade in some distress, it would endure.

For all their success and achievement, the nation's leading forms of popular culture faced serious problems at the start of a new decade. The movies' preliminary assaults on middle-class standards of decency and the embarrassment caused by legal and ethical scandals in television, sports, and music threatened to undermine the popularity of each of these enterprises. During the 1960s, however, all would survive and thrive, either financially or creatively or both.

Behind many of the decade's trends stood the postwar youth culture. Rock and roll music would not have surfaced without teenage record buyers. Hollywood studios recognized the growing potential of income from younger audiences and shaped their output accordingly. Popular culture would increasingly be influenced by the demands, both real and perceived, of the baby boomer generation. As it spread, the youth culture's rebellion against adult authority and norms raised social anxieties.

The powerful and successful studio system was in sharp decline by the mid-1950s. Rocked by anticommunist investigations and labor problems, separated from guaranteed markets by the *Paramount* decision, hurt by migration to the suburbs and television, the motion picture industry faced serious financial problems. Hollywood turned out fewer pictures, which required reducing overhead costs by limiting the number of staff people under contract. Creative personnel were anxious about the loss of job security but enjoyed the freedom to negotiate deals for individual projects.[58] Troubles for the major studios meant more opportunities for independent filmmakers. Although still somewhat limited, film content expanded because of foreign influences and a greater emphasis on youth audiences and their problems.

Television linked up with Hollywood as the movie industry provided filmed programming for TV. The networks gained increased control of their

own product as they shifted away from accepting programs created by advertisers and toward selling commercial time on their own shows. If television
generally defended the conservative political and social status quo and became
more commercialized during the 1950s, its golden age of live programs
stretched through the end of the decade. Protecting news coverage from easy
manipulation, making entertainment more reflective of national diversity,
and overcoming the ethical lapses of quiz show scandals remained challenges
into the 1960s.

Sports would increasingly come to rely on television for its prosperity.
Growing to national proportions, professional leagues operated as economic
monopolies yet faced financial insecurities. The seeds of labor problems grew
slowly but would change the face of the game in the near future. Significant
barriers to equal participation for women and minorities remained, even as
progress became visible.

Rock and roll established itself as a major trend, but the public debated
whether or not it would last. Energized by regional and marginalized segments of the population, the new musical style retreated with the decline of
its first generation of stars and attacks from established interests. Northern
and urban sounds kept rock and roll exciting even as regional differences
faded, creating a tamer and more homogenized version. It seemed as if the
country was catching its breath before pressing on to new challenges.

NOTES

1. Paddy Chayefsky, quoted in Ronald Davis, *Celluloid Mirrors: Hollywood and
American Society since 1945* (Fort Worth, TX: Harcourt Brace, 1997), 179.

2. Shaun Considine, *Mad As Hell: The Life and Work of Paddy Chayefsky* (New York:
Random House, 1994), 161.

3. Rod Serling, quoted in "The Weary Young Man," *Newsweek*, September 28,
1959, 82.

4. Harry Castleman and Walter J. Podrazik, *Watching TV: Four Decades of American
Television* (New York: McGraw-Hill, 1982), 123.

5. Erik Barnouw, *Tube of Plenty: The Evolution of American Television*, 2nd rev. ed.
(New York: Oxford University Press, 1990), 214.

6. Sylvester "Pat" Weaver, quoted in William Boddy, *Fifties Television: The Industry and Its Critics* (Urbana: University of Illinois Press, 1990), 159.

7. Leo Bogart, *The Age of Television: A Study of Viewing Habits and the Impact of Television on American Life*, 3rd ed. (New York: Frederick Ungar, 1972), 1.

8. Keisha Hoerrner, "The Forgotten Battles," *Web Journal of Mass Communication Research* 2 (June 1999), at www.scripps.ohiou.edu/wjmcr/vol02/2-3a-B.htm (accessed May 14, 2002).

9. Nat "King" Cole, quoted in Daniel Mark Epstein, *Nat King Cole* (New York: Farrar, Straus and Giroux, 1999), 276.

10. Barnouw, *Tube of Plenty*, 169.

11. Kathleen Hall Jamieson, *Packaging the Presidency: A History and Criticism of Presidential Campaign Advertising*, 3rd ed. (New York: Oxford University Press, 1996), 95.

12. "Fort Knox or Bust," *Time*, August 22, 1955, 47.

13. "Are TV Quiz Shows Fixed?" *Look*, August 20, 1957, 46.

14. "The Wizard of Quiz," *Time*, February 11, 1957, 44.

15. Charles Van Doren, quoted in William M. Blair, "Van Doren Admits Lying, Says TV Quiz Was Fixed; Loses His Columbia Post," *New York Times*, November 3, 1959, 1.

16. Hans Morgenthau, quoted in Walter Karp, "The Quiz-Show Scandal," *American Heritage*, May/June 1989, 88.

17. John Steinbeck, quoted in David Halberstam, *The Fifties* (New York: Villard Books, 1993), 665.

18. Halberstam, *The Fifties*, 665.

19. Davis, *Celluloid Mirrors*, 21; Paul Monaco, *The Sixties, 1960–1969*, vol. 8 of *History of the American Cinema*, ed. Charles Harpole (New York: Scribner, 2001), 24. Janet Wasko, *Movies and Money: Financing the American Film Industry* (Norwood, NJ: Ablex, 1982), 107, indicates 65 percent of feature films in 1959 came from 165 independent producers.

20. Boddy, *Fifties Television*, 141.

21. Robert Sklar, *Movie-Made America: A Cultural History of American Movies*, rev. ed. (New York: Vintage, 1994), 174.

22. Charles Champlin, *The Movies Grow Up: 1940–1980* (Chicago: Swallow/Athens: Ohio University Press, 1981), 38.

23. John Victor-Smith, quoted in "Film Editors Forum," *Film Comment*, March/April 1977, 25.

24. Gerald Mast and Bruce F. Kawin, *A Short History of the Movies*, 5th ed. (New York: Macmillan, 1992), 318.

25. Mast and Kawin, *Short History*, 373.

26. James Miller, *Flowers in the Dustbin: The Rise of Rock and Roll, 1947–1977* (New York: Fireside, 1999), 88.

27. Thomas Doherty, *Teenagers and Teenpics: The Juvenilization of American Movies in the 1950s* (Boston: Unwin Hyman, 1988), 74.

28. Doherty, *Teenagers and Teenpics*, 157.

29. Randy Roberts, *Winning Is the Only Thing: Sports in America since 1945* (Baltimore: Johns Hopkins University Press, 1989), 49.

30. Roberts, *Winning*, 52.

31. Richard O. Davies, *America's Obsession: Sports and Society since 1945* (Fort Worth, TX: Harcourt Brace, 1994), 74.

32. Branch Rickey, quoted in Roberts, *Winning*, 58.

33. Connie Hawkins, quoted in David Wolf, *Foul! The Connie Hawkins Story* (New York: Holt, Rinehart and Winston, 1972), 50.

34. Glenn C. Altschuler, *All Shook Up: How Rock 'n' Roll Changed America* (New York: Oxford University Press, 2003), 108.

35. Bruce Pollock, *Hipper Than Our Kids: A Rock and Roll Journal of the Baby Boom Generation* (New York: Schirmer Books, 1993), 2.

36. Nick Tosches, *Hellfire* (New York: Grove, 1982), 145–46.

37. Ellen Sander, *Trips: Rock Life in the Sixties* (New York: Scribner, 1973), 1.

38. Charlie Gillette, *The Sound of the City: The Rise of Rock and Roll*, rev. ed. (New York: Pantheon, 1983), 39–40, 64, 190; Steve Chapple and Reebee Garofalo, *Rock 'n' Roll Is Here to Pay: The History and Politics of the Music Industry* (Chicago: Nelson-Hall, 1977), 272.

39. "White Council vs. Rock and Roll," *Newsweek*, April 23, 1956, 32.

40. Reebee Garofalo, *Rockin' Out: Popular Music in the USA*, 2nd ed. (Upper Saddle River, NJ: Prentice Hall, 2002), 6–7.

41. Vance Packard, quoted in David P. Szatmary, *Rockin' in Time: A Social History of Rock-and-Roll*, 3rd. ed. (Upper Saddle River, NJ: Prentice Hall, 1996), 22; Peter Guralnick, *Last Train to Memphis: The Rise of Elvis Presley* (Boston: Little, Brown, 1994), 285.

42. Martin Luther King Jr., quoted in Brian Ward, *Just My Soul Responding: Rhythm and Blues, Black Consciousness, and Race Relations* (Berkeley: University of California Press, 1998), 189.

43. Linda Martin and Kerry Segrave, *Anti-Rock: The Opposition to Rock 'n' Roll* (Hamden, CT: Archon Books, 1988), 19.

44. Jeff Greenfield, *No Peace, No Place: Excavations along the Generational Fault* (Garden City, NY: Doubleday, 1973), 29.

45. Frank Sinatra, quoted in Szatmary, *Rockin' in Time*, 23.

46. Mitch Miller, quoted in "Deejay's Responsibility," *Variety*, March 12, 1958, 53; Nat King Cole, quoted in "Rackets Infest Music Industry, Says Nat Cole," *Variety*, March 25, 1959, 57.

47. "Disk 'Oscars' Brush Off R 'n' R," *Variety*, March 18, 1959, 77.

48. Altschuler, *All Shook Up*, 34.

49. Altschuler, *All Shook Up*, 45.

50. Kerry Segrave, *Payola in the Music Industry: A History, 1880–1991* (Jefferson, NC: McFarland, 1994), 104; Jack Gould, "TV: Assessing Effects of Life under the Table," *New York Times*, November 20, 1959, 63.

51. Segrave, *Payola*, 105.

52. "The No-Payola Sound of Music," *Variety*, December 2, 1959, 1.

53. John Tynan, "A Clean Fresh Wind," *Down Beat*, January 7, 1960, 17.

54. John Moss, quoted in Peter Bunzel, "Music Biz Goes Round and Round: It Comes Out Clarkola," *Life*, May 16, 1960, 120.

55. Peter Mack Jr., quoted in Anthony Lewis, "House Unit Plans Payola Remedies," *New York Times*, May 4, 1960, 34.

56. Oren Harris, quoted in "Rep. Harris Wants Answers on Link of Payola and Radio's 'Juke' Sound," *Variety*, April 13, 1960, 47.

57. Segrave, *Payola*, 143.

58. Davis, *Celluloid Mirrors*, 23–24.

3

New Frontiers: 1960 to 1968

President John Kennedy declared during his January 1961 inaugural address, "The torch has been passed to a new generation." If the new president did much to spark a generation's political activism, he also observed the beginning of fundamental cultural change. Satellites could now relay broadcast signals that allowed live television transmission. The use of technology also led to revolutionary TV coverage of sporting events. The games that television covered looked increasingly different as more racial barriers cracked under the strain of civil rights activism. This era of social change nourished the emergence of the music industry's most successful black-owned company and the careers of numerous African American singers, songwriters, and record producers. The movies changed both in their appearance and in their content. The 1960s were under way.

An important feature of this new era was the international nature of popular culture. For the United States, few recent cultural events came as suddenly and with such success as music's "British invasion." The breakthrough to the American music charts of the Beatles in early 1964 led a flood of other British artists who stood at the forefront of rock and roll popularity for years and even decades. As much as any other event, the British invasion underscored the mutual connection and influence of U.S. and foreign popular culture. This was evident not only in music but also in films, television, and athletic competition.

MOTION PICTURE REVIVAL

The early 1960s found Hollywood on the defensive. The postwar decline in movie attendance continued, competition from other leisure pursuits increased, and some disastrous big-budget failures occurred; these factors combined to shake the major studios. Attendance at the movies, which stood at ninety million people per week in 1946, had fallen to forty million per week in 1960 and would fall further, to only twenty million per week, by 1970. The waning interest reflected not only the intense competition from television but also demographic and social changes in postwar America. The internal migration away from the cities and toward outlying suburbs was critical. As marriage rates increased and the baby boom ensued, suburban life offered affordable space. The vast majority of America's metropolitan growth in the 1960s took place in the suburbs. The expanding economy also offered more leisure time options, with swimming pools, tennis courts, bowling alleys, golf courses, and other sports venues added to an expanding park system. Unless they moved into new areas quickly, before land costs became prohibitive, traditional-style movie houses rarely followed the population. Theaters remaining in downtown areas often existed in economically declining neighborhoods with little commercial appeal after work hours. Owners of many of the large urban movie palaces sold them or converted them to more profitable uses.

Traditionally, Hollywood distributed films in a gradually expanding pattern. Major releases would open in the largest cities at a limited number of first-run theaters. After a set number of weeks the movies shifted to second-run and then third-run theaters and filtered into smaller towns across the country. With this leisurely release strategy, movie reviews and word of mouth could help build an audience for pictures that started slowly. Most advertising went to attract crowds to the small number of first-run theaters, and the studio's money from exhibitors came in gradually over a lengthy period of time. The changing nature of theater ownership would eventually lead the studios to develop a new distribution system to enhance their profits.

The technological innovations of the 1950s represented attempts to stem the loss of the motion picture audience. These proved to be unsuccessful stop-gap measures, however. As movie attendance dwindled, studios produced fewer films. Three-fourths of Hollywood movies lost money in 1961. In 1963 United States–produced feature films reached a postwar low of only 143. In its struggle to find solutions, the American cinema took an increasingly international perspective. The motion picture industries of other nations had gradually made an impression on the United States, but the full impact of this foreign influence became evident only in the 1960s.

Foreign films influenced American tastes, but domestic social changes played an equally important role in transforming U.S. motion pictures in both content and style. Many imports initially appeared in the United States as art films and played to relatively small crowds. The typical moviegoer was just as likely to be aware of other changes on the movie screens. American society was becoming more tolerant toward a greater variety of human experiences, and evolving social beliefs permitted films to handle adult sexuality more extensively and openly. Film historian Paul Monaco called the 1960s "the decade that would witness the most extensive shift in film content in the history of the American motion picture."[1]

The erosion of self-imposed and social restraints on motion picture content that began in the 1950s continued with even greater speed in the 1960s. With trends in film content clearly shifting, in 1961 Eric Johnston, head of the MPAA, suggested replacing the production code seal with a rating system. Theater owners opposed the move largely because the burden of enforcement would fall on them. The existing production code was already outdated by the early 1960s, but Hollywood studios feared pushing the limits because local censorship laws might limit the distribution of their films. Change was coming, however. The film *Splendor in the Grass* (1961) included an extramarital affair conducted without guilt. The production code guidelines further disintegrated when *Tom Jones*, a salacious British film, took Hollywood's picture of the year honors in 1963. *The Pawnbroker* (1965) received the seal of approval despite nudity and prostitution. The following year *Who's Afraid of Virginia Woolf?* smashed existing standards for acceptable language, but even this passed inspection by the National Catholic Office of Motion Pictures.

The effectiveness of the anticommunist blacklist also deteriorated during the new decade. Kirk Douglas openly credited Dalton Trumbo, one of the blacklisted Hollywood Ten, as screenwriter for *Spartacus* (1960), a major picture about a slave revolt against imperial Rome. The American Legion picketed the film over Trumbo's involvement. With President Kennedy among those ignoring the picket lines, the movie achieved critical and financial success. This dealt a severe blow to groups trying to impose political orthodoxy on Hollywood.

The production code finally fell despite continued objections from exhibitors. The Supreme Court closed down most remaining morality watchdogs
with its 1966 decisions making it difficult to enforce obscenity codes; the court
ruled that prior censorship violated constitutional protections. Court rulings
in 1968, however, allowed communities to set local standards. That same year
MPAA president Jack Valenti established a new rating system for films: G for
general audiences; M for mature; R for restricted, no one under age seventeen
admitted without a parent or guardian; and X, no one under age eighteen admitted. This provided the public with a guideline for film content and allowed
filmmakers greater flexibility. Producers who included overt sexuality or violence, however, recognized they were limiting their potential audience.

Foreign influence on the American movie industry was not limited to style
and content. Film companies in the United States increasingly looked beyond
America's borders for profits. Starting in the late 1950s the Hollywood studios
not only increased their marketing to foreign outlets but moved a significant
portion of their production abroad as well, hoping to save money through
cheaper labor, lower production costs, and foreign tax breaks. This was part of
Hollywood's larger strategy of shifting from production and exhibition to financing and marketing motion pictures. Companies saved money by slashing
contract employees from their budgets. Worker conflicts naturally resulted,
but congressional threats and labor pressure failed to stop Hollywood's use of
foreign production sites.

After the *Paramount* decision drove the major studios out of exhibition,
film distribution became more of a concern and a more lucrative aspect of
their business. With RKO having closed in 1958, the major studios in 1960
consisted of Paramount, MGM, Warner Bros, Twentieth Century-Fox, United
Artists, Columbia, and Universal. Beginning in 1958, American films returned
more income from foreign distribution than from domestic sources. This
trend continued throughout the 1960s. Although the majors earned more
money in 1961 than in any year since 1948, half of that came from foreign
sources. Some of this income derived from the expansion of television. In the
early 1960s the number of television sets outside the United States exceeded
the number in the United States for the first time, and people watching those
sets wanted to see American movies.

European governments tried to safeguard their national film industries.
France, Great Britain, and Italy were especially protective, usually through var-

ious subsidies. Some of this money was available to U.S. companies that shot their films in those countries. Americans also invested in foreign film companies, and especially in Britain, some of the movies were so heavily financed or influenced that the resulting pictures were essentially American. In 1960, 40 percent of the movies produced or financed by the Hollywood majors were shot overseas. Several Italian-made films by director Sergio Leone, dubbed "spaghetti westerns" by Americans, made Clint Eastwood a star. Unfortunately for the studios, the lower labor costs of filming abroad did not always translate into lower production costs. Less experienced technical personnel often lost in time and lack of expertise what producers gained from paying lower salaries. Although the majors continued to produce a significant percentage of films in foreign countries, by mid-decade the number was declining.

These transitions in content and production coincided with a major shift in how movies looked. Motion pictures had been made with both black-and-white and color film for several years. By the mid-1950s about half of Hollywood's major movies appeared on color film, but in the following years most continued to be shot in black and white. Not until the arrival of color television in 1963 did color films come to dominate Hollywood production. The major studios saw television as an important future market for their feature films and, with TV now broadcasting in color, believed selling black-and-white movies to the networks would become increasingly difficult. As Paul Monaco observes, "With the arrival of color television, it was promptly assumed that audiences in the future would expect virtually all feature films in color. Hollywood's wholesale shift to color production, then, was essentially a producers' decision based on commercial assessments of future markets."[2]

While movie production adjusted to these changes, film exhibitors faced growing problems by the beginning of the 1960s. With fewer American-made movies being produced, distributors held greater economic leverage, often demanding a minimum fee from theater owners plus a percentage of ticket sales for each motion picture. Operating throughout the decade with an average profit margin of only 3 percent, exhibitors looked for solutions.

A long-term resolution involved building cinemas in shopping centers and malls. These new locations offered easy access to the growing suburban population and plenty of free parking. Because the new theaters usually featured two or more screens sharing a single projection center, they also offered a greater variety of pictures with lower operating costs. These multiscreen units became the standard for building new movie theaters by the mid-1960s. While they provided variety, the new theaters were much smaller, usually no more than a few hundred seats in each auditorium, and lacked the elegance of the golden age movie palaces. These small basic rectangles were a classic example of substance over style.

When the major studios gave up their theaters, new chains developed. During the 1960s General Cinema, with over two hundred theaters, and the National Cinema Corporation emerged as the largest. Already tied in with leisure shopping because of their location, the multitheater corporations improved their chances for profit by buying related businesses. General Cinema, for example, owned soft drink bottling plants as a way of reducing costs for their concession operations, which represented a critical difference between profit and loss.

As mass appeal, or family, films declined, they were replaced by movies that appealed to specific audiences. When the audience fragmented so did movies themselves. Art films, as one example, attracted sophisticated and more educated viewers, but that was a relatively small market. The largest audience was elsewhere. As middle-aged attendance declined, younger people went to the movies in growing numbers. "Cinema," declared *Time* magazine, "has become the favorite art form of the young."[3] The most consistent moviegoers were teens and young adults, especially males. They wanted films with a sense of social alienation and personal rebellion, and filmmakers tried to give them what they wanted. Other themes appeared less frequently as their audiences increasingly stayed home.

With the major studios reducing their output, the earlier trend toward increased independent film production continued. Throughout the 1960s, independent companies produced a significant percentage of U.S. films, while the major studios continued to handle most of the distribution. This combination of independent production and emphasis on young audiences resulted in such fare as American International Pictures' *Beach Party* (1963), *Bikini Beach* (1964), and *Beach Blanket Bingo* (1965), featuring Annette Funicello and Frankie Avalon. The emphasis on young audiences did not immediately solve the industry's problems, but it did reinforce the notion that youth represented a powerful economic force.

Two films that became surprisingly big hits set the stage for major changes in Hollywood film production over the next several years. *Bonnie and Clyde*

(1967) was directed by Arthur Penn and starred Warren Beatty and Faye Dun-away. It reflects French new wave influences as it combines violence, comedy, and romance. The story revolves around Bonnie Parker and Clyde Barrow, two real-life criminals who committed robbery and murder in the early 1930s. They finally meet death in a violent ambush, filmed in slow motion. Penn turns the traditional view of criminal behavior upside down, however, por-traying their bored disrespect for the law as glamorous rebellion. That ap-proach had great appeal in the countercultural 1960s. Dustin Hoffman stars in Mike Nichols's *The Graduate* (1967), the year's top moneymaker. The story builds around a love triangle between recent college graduate Benjamin Brad-dock, Elaine Robinson, and her mother. What connected with young audi-ences was each character's anxiety and struggle over conforming to social expectations. At the film's conclusion, both Benjamin and Elaine reject those expectations for a chance at happiness. These films contributed to the first major rise in movie attendance since 1946. The 1967 surge in ticket sales proved to be an exception to the trend, however, as the following year atten-dance dropped to a record low.

In the new era, a producer often brought together the different essential el-ements of a movie, including a script, actors, and director, and took the pack-age to a studio for funding and distribution. Without the old studio system to guarantee outlets and continued production, which enabled studios to cover films that lost money with hit movies, financial risks increased and producers grew more cautious. This led companies to take fewer risks with production.

With the major studios cutting their payrolls, actors looked for ways to protect themselves. In 1960 the Screen Actors Guild (SAG) called a strike against the major studios, demanding residual payments for films that ap-peared on television. The organization negotiated a deal with the studios that March: SAG would be paid $2.25 million and guaranteed 6 percent of pro-ducers' net revenues on television rights for all post-1948 movies.

The major Hollywood studios increased their involvement in television production during the 1960s. Early in the decade they produced some films for release on television rather than in theaters, and by the early 1970s TV broadcast more premiere films than movies previously released in theaters. Although much of the movies' audience stayed home to watch television, much of that programming was now supplied by Hollywood, despite some networks' efforts to produce their own films in the late 1960s.

Even while the film industry was experiencing significant upheaval during the 1960s, movie studios produced several outstanding features. *Lawrence of Arabia* (1962) was an epic story of T. E. Lawrence, a British military officer who helped organize Arab tribes against the Turks during World War I. The vast Arabian desert held a mystical allure for the troubled Lawrence and provides a majestic backdrop for the film. Billy Wilder directed *The Apartment* (1960), a cynical yet comical film about corporate America. Bud Baxter climbs the corporate ladder by making his apartment available to his superiors for their adulterous affairs. When a woman he cares for is seduced by his boss and attempts suicide, Baxter questions his life and gives up his job. Alfred Hitchcock's *Psycho* (1960) is a modern suspense classic of a psychotic murderer at an isolated motel. It served as a profitable precursor to more gruesome horror films a decade later.

America's civil rights movement provided a poignant context for films that addressed racial issues. *To Kill a Mockingbird* (1962) stars Gregory Peck as Atticus Finch, a white lawyer who heroically defends a black man wrongly accused of rape in the segregated Deep South. The story is told through the eyes of his young daughter, Scout, who recognizes the violent racism of her society and admires her father's stand against it. Sidney Poitier plays a Philadelphia detective and Rod Steiger a Mississippi sheriff in 1967's *In the Heat of the Night*. Steiger begins to overcome his bigotry while working with Poitier to solve a murder case in the charged racist atmosphere of his Mississippi town. *Guess Who's Coming to Dinner* (1967) deals with interracial marriage and the challenges this presents to two families.

Several movies of the 1960s address concerns about the Cold War and the national security state. Peter Sellers stars as three characters in the Stanley Kubrick film *Dr. Strangelove* (1964). This dark comedy centers on immature men whose sexual dysfunctions and conspiracy theories about communism lead the world to nuclear annihilation. *Fail Safe*, also from 1964, deals with nuclear catastrophe in a more serious manner. John Frankenheimer directed two films about threats to national security. *The Manchurian Candidate* (1962) details a plot by communists disguised as ultraconservatives to gain the presidency through an assassination by a brainwashed Korean War veteran. *Seven Days in May* (1964) explores a planned military coup of the United States. In both films the plots are thwarted at the last minute.

Gregory Peck in To Kill a Mockingbird *(Library of Congress)*

Two of the best films of 1960 focus on the clash between traditional values and modernism in the 1920s. Burt Lancaster plays the title character in *Elmer Gantry.* Gantry is a Midwestern revivalist caught up in the anxieties brought about by industrialization and immigration. Stanley Kramer's *Inherit the Wind* tells the story of the Scopes Trial on the teaching of evolution.

Musicals enjoyed a resurgence in the first half of the 1960s. Three won Academy Awards for best picture, all based on Broadway plays. *West Side Story* (1961) is adapted from Shakespeare's *Romeo and Juliet.* Set in modern New York City, it replaces feuding families with street gangs. In *My Fair Lady* (1964), Professor Henry Higgins turns a poor Cockney street vendor, Eliza Doolittle, into a "proper" English lady. *The Sound of Music* (1965) stars Julie Andrews as a governess who wins the affection of the seven von Trapp children and their widowed father in Austria as World War II approaches.

By 1968 the motion picture industry had rebounded from economic problems in the early 1960s. Fearing risk because of the continued decline of attendance and the erosion of their traditional urban base, studios produced fewer films than ever before. The cumulative influence of foreign films and changing social values eventually brought more realism and diversity to the public, which necessitated a ratings system to guide consumers. Theater owners chased an increasingly young constituency with a building boom of suburban theaters. The major studios crafted several large-scale successes even as independent companies produced a much larger share of Hollywood's output. The movies had survived a financial crisis. Television faced a different challenge.

THE VAST WASTELAND

Television's golden age appeared to be over by the 1960s. Network programming was under attack from numerous sources. *Time* magazine called the 1960–1961 TV season "the worst in the 13-year history of U.S. network television."[4] The end of *Playhouse 90* in 1960 effectively closed the era of live drama. Critics who perceived a decline in television's quality often blamed growing commercialism: advertisers controlled scripts, censored controversial topics, and integrated their products into the stories. Director John Frankenheimer echoed this judgment: "Television today is not an art form. It's a supermarket. It exists to sell cigarettes, gas, lipstick. . . . It was fun while it lasted. But it's over."[5] ABC executive Daniel Melnick claimed that the worst TV programs required a writer "who doesn't have a burning desire to make an original statement."[6] The view that television had abandoned the public interest for the unrestrained pursuit of private profit led some to call for government intervention.

President John Kennedy's administration posed potentially the greatest threat of regulation to television broadcasters since the government's freeze on granting licenses. The clearest indication of this threat came from Kennedy's appointee as chair of the Federal Communications Commission, Newton Minow, during a May 9, 1961, address to the National Association of Broadcasters. After highlighting his views of television's best achievements, he turned his attention to its shortcomings. "When television is bad, nothing is worse," he declared. Television programming was "a vast wasteland." "You will see," he went on, "a procession of game shows, violence, audience participation shows, formula comedies about totally unbelievable families, blood and thunder, mayhem, violence, sadism, murder, western bad men, western good men, private

eyes, gangsters, more violence, and cartoons. And endlessly, commercials—
many screaming, cajoling, and offending."[7] He challenged the broadcasters to
improve their programming and warned them that license renewals would no
longer be automatic.

Minow's criticisms evidently made an impression. Although the fall television schedules had been set prior to this challenge, all three networks made
slight adjustments. They retrieved a handful of respected but low-rated programs planned for cancellation and altered several episodes of other programs
to reduce violent content. Broadcasters also increased the number of public
affairs shows, and the networks combined aired 254 hours of documentaries
during the 1961–1962 season—the most in television history. Throughout the
Kennedy years, in fact, experiments in documentary forms provided unprecedented access to national and world leaders and events.

The networks produced several new thoughtful dramas and clever comedies in the 1961–1962 season. *Dr. Kildare* and *Ben Casey* were medical dramas;
The Defenders focused on legal stories; while *The Dick Van Dyke Show* and,
starting the following year, *The Lucy Show* were witty comedies. Within a couple of years shows featuring a teacher, *Mr. Novak*, and a social worker, *East
Side/West Side*, appeared to critical praise, though not overwhelming popularity. Writers on various programs developed story lines that often dealt with
contemporary social problems without feeling obligated to resolve them
within the show's weekly time frame.

The majority of new programs continued to fall outside the categories of
social relevance and public edification. *The Flintstones* began a three-year run
in the top thirty during the 1960–1961 season. This was the first animated
telefilm to break into prime time. An even bigger success, although critics dis-
agreed on whether it constituted quality programming, was *The Beverly Hillbillies*, the top-rated show for the two seasons from 1962 to 1964. The show's
premise has a poor, backward Ozark family accidentally discover oil on their
property and move to a Beverly Hills mansion, where they maintain their old
speech patterns, dress, and provincial view of life. The *Beverly Hillbillies* remained in the top twenty through 1970. Despite this infusion of new topics,
old standards remained extremely popular. New westerns such as *The Virgin-
ian* and *Branded* competed for viewers with the highly rated *Bonanza* and
Gunsmoke. Still, as Minow observed, "The blood on the living room floor isn't
as deep as it was a year ago."[8]

Most of these changes proved to be only temporary. Fewer action shows and new dramas brought some reduction in screen violence until Lyndon Johnson assumed the presidency after Kennedy's assassination in November 1963. Johnson, who had made a small fortune from broadcasting, did not share Minow's enthusiasm to oversee TV content. Kennedy's death brought a brief period of finger-pointing from critics who connected television's reliance on aggression to resolve problems with an increasingly hostile American culture. Even this, however, did not last long. As historian Mary Ann Watson observes, "Programming executives were not about to be shamed into soul-searching by a few dour columnists."[9] With a more sympathetic man in the White House, "the networks appeared to have exhausted their reserves of moral courage."[10]

Although entertainment continued to dominate programming, television news received increased attention and achieved greater prominence in the early 1960s. In July 1962 Telstar became the first communications satellite capable of relaying television signals, which made live transmission possible. Satellite communication expanded rapidly, largely through public funding by Congress. This technology permitted more immediate television coverage of news events. All three networks increased their evening news programs from fifteen to thirty minutes in 1963, and that same year a Roper poll indicated that more Americans received their news from TV than from any other source.

The televised images of the nation's most serious confrontations played a significant role in the outcome of those conflicts. The modern civil rights movement, which centered on the efforts of African Americans to achieve legal equality, was transmitted and occasionally abetted by television coverage. For many Americans the most vivid images of the movement appeared on their TV screens. Pictures of snarling police dogs and high-pressure water hoses turned on black demonstrators, many of them children, generated emotional and moral support of the movement as no other medium could. The massive August 28, 1963, march on Washington, highlighted by Martin Luther King Jr.'s "I have a dream" speech, received wide, and sometimes live, coverage.

The nation's changing racial climate encouraged producers to create opportunities for racial minorities on camera. The shift was gradual and often subtle, like including blacks in background crowds, but some advances were more significant. Ossie Davis appeared as a prosecutor on *The Defenders*, Ed

Sullivan featured acts by black entertainers, a few shows built episodes around black characters, and NBC canceled its coverage of a college football all-star game that barred black athletes. The networks all added black news reporters. The changes, however, drew resistance from some advertisers, southern affiliate stations, and members of Congress. Some southern affiliates would not air episodes of *East Side/West Side* that featured stories of African Americans. Senator Strom Thurmond (R-SC) disapproved of TV's sympathetic treatment of civil rights activists, and fellow legislators tried to stop distribution of a U.S. Information Agency film of the march on Washington. ABC's broadcast of a one-hour special in October 1963 on the showdown over racial integration at the University of Alabama between President Kennedy and Governor George Wallace—*Crisis: Behind a Presidential Commitment*—was delayed by problems with finding a willing sponsor. That only eleven of the 23,600 employees in New York's top ten advertising agencies were black helps explain the lack of urgency in advancing civil rights on television.[11]

Eventually entertainment programming began to reflect the nation's changing racial climate. In the early 1960s occasional TV episodes dealt with racial prejudice, but by mid-decade African Americans had made visible gains on network television. Bill Cosby costarred on *I Spy* (1965) as a highly educated American spy, and Greg Morris costarred on *Mission: Impossible* (1966) as a secret agent electronics expert. Diahann Carol starred as *Julia* (1968), a widowed mother working as a nurse, in the first program to feature a black woman. Clarence Williams III played a special youth police member as part of an ensemble cast on *The Mod Squad* (1968), and Lloyd Haynes and Denise Nichols costarred as part of the cast of *Room 222* (1969), a teacher and counselor, respectively, in a middle-class high school. With the possible exception of *The Mod Squad* role, these black characters, as well as their white colleagues, were all hardworking middle-class believers in the American system. Ironically these characters appeared at a time of increasing racial discontent and challenges to the dream of a racially integrated and color-blind society, following the assassination of Martin Luther King Jr.

Television also played a significant role in political campaigns. The 1960 presidential race provided ample evidence of the medium's power to shape national decisions. The visual image of a youthful, handsome, eloquent John Kennedy matched against a plain, stiff, and perspiring Richard Nixon helped tip the balance toward the Democrat. Political commentator Russell Baker claims

Walter Cronkite and John Kennedy (Library of Congress)

of the first Kennedy-Nixon debate, "That night television replaced newspapers as the most important communications medium in American politics."[12]

During the 1964 presidential election campaign, the Democrats' advertising agency emphasized short TV ads that would not intrude on or preempt entertainment shows. These focused on Republican candidate Barry Goldwater without mentioning his name, targeting his apparent acceptance of using nuclear weapons and his criticism of Social Security, among other issues. Some of the ads themselves, especially the "daisy girl" spot, which pictured a child followed by a nuclear explosion, became news items and received enormous publicity. A Republican campaign film, "Choice," attempted to link the Democrats to a rise in sexual immorality and racial and teenage rioting and included staged shots that implied President Johnson was guilty of drunk driving. Democratic protests and network anxieties caused Goldwater to cancel the planned airing on NBC, though local showings took place around the country. The Democrats turned the film against the Republicans and won a landslide victory at the polls.

One of television's milestones was its coverage of President John Kennedy's assassination. With remarkable continuous national coverage, the networks allowed millions of Americans to watch the tragic yet orderly transition of their government. Images of Jacqueline Kennedy's blood-spattered clothing, the horrific murder on live television of accused assassin Lee Harvey Oswald, and the funeral procession led by a riderless horse became part of the national consciousness. The networks did not run commercials during their four-day coverage. Its professional and solemn attention to the weekend's events "cemented television's role as national information source and national unifier."[13]

For network executives the tensions between entertainment and news divisions grew increasingly strained. News and documentaries produced far less profit than dramatic shows and often lost money. Struggles over programming grew more intense. At CBS, for example, president James Aubrey wanted to eliminate *CBS Reports* if it could not air at a profit, and another executive told a newly hired producer to concentrate on satisfying the mass audience rather than creating art: "Your job is to produce shit."[14] Local stations often reinforced this attitude, as they, too, would benefit from the additional dollars that entertainment sponsors brought in.

At the same time subjects covered in the news often found their way into television entertainment programs. The Bay of Pigs invasion, the Cuban missile crisis, the erection of the Berlin Wall, and the public revelations of American covert operations in various parts of the world all heightened Cold War tensions in the early 1960s. Television, usually rationalizing U.S. actions as necessary in the face of communist aggression and deceit, injected espionage into numerous story plots. New spy shows, both dramas and comedies, appeared on the network lineups in mid-decade. The most popular included *The Man from U.N.C.L.E.*, *Get Smart*, *I Spy*, and *Mission: Impossible.* Episodes invariably justified American actions, even illegal or ethically questionable actions; demonized "enemy" motives and plans; and often disparaged the government's domestic critics. The perspective running throughout these shows was that the danger and depth of the opposition's malevolence required an American response in kind.

The nation's march toward war in Vietnam was accompanied by several military-oriented shows that utilized the popularity of World War II. Dramatic series like *Combat* (1962), *Twelve O'Clock High* (1964), and *Rat Patrol* (1966) mixed with comedies like *McHale's Navy* (1962) and *Hogan's Heroes* (1965). The concept of defeating malicious opponents through violent destruction spilled generously into children's programs as well, frequently supported by commercials pushing warlike toys. Concerned viewers seeking a careful analysis of America's global interests would have been hard-pressed to find it on their television sets. Government policy received a real boost, whether intentional or subliminal, from TV programming.

Special interest groups sometimes enjoyed portrayals as positive as those of the government's policies. Professional organizations used television to shape their public image. Groups like the American Medical Association (AMA) often served as consultants for the networks. Television producers hoped to achieve more accurate portrayals on their shows, while physicians and other groups wanted to influence the depiction of their professions and affect the public perception of them. No group liked to be associated with negatives such as incompetence or criminal activity. The AMA had, in fact, established an advisory committee to inform and influence the entertainment industry in 1955. This committee played a particularly important role in consulting during the early 1960s when *Dr. Kildare* and *Ben Casey* enjoyed wide popularity. An AMA spokesman called the shows "the best public relations the AMA ever had," as the organization worked to hold back Social Security medical care.[15] The lead characters on these shows were committed, skilled, compassionate, and virtuous and were as unchallenged in their profession as suburban fathers were in their television homes. If controversy arose, physicians were invariably presented as on the side of justice and competence. *The Nurses*, a program debuting in 1962, used independent nurses rather than professional advisers and included more controversial episodes, such as one where doctors harass a nurse who supports Medicare.

Other professions made comparable efforts. The American Bar Association provided advisers to programs that featured courtroom action, such as *Perry Mason* and *The Defenders*. Since lawyers confronted one another in court on these shows, those on the losing side presented a less-glowing image of lawyers than that of physicians. Producers also consulted with representatives from the National Education Association for shows such as *Mr. Novak*. While writers wanted to use character flaws to create drama, professional advocates favored untarnished champions. As Mary Ann Watson observes:

Of all the ways in which Americans learned about and formed opinions about professions and their practitioners in the postwar era, the most persuasive messenger was television. In the 1960s, organized attempts to influence the medium's storytelling—some successful and some ignored—became routine as it became obvious that in the real world, familiar images mattered.[16]

President Kennedy labeled his domestic political programs the "New Frontier," but the phrase could also apply to some of the changes taking place in popular culture. A potential explosion of cable television involved pay TV. Most cable companies charged fees to install their system and monthly bills for their entire package of programming. Pay TV required subscribers to select and pay for premium channels on an individual basis. In the late 1950s, an early attempt to develop a pay system failed in Texas as local broadcasters fought back by increasing the number of films they aired. In 1963 Subscription Television (STV) broke into major urban areas by offering films and baseball games to the Los Angeles and San Francisco areas. Subscribers would purchase programs they selected by telephone, including events not available from the networks. The networks feared losing desirable programming to cable systems, and theater owners worried pay TV could reduce movie attendance. Motion picture theater owners led a campaign to preserve "free" television, initiating a 1964 referendum in California that banned fees for transmitting TV signals into homes. The public passed the measure, but the courts overturned it the following year. By then STV was bankrupt. The availability of more broadcast channels and FCC restrictions in the mid-1960s severely limited cable's expansion.

The stakes were high because the television industry continued to be highly profitable, even in previously marginal time slots. Saturday morning programming yielded growing profits built around the shift of toy makers to year-round advertising. They served as the primary sponsors for children's cartoons. Greater profits from weekday morning and daytime programming came when drama series expanded to thirty minutes. By 1964 they achieved the popularity earlier bestowed on the older radio serials. Daytime dramas also became the foundation of New York television production. Early morning, with NBC's *Today* show, and late night, with NBC's *Tonight Show*, hosted from 1962 by Johnny Carson, brought in rising profits. There seemed to be no time slot that couldn't operate profitably if you could fill it with entertainment. The rising popularity of professional football made even Sunday afternoons extremely profitable. CBS's purchase of the New York Yankees baseball team in 1964 only strengthened the link between sports and television.

Most television growth continued to occur on sponsored network shows, and commercial advertisements increasingly intruded onto TV screens. During one typical 1964 morning, Erik Barnouw counted forty-one commercial ads and five program promotions during a two-hour period on New York's WCBS. The National Association of Broadcasters (NAB) proudly claimed that self-regulation of content was sufficient, but critics found its rules on such matters as televised violence and time devoted to commercials to be vague, without adequate enforcement mechanisms, and widely disregarded. A 1963 Federal Communication Commission survey found that 40 percent of TV stations exceeded the NAB codes on limits for commercials. When commission chairman E. William Henry suggested in 1964 that the FCC adopt the NAB's own standards of evaluation during license renewal procedures, the television industry and House of Representatives combined to ban the commission from taking any action to limit commercial time on TV. The influx of advertising money by the mid-1960s made television enormously profitable.

By mid-decade families with children watched sixty hours of television per week. Prime-time TV provided an escape from the public turmoil often raging outside viewers' walls. Hollywood's leading studios were by then an integral part of creating telefilms. Leading half-hour shows cost over seventy-five thousand dollars per episode to produce, and sixty-minute programs cost more than twice as much. The creative talent, especially writers, increasingly had to contend with network executives, advertising agents, and sponsors who wanted to influence the final product. Topical trends included characters with magic powers (*I Dream of Jeannie*, *Bewitched*), heroic animals (*Flipper*), and wholesome families, including endearing monsters in *The Addams Family* and *The Munsters*. Several series focused on rural life. The respected *Andy Griffith Show*, which debuted in 1960, was gradually joined by *Petticoat Junction* (1963), *Gomer Pyle, U.S.M.C.* (1964), and *Green Acres* (1965). *That Was the Week That Was* provided the networks' first show dealing with current political satire, though it faded rather quickly. Another program perhaps ahead of its time was *Star Trek*. During its three-year run beginning in 1966, it ranked no higher than fifty-two in annual ratings. Shows with multiple sponsors had almost totally replaced single-sponsor programs. Foreign use of U.S. shows brought in growing profits. Earnings from American programs used overseas rose from thirty million dollars in 1960 to over seventy-five million dollars in 1965, and U.S. shows dominated prime-time viewing in many countries around the world.

Television remained, however, the most conservative entertainment medium, even in the middle of the post–birth control pill sexual revolution. On *The Dick Van Dyke Show*, Rob and Laura Petrie, played by Van Dyke and Mary Tyler Moore, provided more romantic spark than previous TV couples, though they still slept in separate beds. Moore even broke with standard practice by having her character wear pants at home, but only after sponsors warned against them being too tight. Sex rarely intruded on regular programming, but throughout the decade assaults on conventional behavior did take place. *Peyton Place* debuted in 1964, a drama featuring a small town with an ample amount of nonmarital sex and gossip. Promiscuous behavior, however, generally had negative consequences for those involved. Most shows continued to adhere to a standard of no sexual activity before or outside of marriage. Television even tried to keep sexuality out of the popular music that appeared on its screens, with Ed Sullivan and others changing or eliminating the sexually suggestive lyrics of artists like the Rolling Stones.

Eventually, however, even TV experienced the sexual revolution, although in relatively modest form. *Rowan and Martin's Laugh-In*, which debuted in 1968 and quickly claimed the number one rating, included comic lines painted on the bodies of bikini-wearing cast members Goldie Hawn and Judy Carne, as well as a regular barrage of sexually suggestive humor. *Love, American Style* frequently dealt with sexual affairs within comedic sketches, while *M*A*S*H* examined sexual issues with both comedy and sophistication.

Despite the increased number of married women moving into the workforce, television's picture of women remained primarily that of wife and mother. By 1960 nearly one-third of married women in the United States worked outside the home, but women often felt social expectations to end their careers after marriage. According to Margaret Mead, "TV more than any other medium gives models to the American people—models for life as it is or should be or can be lived."[17] In the early 1960s TV wives, when offered opportunities outside of nurturing their families, invariably turned them down as less important. The rare TV career woman, such as the character Sally

Rogers—played by Rose Marie—on *The Dick Van Dyke Show*, spent much of her time looking for love and marriage, achieving career success only by giving up what she really wanted. The stirring women's movement of the 1960s and books such as Betty Friedan's *The Feminine Mystique* revealed doubts and dissatisfaction among women about their life choices, which some found limiting and unfulfilling. "Television badly needs some heroines," wrote Friedan in 1964.[18] What turned up instead were women with magical powers: a witch in *Bewitched* and a genie in *I Dream of Jeannie*. Despite their advantages over mortals, these women accepted the authority of the men in their lives. Ironically television usually made these women more intelligent, creative, and rational than their male counterparts.

THE WAR ON TV

The growing Vietnam War encroached more deeply into television than other cultural outlets, primarily through TV's news divisions. Television networks increased their news crews in Vietnam as the U.S. military involvement escalated. TV news reporters, as well as newspaper writers, encountered some disturbing situations in covering the war. While civilian and military officials expected the press to work cooperatively toward their goals, reporters were more interested in providing an objective evaluation of the situation. Even during the early years, when correspondents were generally strong supporters of American efforts, reporters received deceptive information and observed illegal or officially denied activities. Still, as Erik Barnouw observes, "the sense of involvement in a dubious enterprise was resisted by newsmen, as by combatants."[19]

Perhaps the most controversial televised report in 1965 was CBS correspondent Morley Safer's coverage of a Marine patrol that showed a soldier lighting Vietnamese huts on fire with his cigarette lighter. Over one hundred huts burned during the village sweep, and the scene drew criticism of both the war and the network for portraying Americans in such a bad light. In general, however, television provided a much narrower range of debate over the war, thereby bolstering government policy. Even when field reporters began to question official statements about the war's progress, network executives continued to filter out nearly everything that might appear critical of the government.

As questions and criticism of U.S. policy emerged, especially from within Congress, television relayed those doubts to the public. The most dramatic of these early events was live coverage of the Senate Foreign Relations Committee's hearings on the war in February 1966. Chaired by Senator J. William Fulbright, the committee heard testimony from both defenders and critics of existing policy. NBC and CBS covered the initial witnesses, but CBS president John Schneider cut away from live coverage with the appearance of George Kennan, one of the creators of the Cold War containment policy but a critic of the nation's Vietnam strategy. Fred Friendly, president of CBS News, resigned in protest, calling TV "the profit machine—whose only admitted function was to purvey six one-minute commercials every half-hour."[20] Nevertheless, either as a political statement or to bring in additional revenue, many network affiliates carried only portions of the testimony or none at all.

Friendly's protest reflected broader dissatisfaction with the war. The Vietnam War supplanted civil rights as the nation's dominant issue by the mid-1960s. Television relayed pictures of Buddhist monks setting themselves on fire, U.S. soldiers burning civilian huts, student protests in America, and napalm victims. The unrelenting coverage eventually contributed to American war weariness and questions about presidential war policies.

North Vietnam's Tet Offensive in early 1968, again dramatically captured on television, was the war's turning point. The shock caused by the offensive helped convince many Americans that the war should not continue. Some reacted instinctively to sights like a South Vietnamese officer shooting a bound prisoner in the head. Others received more gentle persuasion. When the Senate Foreign Relations Committee held new hearings on the war in February, the televised meetings revealed the 1964 Gulf of Tonkin incident as a highly questionable rationale for American policy.

Respected newscaster Walter Cronkite's analysis of the war sent additional ripples across the country. Typically news anchors had maintained a distant objectivity when reporting the war, and Cronkite had a reputation for integrity exceeded by none. He traveled to Vietnam during the Tet Offensive and returned with a special half-hour broadcast. His report concluded with this chilling observation: "It seems now more certain than ever that the bloody experience of Vietnam is to end in a stalemate. . . . It is increasingly clear to this reporter that the only rational way out then will be to negotiate, not as victors, but as an honorable people who lived up to their pledge to defend democracy, and did the best they could."[21] President Johnson felt that Cronkite's televised statements marked a turning point for public opinion. Nevertheless, some observers criticized television news executives for encouraging and covering dissenting views.

Networks only rarely discussed Vietnam beyond mentions on newscasts. An exception was CBS's 1967 special *Morley Safer's Vietnam*. CBS also commissioned a film by Felix Greene entitled *Inside North Vietnam*. The contents proved controversial enough that the network decided to air only brief excerpts during its news program. National Educational Television (NET) encountered resistance when it decided to run part of the film in 1967. Members of Congress were among those who attacked NET for running what they termed "communist propaganda."[22]

The attack on educational television highlighted an important transitional phase for that system. Public television's decentralized structure had contributed to its slow growth. Momentum built when New York acquired its first noncommercial station in 1962 and Congress required that, beginning in 1963, all new TV sets be able to receive both VHF and UHF channels. With the networks closely tied to the interests of the national government, more voices called for an increase in noncommercial TV. In early 1967 the Carnegie Commission on Educational Television called for federal funding of public television. Shortly thereafter, the Ford Foundation helped launch a Public Broadcast Laboratory (PBL) that provided a weekly series for the roughly one hundred noncommercial stations around the country. Beginning in November, PBL offered experimental programming such as underground films, off-Broadway theater, and countercultural messages that often attracted controversy.

Even as the private sector was moving forward, Congress responded to the Carnegie report with unusual speed. With strong support from President Lyndon Johnson, Congress passed the Public Broadcasting Act in November 1967, creating the Corporation for Public Broadcasting to establish policy and the Public Broadcasting System as the "network" to broadcast the programming. Federal dollars joined public, corporate, and private foundation money to make the system work. Although public television would usually draw a small audience compared to commercial stations, it became widely recognized for the quality of its children's programs, such as *Sesame Street*, which debuted in November 1969.

Most television executives felt threatened by greater public demands for access to the airwaves. In 1967 the FCC, through its "fairness doctrine" designed to serve the public interest, agreed that the appearance of cigarette advertisements on TV warranted free "public service" messages produced by health organizations. These and other attacks on the health problems promoted by cigarette smoking led Congress in 1970 to prohibit cigarette advertising on TV. Other groups demanded a right to address a variety of issues based on the fairness doctrine, and the FCC required cable companies to provide "public access" channels to deal with local concerns.

The 1968 presidential campaign brought another wave of national introspection. Concerns about the impact of constant exposure to TV violence resurfaced with the outbreak of racial violence and the murders of Martin Luther King Jr. and Robert Kennedy. As they had done after President Kennedy's death, and would do in reaction to real-life violence in the future, networks postponed episodes or revised scripts that were especially violent or close to recent events, implicitly acknowledging TV's impact on social attitudes. More than one hundred workers in the television industry took out a trade journal ad pledging to work to change "a climate for murder."[23]

Television's role in the presidential campaign climaxed during the Democratic convention in Chicago. Mayor Richard Daley's heavy-handed restrictions on public dissent and an unusually large and aggressive police presence combined with thousands of protesters to produce an often violent and dramatic confrontation. Initial street confrontations, under the watch of TV cameras, brought chants from countercultural demonstrators: "The whole world is watching. The whole world is watching." As film footage and stories of the bloody battles—later described by a government investigation as "a police riot"—made their way to television screens and the convention floor, Senator Abraham Ribicoff referred to "Gestapo tactics on the streets of Chicago." News reporters and photographers were among those attacked by the police.[24]

The continued concern about televised violence led to several studies, including those by the U.S. Public Health Service and the Senate Subcommittee on Communications. President Johnson appointed Milton Eisenhower to head a National Commission on the Causes and Prevention of Violence. That commission's report concluded, among other things, that televised aggression "encourages violent forms of behavior and fosters moral and social values about violence . . . which are unacceptable in a civilized society."[25] Television executives continued to reduce violent acts in programming, with CBS announcing a 30 percent reduction in prime-time violence for its upcoming season.

Television was also a battleground for contesting the nation's cultural values. With the struggle over civil rights and the Vietnam War at its center, the 1960s counterculture challenged commercial television's depiction of the acceptable American lifestyle. Despite resistance, various modes of popular culture felt the counterculture's influence. A classic confrontation took place on *The Smothers Brothers Comedy Hour*. Tom and Dick Smothers, a young comedy and folk singing team, injected political and social issues into their act that created an ongoing battle with CBS executives. Censors consistently fought material regarding sex, drugs, religion, and race that might be offensive and eliminated antiwar references. When the previously blacklisted Pete Seeger appeared on the *Smothers Brothers* program in September 1967, CBS edited his antiwar song "Waist Deep in the Big Muddy" out of the program. The publicity resulting from this decision led to a second appearance by Seeger the following February. This time the network left the song in. Despite the show's continued popularity, CBS canceled it in April 1969.

Like the movies, television weathered serious criticism in the early 1960s. By 1968 it had emerged as perhaps the dominant provider of both entertainment and news coverage. As it grew, it helped carry other forms of popular culture with it.

THE SPORTS EXPLOSION
Professional leagues experienced enormous growth during the 1960s. Major League Baseball grew from 16 to 26 teams; the National Hockey League from 6 to 21 franchises; the National Basketball Association from 8 to 23 teams; and the National Football League from 11 to 27. Both soccer and tennis formed leagues for play in the United States, but neither drew more than a small fan base, and they attracted little national attention, certainly nothing on the level of the major sports.

Despite TV's slow acceptance of some social changes, it accelerated the growth of spectator sports. Historian Benjamin Rader accurately observes, "Nothing was more central to the history of organized sports during the second half of the twentieth century than television."[26] By the early 1960s new techniques and improved technology made televised sports coverage more attractive to viewers. Over the years the success of sports programming led networks to pay increasing sums of money for broadcast rights, creating enormous revenues for team owners. As professional leagues became more reliant on TV money for their profits, viewers at home became at least as important as fans at the stadium. In order to get those viewers, and the commercial sponsors that paid their bills, television producers created a more entertaining package. However, they also altered the games they covered, changing rules, adding time-outs, and making championship playoffs and tournaments longer. By frequently showing the country's best athletes, national television also contributed to declining interest in local amateur teams.

Television's maturity in the 1960s played a significant role in the growing popularity of American sports. Professional football in particular benefited from the exposure. The National Football League's owners and commissioner negotiated as a single economic unit and signed a television contract that divided the income equally among all NFL teams. This revenue sharing proved to be one of the single most important ingredients in the league's success in the coming decades. The league also agreed to television blackouts to protect local live gates.

No one had a greater impact on sports television than Roone Arledge. Moving to ABC in 1960, the twenty-nine-year-old became the producer for the network's football games and changed the way TV covered football. Arledge transmitted the pageantry of college football, not just the game itself, hoping that "if they didn't give a damn about the game they still might enjoy the program."[27] He instituted original technical changes that put the viewer in the game atmosphere, such as isolated cameras, split screens, remote microphones, and halftime shows that emphasized first-half highlights and detailed game analysis. He used more cameras to cover college football than anyone before him: aerial shots, campus tours, close-ups from hand-held cameras, and attention to coaches, sideline activities, cheerleaders, and fans in the stands—the same things people watched when they were in the stadium and on campus. His field microphones picked up the on-field collisions and shouts from the players. Arledge also brought the development of instant replay in 1960. The ability to rerun a previous bit of action in slow motion allowed a closer look at exciting or controversial plays and a greater appreciation of the skills of the athletes. He drew larger audiences through competent and innovative coverage, integrating entertainment values into the competitions, and bringing out the human drama and personalities involved. Arledge's new approach to covering sports, entertaining both fans and neutral viewers, quickly moved ABC into the leadership position of sports television and was a major contributor to the network's rise to the top in the ratings race.

Arledge expanded from college football to televising leading sports events all year long. In 1961 he introduced *Wide World of Sports*, an award-winning program whose introductory slogan, "the thrill of victory and the agony of defeat," became part of the sporting language. The weekly series covered events around the world, focusing on exotic venues and interesting personalities. The prerecorded shows could be edited to maintain the attention of viewers. The events themselves were a collection of mainstream and marginal sports and games, from boxing, track, and skiing to cliff diving, demolition derby, and barrel jumping.

With the exception of football, the almost daily game schedules of the major sports leagues had hindered the expansion of professional franchises outside the East and Midwest. By the early 1960s, however, several factors combined to make major professional spectator sports truly national through the geographic expansion of franchises. The arrival of commercial jets in the mid-1950s made travel much easier, and television needed teams in the West and South to attract larger audiences in those regions. The rapid increases in television revenue to sports leagues and beneficial tax laws that encouraged investment in sports teams also made new franchises more attractive. The American population and economic base underwent important shifts in the 1960s and beyond, moving from older industrial sites in the Northeast and Midwest to the warmer locations and service-oriented industries of the West and South. The growing Sun Belt cities often saw a professional sports team as a badge of having "arrived" on the national scene. To get a major league team, city administrations often made deals with team owners that benefited the owners at the expense of the local community.

Major League Baseball, having shifted franchises in the 1950s, expanded in the early 1960s. At least part of the motivation was to keep the newly formed, but short-lived, Continental League from dominating important television markets. The American League shifted a team from Washington, D.C., to Minnesota and added new franchises in Washington, D.C., and Los Angeles in 1961. The following year the National League put new teams in New York and Houston. Four years later the Milwaukee Braves moved to Atlanta, adding yet another southern city to the major league ranks.

The Vietnam War's impact on sports was less dramatic than its impact on other aspects of the nation's culture. Unlike in World War II, famous athletes did not give up their careers for military service. Many professional teams protected their investments by having players added to National Guard or reserve units. A general with the Maryland National Guard revealed in a national magazine, "We have an arrangement with the [Baltimore] Colts. When they have a player with a military problem, they send him to us."[28] A Detroit army reserve unit took two members of the Detroit Lions in exchange for tickets on the fifty-yard line and honor guard duties at home games. Since men wanting to avoid the draft filled National Guard and reserve slots during the war's peak years, there were often long waiting lists to get in. Pro teams exerted their influence to bypass these lists if necessary. In this sense professional athletes represented yet another privileged class. As Myra MacPherson concludes, "The National Guard and reserves became such a dodge for professional football players that if there had been a call-up there scarcely would have been a football season."[29]

For some members of the Vietnam generation, sports no longer represented the positives of competition and virile national values. Instead they epitomized the racism, gambling, cheating, violence, and crime so visible in the larger society. Players who challenged the stereotype of the contented athlete usually received heated criticism for doing so. Increasingly college and professional athletes defied established clothing and hairstyles. Others went much further. Pro football player Dave Meggyesy exposed the academic fraud and medical abuse that occurred during his college career, as well as racial and class tensions. By the late 1960s he was actively organizing against the Vietnam War. "It is no accident," he wrote in 1970, "that some of the most maudlin and dangerous pre-game 'patriotism' we see in this country appears in football stadiums. Nor is it an accident that the most repressive political regime in the history of this country is ruled by a football-freak, Richard M. Nixon."[30] Oakland linebacker Chip Oliver was another NFL player who quit the game, claiming, "Pro football . . . dehumanizes people."[31] Some college football stars gave up the game as well. Baseball pitcher Jim Bouton's published diary of his 1969 season with the New York Yankees was equally controversial. His publicizing of drug use and womanizing and criticisms of baseball stars and a range of team owners and administrators did not endear him to the sport's establishment. His observations embraced a variety of the decade's most controversial topics:

"You *could* talk about the war in Vietnam, only you had to say, 'Look at those crazy kids marching in the street. Why don't they take a bath?' If you said things like, 'We've got no right to be in Vietnam,' . . . you were *wrong*."[32] A teammate claimed management treated ballplayers like children: "Right now baseball is about twenty years behind the most puritanical of freshman girl dormitories."[33] Bouton, too, observed racism and an uncomfortable link between organized sports and overzealous patriotism. These cultural shifts related to other important trends.

The economics of sport changed drastically during the 1960s. Civil rights concerns and other kinds of social activism affected many areas of American life by mid-decade. For professional athletes this sometimes translated into efforts to acquire greater control over their working conditions. Although players often enjoyed comparatively high salaries, restrictive contract clauses and baseball's antitrust exemption severely limited the bargaining power typically open to workers in other unionized occupations. With greater competition among team owners for talented athletes and more effective players' unions, professional athletes began to rebel and demand a greater share of sports' financial gains. The turbulent times almost guaranteed a direct attack.

One of the early warnings came from the West Coast. The star pitching duo of Sandy Koufax and Don Drysdale refused to sign their 1966 contracts with baseball's Los Angeles Dodgers and hired an agent to negotiate for them. Given their obvious talent and their importance to the club's success, they rebelled at what they felt were undervalued salaries. Koufax's rationale for the holdout was "to convince them that they would have to approach us not as indentured servants but as coequal partners to a contract, with as much dignity and bargaining power as themselves."[34] Dodger owner Walter O'Malley reluctantly conceded, agreeing to a salary of well over one hundred thousand dollars for each player. That same year Marvin Miller became the head of the Major League Baseball Players' Association and worked to turn the group from a loosely organized and ineffective collection of players into a true union.

Television revenue caused rapid increases in the value of sports franchises and also fueled the swift rise of player salaries. New team owners were almost by necessity, then, rich business executives who did not need their teams to generate income but who welcomed the notoriety attached to a professional team. A new generation of owners seemed less connected to their cities than previous generations. Knowing that many cities, or at least some of their key political and business leaders, were desperate to keep or entice a major league sports team for its perceived economic benefits or prestige, owners often used the threat of moving to extract extremely generous tax breaks, new stadiums, and other lucrative concessions from city governments. In most cases taxpayers shouldered the burdens of new stadium construction and other improvements to lure privately owned sports franchises. The craving rose even to the federal level. New Orleans received an NFL franchise in 1966, shortly after two Louisiana congressmen helped smooth the league's merger with the AFL by voting for an exemption from antitrust laws.

The impact of TV income was perhaps most clearly evident in the remarkable increase in pro football's popularity throughout the 1960s. One of the keys to the pro game's health was a competitive balance based largely on sharing finances. NFL teams gave 40 percent of their ticket income to visiting teams and split national television income evenly across the league. Franchise owner Art Modell once described the arrangement as "28 Republicans who vote socialist."[35] The money paid by the networks to televise football rose considerably during the decade. It also kept the NFL's new competitor alive. The American Football League began play in 1960 with eight teams. ABC televised the league's early years, but when NBC gave the AFL forty-two million dollars for its rights in 1964, player salaries began to climb dramatically. In 1965 the New York Jets signed University of Alabama quarterback Joe Namath to a three-year contract worth $420,000, an unheard-of amount at that time.

Rising player salaries was a key motive in the two leagues' decision to merge. They agreed on a common player draft and to keep Pete Rozelle as NFL commissioner and began a championship game between the two in 1967. The AFL became the American Football Conference of the NFL in 1969. The first two championship games, known as "Super Bowls," were one-sided victories for the NFL's Green Bay Packers, but Namath's New York Jets pulled a huge upset in 1969, defeating the Baltimore Colts 16–7.

The Green Bay Packers ruled professional football, winning five NFL titles from 1961 to 1967. Three Packers, quarterback Bart Starr and running backs Jim Taylor and Paul Hornung, won player of the year honors. Their coach, Vince Lombardi, achieved legendary status. Other league MVPs included running back Jim Brown of Cleveland, the NFL rushing leader in eight of his nine seasons, and quarterbacks Y. A. Tittle and Johnny Unitas. Lance Alworth of the

San Diego Chargers would later become the first AFL player inducted into the pro football hall of fame.

Some of the most impressive feats in baseball history took place in the early and mid-1960s. Roger Maris broke Babe Ruth's single-season home run record, hitting sixty-one for the 1961 New York Yankees. Frank Robinson became the only player to win most valuable player awards in both leagues, with the Cincinnati Reds in 1961 and the Baltimore Orioles in 1966. Pitching became increasingly dominant in the sport. Sandy Koufax was the game's premier pitcher, leading the National League in earned run average (ERA) from 1962 to 1966, throwing four no-hitters, and becoming the first player to strike out over three hundred batters in three separate seasons. Bob Gibson's 1.12 ERA in 1968 was the lowest in major league history. That same year Denny McLain became the first pitcher to win at least thirty games since 1934, and Don Drysdale pitched a record 58 2/3 consecutive scoreless innings. One of the game's great moments occurred when Bill Mazeroski's dramatic home run in the ninth inning of the seventh game gave the Pittsburgh Pirates the 1960 World Series over the Yankees. Major League Baseball had three multiple champions during this period, the New York Yankees, Los Angeles Dodgers, and St. Louis Cardinals.

The Boston Celtics continued to dominate professional basketball, winning all but one NBA championship between 1960 and 1968. Among the best pro players through the 1960s were five-time league MVP Bill Russell; Oscar Robertson, who averaged double figures in the three major statistical categories during the 1961–1962 season (30.8 points, 12.5 rebounds, 11.4 assists); and Wilt Chamberlain, who scored one hundred points in a single game and averaged fifty points per game for a season. Robertson, Elgin Baylor, Chamberlain, and Jerry West each attained first team all-pro status at least a half-dozen times.

Remarkable champions appeared in other sports as well. The National Hockey League's Canadian franchises won every championship but one between 1960 and 1968, with Toronto and Montreal each taking four. Detroit's Gordie Howe and the Chicago Blackhawks' Bobby Hull and Stan Mikita were honored with two MVP trophies each in the 1960s. In horse racing, Kelso was a five-time horse of the year, Damascus set a new earnings record for a single year, and Buckpasser twice led the nation in money won. A. J. Foyt captured the most famous auto race in America, the Indianapolis 500, three times during the 1960s.

Athletic competition continued to play in front of an admiring public. The Professional Golfers Association (PGA) enjoyed some of the sport's best and most entertaining players during this era. Much of golf's broader appeal during the 1960s came with the success of Arnold Palmer. Known for charging from behind to win, Palmer captured seven major tournaments from 1958 to 1964. His appealing personality won many new fans to the game, and his income from product endorsements made him the highest-paid athlete in the world. Jack Nicklaus ultimately surpassed Palmer's achievements, becoming perhaps the greatest golfer in history. Nicklaus won his first major event at the 1962 U.S. Open, and his 1986 victory at the Masters was his record eighteenth major tournament title. Challenging these two during most of the 1960s and 1970s, South African Gary Player claimed nine majors. Until 1961 the PGA formally excluded nonwhites but finally admitted minorities under public and legal pressure. Hispanic Lee Trevino became one of the tour's best and most popular players in the late 1960s and ended his career with wins in six majors. Professional women's golf grew much more slowly, offering significantly more prize money only in the late 1970s. Kathy Whitworth was the women's tour player of the year seven times between 1966 and 1973.

Tennis also captured new fans with the opening of tournaments to professional players in the 1960s. By the end of the decade the major tournaments at Wimbledon and Forest Hills were open to professionals as well as amateurs. By allowing all the best players into the most prestigious tournaments, which had previously been limited to amateurs, tennis broke out of a period of stagnation. Billie Jean King emerged as the world's top-rated woman player in 1966. Televised tennis ratings in the early 1970s tripled, with American and Australian stars competing for dominance.

College sports grew as spectacularly as their professional counterparts. College football's popularity exploded during the 1960s, allowing it to thrive as never before. National attendance grew from twenty to thirty million during the decade and to forty million in the 1970s. This popularity coincided with the switch to two-platoon football—one group of players on offense and a second on defense—allowing more sophisticated offenses and higher-scoring contests. As a televised sport, college football was more popular than baseball and basketball, trailing only professional football by the late 1970s.

With no national championship for the largest schools, the national polls and a handful of postseason bowl games decided the top college teams, a controversial method still hotly debated. The Rose Bowl in Pasadena, California (first held in 1902), Orange Bowl in Miami (1933), Sugar Bowl in New Orleans (1935), and Cotton Bowl in Dallas (1937) were the most important through the 1960s, all played annually on New Year's Day. Their outcomes often determined the polls' top choice. National champions included Alabama, University of Southern California (USC), Ohio State, and Texas. Among the decade's most memorable games, both between the two top-ranked teams in the country, were USC's 42–37 shoot-out over Wisconsin in the 1963 Rose Bowl and Notre Dame and Michigan State's 10–10 tie in 1966. Ohio State's undefeated 1968 squad received recognition as the best team of the decade. The era's most notable players included Ernie Davis of Syracuse, Dick Butkus of Illinois, Navy's Roger Staubach, Michigan State's Bubba Smith, and Mike Garrett and O. J. Simpson of USC.

In the early part of the decade the Midwest dominated college basketball. Ohio State, led by two-time national player of the year Jerry Lucas, captured the 1960 title but lost the next two championship games to in-state rival Cincinnati. Cincinnati fell in overtime in their third straight trip to the final game, losing to Loyola of Chicago in 1963. The power shifted west as UCLA won four national titles between 1964 and 1968. Notable All-American players included Cincinnati's Oscar Robertson, West Virginia's Jerry West, Bill Bradley of Princeton, and Michigan's Cazzie Russell.

The January 20, 1968, contest between top-ranked UCLA and second-ranked Houston was a landmark for the college game. Both teams were undefeated, and UCLA owned a forty-seven-game winning streak. The record attendance in Houston's Astrodome, the nation's first enclosed athletic stadium, exceeded fifty-two thousand fans, but it was also the first regular season college game televised nationally. The game featured college basketball's top two players. UCLA's Lew Alcindor was hampered by an eye injury, and Houston's Elvin Hayes scored thirty-nine points as Houston prevailed 71–69. UCLA gained revenge in the championship semifinals, shutting down Hayes and winning by thirty-two points.

Universities received financial benefits from this popularity but also incurred higher costs, both financial and otherwise. ABC paid three million dollars for college football rights in 1964, a sum that rose to twenty-nine million dollars in 1981. From there fees escalated dramatically, but the Supreme Court declared the system of collective agreements in violation of antitrust laws, allowing each school to negotiate its own deals. As with other college sports, the drive for national recognition brought more spending on athletic facilities and recruiting of top athletes and coaches, as well as a large support staff. The ratio of players to coaches in college programs, which was thirty to one in 1966, dropped to eight to one in 1973. Increasingly at large schools, coaches specialized in one sport and had no academic teaching responsibilities. For players this meant their sport became a full-time job, in addition to their schoolwork. Athletic booster organizations sometimes provided top athletes with money or gifts, the use of cars or apartments, or other enticements. Coaches, administrators, or faculty sometimes kept athletes academically eligible through easy courses or falsified transcripts. The NCAA, with only a small investigative staff, found it impossible to keep up with activities at over nine hundred schools under its jurisdiction.

BLACK, WHITE, AND GOLD

Race remained among the most important issues within sports. Athletic teams and competitions, especially in the South, remained racially segregated well into the 1960s, and Deep South teams often declined invitations to football bowl games or the NCAA baseball and basketball tournaments if that meant playing against integrated teams. White segregationists correctly feared that the integration of sports would have an impact far beyond athletic contests. Playing integrated teams in the North would open the door to integrated teams traveling in the South. Southern universities often integrated their classrooms before their athletic teams.

Segregationist practices gradually eroded in the late 1950s and early 1960s. Mississippi State University is a case in point. Through the early 1960s, the state's segregated university sports teams would not play integrated teams under an unwritten agreement with the Mississippi state legislature, which threatened school funding should they do otherwise. Mississippi State's all-white basketball team won the Southeastern Conference (SEC) championship in three of the four years from 1959 to 1962, but university administrators declined to participate in the NCAA national tournament each time. James Meredith's integration of the University of Mississippi in fall 1962 helped change the state climate, and as the Mississippi State basketball team rolled toward its third consecutive league championship during the 1962–1963 season, Coach "Babe" McCarthy solicited public support for his team's participation in the national tourney. With many students, fans, faculty, and alumni voicing their support, university president Dean Colvard accepted the tournament's invitation to play. Segregationist politicians and newspapers strongly disapproved. The state's higher education governing board voted to allow the team to play, but a state senator obtained a temporary injunction prohibiting Coach McCarthy, President Colvard, and the board members from taking the team out of the state. The president and coach, along with a few other officials, slipped out of the state to avoid being served with the injunction. The following morning the basketball team also sneaked away, and a state supreme court justice later overruled the injunction.

Mississippi State played a March 15 game against Loyola University of Chicago, which started four black players. The hard-fought game occurred without any racial incidents, and players on both teams displayed fine sportsmanship. Loyola triumphed 61–51 and went on to win the national championship, upsetting Cincinnati's bid for a third straight title. Mississippi State won its regional consolation game against Bowling Green and finished the season ranked seventh in the country. The team's actions effectively led to the ending of Mississippi's unwritten law. Sports had proven a more acceptable channel for racial integration than public schools or voting rights but eased the transition in those areas as well.

If many northern and West Coast colleges and universities recruited African American athletes in a variety of sports, southern schools, led by the Southeastern, Atlantic Coast (ACC), and Southwest (SWC) conferences, maintained all-white programs well into the 1960s. A pivotal event in hastening integration was the 1966 college basketball championship game between all-white Kentucky and Texas Western (later the University of Texas at El Paso). Adolph Rupp, Kentucky's renowned coach, refused to recruit black players. Like many other white segregationists, he believed blacks lacked the discipline and intelligence to play championship basketball, despite their physical talent and the performance of black players on previous NCAA championship teams. Forty-two percent of major college teams had no black players in 1966. Texas Western started five black players and upset Kentucky 72–65.

The major southern athletic conferences integrated during the mid-1960s. In 1965 Maryland broke the ACC color barrier and Houston did the same in the SWC, both in basketball. The University of Kentucky was the first SEC school to admit African American students, in 1949, but some schools were not integrated until the 1960s. Kentucky was also the first to recruit black athletes, signing two football players in 1966. Black athletes first reached varsity status—freshmen were not eligible for varsity teams at that time—during the 1967–1968 school year, when seven African Americans played at four SEC schools. Vanderbilt's Perry Wallace was the conference's first black basketball player.

Sports provided an important stage for America's historic and continuing racial conflicts. Black athletes were among the most visible civil rights dissenters during the 1960s. Cassius Clay was a gold medal–winning boxer at the 1960 Rome Olympics who became the heavyweight champion after upsetting heavily favored Sonny Liston in 1964. This talkative self-promoter surprised people shortly afterward, converting to the Black Muslim faith and changing his name to Muhammad Ali. The changes made him a constant subject of controversy, as did his flamboyant boxing tactics, which embarrassed opponents. When the military drafted Ali, he claimed exemption on the basis of his religious beliefs. Boxing commissions stripped him of the heavyweight title in 1966 and refused to allow him to box. While his draft case made its way through the courts, he symbolized African American resistance to racial discrimination and opposition to the Vietnam War.

In 1967, Harry Edwards, a sociologist at San José State College, organized an effort by African American athletes to boycott the 1968 Olympics. The action would serve as a visible protest over many issues affecting black Americans, both athletic and nonsports-related. Their first action was a boycott of the annual New York Athletic Club track and field meet at Madison Square Garden in 1967. This was a prestigious meet, but the sponsoring club had no black members. Most black athletes pulled out, as did the Soviet team and numerous other white athletes. The Olympic boycott, however, was not a success, with relatively few world-class athletes willing to give up the biggest competition of their careers. A few black performers made sporadic but highly publicized demonstrations at the games, but others countered with traditionally patriotic gestures.

Black athletes, and blacks in general, achieved greater success and acceptance in American society as time progressed. Arthur Ashe became the first black male on the tennis circuit in 1963 and won U.S. Open and Wimbledon tennis championships in 1968 and 1975 respectively. Golf opened up more slowly, but Charlie Sifford and Lee Elder appeared on the PGA tour in the

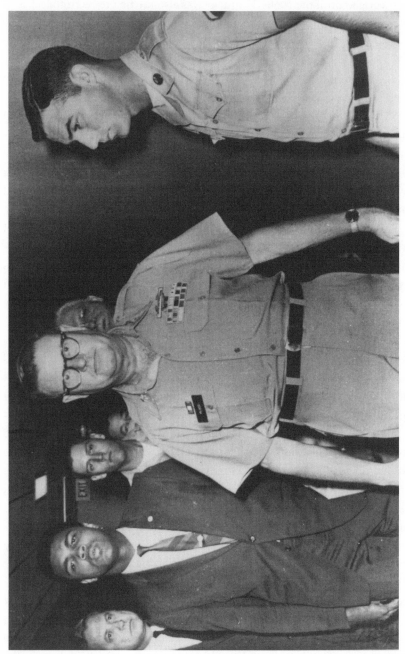

Muhammad Ali (second from left) refuses military induction (Library of Congress)

late 1960s. Sports provided a powerful medium to focus attention on racial issues in America and in the process help break down stereotypes and social barriers.

Prejudicial views of African American mental abilities continued, however. The attitude that black athletes possessed physical skills but lacked intelligence and discipline kept them out of certain decision-making positions: quarterback in football, point guard in basketball, pitcher and catcher in baseball. Those attitudes eroded over time but did not disappear quickly. The NBA in particular opened up to talented black athletes, and by 1970 over half of the league's players were African American.

The issue of race in sport was not limited to the United States. Politics continued to affect the Olympic Games. South Africa's white minority imposed a harsh, discriminatory system of racial segregation known as "apartheid" on the country's black majority. Under pressure from several African nations, the International Olympic Committee (IOC) prohibited South Africa from participating in the 1964 games, but it agreed to readmit the South Africans in 1968 pending minor athletic changes. Most other African nations, as well as other countries and many African American athletes, threatened to boycott the games, until the IOC reconsidered and denied South Africa once again. Not until South Africa replaced its racial policies did it finally return to compete in 1992.

The Olympic Games continued to thrive despite increased political intrusions. The 1960 games were the first to have extensive television coverage. CBS aired eighteen hours of the Squaw Valley Winter Olympics without commercial sponsors and had surprisingly high ratings. For the summer games in Rome, Italy, all the network's twenty videotaped broadcast hours attracted advertisers. The U.S. team in Rome featured track sprinter Wilma Rudolph, who won three gold medals, while hurdlers Lee Calhoun and Glenn Davis both won their events for the second consecutive Olympics. Christine Von Saltza earned three gold medals in the swimming pool. The victorious basketball team, which included Jerry Lucas, Oscar Robertson, and Jerry West, kept the United States undefeated in Olympic competition. The 1964 summer games took place in Tokyo. Swimmer Don Schollander was the U.S. star, winning four gold medals. The biggest surprise winner was unknown long-distance runner Billy Mills, who ran the best time of his life in defeating the world's elite in the ten thousand meters.

The Mexico City games in 1968 opened under ominous circumstances. The potential boycott over South Africa threatened, and the Soviet Union had crushed Czechoslovakia's efforts at political reform earlier in the year. Most critically, not long before the games opened, massive Mexican student protests brought brutal retaliation that resulted in more than 250 deaths. Politics attracted much of the media's attention, but several athletic performances stood out. Swimmers Debbie Meyer and Charles Hickcox each won three gold medals. On the track, Al Oerter won his fourth consecutive Olympic discus title, while sprinter Wyomia Tyus was a repeat winner of the women's one hundred meter race. Lee Evans set a record in the four hundred meters that would stand for nearly twenty years, and Dick Fosbury revolutionized the high jump, winning gold by going over the bar head first and backward. Bob Beamon astounded the sporting world by demolishing the world record in the long jump. His jump of 29 feet, 2 1/2 inches broke the existing record by over twenty-one inches.

Americans struggled to match the success of European nations in the decade's Winter Olympics. Figure skating was their most consistent strength. Carol Heiss and David Jenkins skated to victory in 1960 at Cortina, Italy, and the graceful Peggy Fleming took the country's only gold at the 1968 games in Grenoble, France. A major upset by the hockey team gave the United States a third gold medal in 1960 at Squaw Valley, California. At the 1964 winter games in Innsbruck, Austria, speed skater Terry McDermott earned the lone American victory.

American sports prospered financially at the same time they began breaking down race and gender barriers. Franchise expansion and television dollars combined to bring college and professional contests to the center of public attention. This growing popularity coexisted with new challenges to the role of sports in the increasingly unstable years of the Vietnam era. Sports could be both gloriously uplifting and deeply troubling.

MUSIC MIGRATION

At the beginning of the 1960s rock and roll was in a period of transition. Some of its most popular sounds carried over from the 1950s. The group singing of doo-wop and the reemergence of female stars in the girl groups competed with the smooth, pop-oriented teen idols. Within a few years these were all challenged, and largely eclipsed, by West Coast surf music and Motown soul from the Midwest. The years between rock's first generation and the British invasion produced some of the best and worst music of the rock and roll era.

Doo-wop music rode a second wave of popularity in the early 1960s, but that style was surpassed by the girl groups. These artists represented the return of female singers to the pop charts. During the three years before the rock era began in 1955, women sang about 30 percent of the annual top-fifty pop singles, but in both 1957 and 1958, they sang less than 10 percent. From 1962 to 1964 women recorded at least 25 percent of the top-fifty pop singles, their strongest showing in the rock era's first twenty years. The most successful of these female vocal groups—the East Coast–based Shirelles, Crystals, Ronettes, Chiffons, and Shangri-Las; and Motown groups like the Marvelettes, Martha and the Vandellas, and the Supremes—all placed at least five songs in the pop Top 40 between 1960 and 1966. Like the male-dominated doo-wop groups, the girl groups often began recording as high school students and sang of idealized romance.

Occasionally these young group members wrote their own material, but they frequently benefited from New York professionals centered in the Brill Building. Talented songwriting teams like Carole King and Gerry Goffin, Ellie Greenwich and Jeff Barry, Barry Mann and Cynthia Weil, and others turned out some of the period's most memorable songs. Producer Phil Spector put his personal imprint on many of the records by creating what he called "little symphonies for kids," but what was popularly known as the "wall of sound." Perhaps the most famous of all rock and roll producers, Spector recorded layers of instruments on his songs that created a huge sound that outshone the various artists he recorded. He was most influential during the first half of the 1960s, turning out hit singles on a regular basis but ignoring albums, which he considered "two hits and ten pieces of junk." Known as a demanding perfectionist, Spector "worked his orchestra like a drill sergeant, tinkering with arrangements and textures until he heard exactly what he wanted. The guitarists' hands bled, and the other musicians slumped from fatigue in the heat of the cramped, airless studio"[36]

The more conservative teen idol sound that flourished in the late 1950s and early 1960s had as much in common with older pop crooners as with earlier rockers. Several popular teen idols came from the Philadelphia area, recorded on local labels, and received regular exposure on *American Bandstand. Bandstand* host Dick Clark initially had financial interests in some of these record companies, but his careful presentation of rock and roll as wholesome fun for respectable teens helped him avoid negative repercussions from this conflict of interest.

Among the teen idols, Ricky Nelson, the youngest son on TV's *The Adventures of Ozzie and Harriet*, injected a polished rockabilly sound into some of his records, and Paul Anka wrote a number of memorable songs for various artists. Most teen idols, however, did not play an instrument, write songs, or have more than an adequate voice. Several either began as actors or moved into acting. In addition to Nelson and Anka, among the most popular were Connie Francis, Bobby Vinton, Bobby Rydell, Bobby Vee, Frankie Avalon, Fabian, and Shelley Fabares. A rare nonwhite face in this group was Chubby Checker, whose dance hit "The Twist" reached number one on the pop charts on two different occasions.

One of the styles that helped dislodge the teen idols while maintaining a comfortable suburban feel was surf music. Surfing was a fringe sport enjoyed in relatively few areas of the United States, but for a brief time in the early 1960s a musical sound associated with the water, beaches, and cars of Southern California swept the country. Many of the early surf hits were instrumentals featuring a distinctive guitar sound that simulated riding the ocean waves. Dick Dale acquired the title "King of the Surf Guitar" with an innovative rapid picking style borrowed from Middle Eastern stringed instruments and the use of reverberation. Dale's recording success was more regional than national, but his playing style influenced numerous electric guitarists and was reflected in hits by the Ventures and the Surfaris, among others.

Surf music as a national phenomenon peaked with the vocal group the Beach Boys. In addition to surf sounds, however, the Beach Boys incorporated the guitar influence of Chuck Berry and the vocal harmonies of the Four Freshmen into their music. Hits like "Surfin' USA" and "Surfer Girl" established their reputation, but the Beach Boys soon expanded their interests. Brian Wilson, one of three brothers in the group, was the primary songwriter and creative leader, crafting songs like "Good Vibrations" and the influential album *Pet Sounds*. Ultimately the Beach Boys became the most popular American group of the rock and roll era. Among other surf groups, only Jan and Dean scored more than a couple of hits.

Challenging the popularity of West Coast music in the early 1960s were the soul sounds of the Midwest and East Coast, especially the Motown music of Detroit. The Motown Record Company, founded by Berry Gordy Jr. in 1959, would grow into the largest black-owned company in America, encompassing music publishing, artist development, and multiple record labels. Motown signed a wealth of young musical talent from the Detroit area and supported the artists with creative writers and producers, plus a choreographer and a finishing school owner to train the performers to speak, move, and dress in ways that would appeal to a broad and affluent audience.

The list of Motown's best artists matches any other company's: the Miracles ("Shop Around"), Marvin Gaye ("I Heard It through the Grapevine"), the Marvelettes ("Please Mr. Postman"), the Supremes ("Baby Love"), Mary Wells ("My Guy"), Martha and the Vandellas ("Dancing in the Street"), the Temptations ("My Girl"), Stevie Wonder ("Fingertips—Pt. 2"), the Four Tops ("I Can't Help Myself"), and the Jackson 5 ("I Want You Back"). Songwriters Barrett Strong, Norman Whitfield, Brian Holland, Lamont Dozier, Eddie Holland, and Gordy himself, as well as performers like Marvin Gaye, Smokey Robinson, and Stevie Wonder, wrote some of the era's best songs. The house band, the jazz-trained Funk Brothers, are among the industry's legendary backup musicians and contributed enormously to the success of Motown's records. Behind it all was Gordy's desire to present a polished version of soul music that would appeal to the broadest possible audience, which meant white as well as black Americans. In this he was immensely successful.

A grittier style of soul music rolled out of the South. Stax Records in Memphis—formed under another name in 1957—and its subsidiary label Volt developed a sound that other companies sought out, built around their interracial house band, Booker T. and the MGs. Stax produced hits on its own labels by the MGs and Otis Redding, and its studio recorded some of Atlantic Records' biggest hits by Wilson Pickett and Sam and Dave. The New York–based Atlantic also used Fame Studio in Muscle Shoals, Alabama, to record Pickett and Aretha Franklin. Ironically, the black-owned and -operated Motown produced a smoother and sweeter sound that held greater appeal to white audiences, while the rougher southern soul sound, referred to by some as more "authentically" black—a rather dubious characterization—was white-owned and backed by interracial groups of musicians, although the singers themselves were nearly always black. These artists were more likely to draw on James Brown, Sam Cooke, Ray Charles, and Jackie Wilson as musical models.

Socially conscious lyrics drawn from American folk music represented an equally important contribution to the music of the 1960s. Folk music developed

from songs passed along by oral tradition, and songs often changed as new performers adapted the music to fit their own styles. As these songs were written
down, their form became more fixed. American folk styles varied widely around
the country, but the acoustic stringed instruments used in the Appalachian region, drawn largely from British and Irish traditions, made the biggest impact
on the development of rock and roll.

Twentieth-century American folk music often dealt with social issues like
labor unions and civil rights, but like blues and country music, folk only occasionally crossed over to pop audiences. The virulent anticommunism of the
early Cold War years had significantly inhibited the music's dissenting role. A
more commercial and apolitical brand of folk music enjoyed a revival in the
late 1950s. Groups like the Kingston Trio and the Brothers Four projected a
wholesome image and enjoyed great success, especially among college-age
record buyers. Starting in 1963 folk concerts appeared on the new television
show *Hootenanny*. This success also attracted mainstream attention for more
traditional artists like Joan Baez and Peter, Paul, and Mary, whose music focused more on social concerns. Out of this revival would emerge a singer who
shook up both folk music and rock and roll, Bob Dylan.

By the end of 1963 rock and roll music had come to dominate the popular
music charts. It remained, however, an interesting assortment of styles, as
some of the year's number one hits attest: teen idol Bobby Vinton's crooning
"Blue Velvet," the Angels' girl group warning "My Boyfriend's Back," surf
group Jan and Dean's "Surf City," and Little Stevie Wonder's Motown hit "Fingertips—Pt. 2" fought for chart space with the Singing Nun's folk song "Do-
minique," the Japanese-language tune "Sukiyaki" by Kyu Sakamoto, and Steve
Lawrence's pop standard "Go Away Little Girl." No one in America yet saw the
coming wave from across the Atlantic Ocean.

THE BRITISH INVASION
The international connection of American popular culture was readily apparent in rock and roll. The "British invasion" occurred when America's own raw
and enthusiastic musical styles, usually blues and rockabilly, mixed with
British folk and pop music and returned to U.S. shores. British artists had
never broken through to American audiences in any significant ways before—
not one British artist reached the American top ten in 1963, and only two had

hit the top position since 1954—but the United States remained a potentially lucrative market.

The group responsible for opening up America to British acts was the Beatles. After years of polishing their music in their hometown of Liverpool and in Hamburg, Germany, the Beatles became Britain's most popular group in 1963, a phenomenon termed by the press as "Beatlemania." By that time the band had evolved into its permanent lineup of John Lennon, Paul McCartney, George Harrison, and Ringo Starr. Capitol Records, the Beatles' U.S. distributor, did not think their sound would appeal to American audiences and failed to promote their records with any enthusiasm. In fact it leased the record rights to small independent labels. In January 1964, however, Capitol's parent company launched a publicity campaign that accompanied a trip by the group to the United States, and Capitol finally pushed an American version of the Beatles' second album. By the first week of April the Beatles held the top five spots on the pop singles chart, a staggering and unprecedented accomplishment. Their appearances on TV's *Ed Sullivan Show* were the most watched event in TV history to that time, with over seventy-three million people viewing on February 9. Beatlemania had come to America.

Beatlemania achieved global proportions and extended well beyond music. Shortly after they first arrived in the United States, the Beatles' popularity stirred behind the iron curtain. Public desire for their records deeply disturbed Soviet authorities, who viewed the new Western music as a threat to their control. Communist officials tried repressing rock and roll with a heavy hand but ultimately failed to contain it. At least one scholar on the subject believes rock "altered the very policies and structures of Soviet-bloc governments."[37]

The Beatles' earliest albums contain a few covers of songs by American influences such as Carl Perkins, Chuck Berry, Buddy Holly, and some of the Brill Building teams. Lennon and McCartney, however, wrote the vast majority of the group's recorded work, complemented by some fine George Harrison songs. The Beatles' initial hits, like "I Want to Hold Your Hand," followed typical themes of youthful romance, but each succeeding album revealed music of greater maturity and complexity. Meeting Bob Dylan stimulated more reflective lyrics, while Harrison's interest in Eastern music brought in new instruments like the sitar. Most importantly the group experimented in the recording studio, using it almost as an instrument itself. The result was a series of critically and popularly acclaimed albums: *Rubber Soul* (1965), *Revolver* (1966), and *Sgt. Pepper's Lonely Hearts Club Band* (1967). The *Sgt. Pepper* album became the most praised in rock's history. Built around the theme of a circus concert, it included psychedelic songs, a vast array of sound effects from pipe organs to animal noises, and lyrics with personal and social content.

About the only misstep to threaten the Beatles' popularity was a statement John Lennon made during a meandering interview with a British reporter in March 1966. When asked to comment on religion, he remarked, "Christianity will go. . . . We're more popular than Jesus now." Although ignored in Britain, Lennon's observation on religion appeared that July in an American teen magazine and drew an immediate negative reaction. Numerous radio stations stopped playing Beatles records, and several groups organized record burnings to express their disapproval. In August, prior to the Beatles' American tour, Lennon offered a halfhearted apology: "I'm not saying that we're better or greater or comparing us with Jesus as a person."[38] The controversy died down, but it demonstrated the broad social influence of rock and the Beatles.

The Beatles stopped touring after 1966, tired of performing concerts where fan noise was so loud they couldn't hear themselves play, and recording music too complex to be effectively reproduced on stage. By the time the group disbanded in 1970 it had placed twenty songs at the top of the American pop charts, more than any other artist, and become the most successful of all rock and roll groups. Not only that, but the Beatles' success cleared the way for a flood of other British artists.

While rockabilly and other forms of early American rock and roll became popular in Great Britain, the blues also attracted its share of British imitators. Centered primarily in London, British bands tried to duplicate the original blues sound rather than create a smoother version, as American cover artists usually did. This love of blues music and blues-based rock and roll became a significant strand of the British invasion. The most popular of England's blues-based groups was the Rolling Stones, formed in 1962 by Mick Jagger and Keith Richard, and ultimately joined by guitarist Brian Jones, bass player Bill Wyman, and drummer Charlie Watts. The group members played up their differences from the Beatles, projecting a more rebellious image in both their appearance and their music. Jagger and Richard developed into one of rock's best songwriting teams, providing the Stones with a steady flow of creative material as they tried to keep up with John Lennon and Paul McCartney. Sensing the commercial possibilities of the Beatles' style of pop-oriented rock, many blues-oriented bands moved in that direction while retaining some of their original influences. Among these were the Animals, the Yardbirds, and the Spencer Davis Group. Perhaps the most gifted British blues guitarist was Eric Clapton, who played in several groups, including the Yardbirds, John Mayall's Bluesbreakers, Blind Faith, and, most famously, Cream.

After the Beatles broke open the American market, dozens of British acts followed in the British invasion. The most popular 1964 hit makers were the Rolling Stones, Herman's Hermits, the Dave Clark 5, the Animals, and the Kinks. Within the next few years, the Hollies, the Yardbirds, and the Who crashed the U.S. charts several times. These eight groups alone combined to put over 130 songs in the American Top 40. They offered a wide variety of sounds, from Herman's Hermits' pop tunes of innocent teen romance ("Mrs. Brown You've Got a Lovely Daughter") to the blues-based riffs and bad boy image of the Rolling Stones ("Satisfaction") and the powerful guitar work and social commentary of the Kinks ("You Really Got Me") and the Who ("My Generation"). From the Beatles' arrival until the end of the decade, British artists recorded 28 percent of America's number one pop hits.

Folk music rivaled the British invasion as a major influence on rock and roll in the early 1960s. The most prominent figure in this regard was Bob Dylan. Dylan arrived in New York City from Minnesota in 1961 and quickly became part of the folk scene in Greenwich Village. Styling himself after Woody Guthrie, Dylan wrote lyrics that focused on many of the nation's important social issues: the testing of nuclear weapons, civil disobedience to end racial segregation, and the drift toward military conflict. Many of his songs were direct, while others were more abstract. Although widely admired within the folk community, Dylan's unusual nasally vocal style and pointed social criticism limited his crossover appeal. His commercial success grew in 1963 when Peter, Paul, and Mary hit the top ten with two of his songs and a concert tour with Joan Baez gave him greater visibility.

By 1964 Dylan's first few albums had established his reputation as an important protest singer, and his meeting with the Beatles that year foreshadowed significant changes for both. Dylan's carefully crafted lyrics on adult themes beyond romance pushed the Beatles, and many others, to introduce more sophisticated lyrics and social and political themes into pop music. In 1965 Dylan

Bob Dylan (Library of Congress)

angered many of his folk followers by shifting to electric instruments and a rock beat. The new style, however, gave Dylan his first major hit, "Like a Rolling Stone," and the pairing of electrified rock with socially conscious lyrics launched the style known as "folk rock." Dylan's new music also moved away from overt protest and toward personal rebellion and introspection. Critics often point to his three albums from 1965 and 1966, *Bringing It All Back Home*, *Highway 61 Revisited*, and *Blonde on Blonde*, all hitting the top ten on the album charts, as the high point of Dylan's creativity. While Dylan never matched the commercial heights of other top artists—he had a dozen Top 40 hits and fourteen top-ten albums by 1980—his lyrics earned him the title "Voice of a Generation," a label he did not want and sometimes impolitely rejected. A serious motorcycle accident in 1966 delayed his next album until 1968.

The Byrds emerged as the most successful folk rock group, both creatively and commercially. Their version of Dylan's "Mr. Tambourine Man" actually preceded "Like a Rolling Stone" on the charts and went all the way to number one. Most of the Byrds came out of the folk tradition, and their new sound emphasized a distinctive twelve-string guitar and soaring vocal harmonies. As the decade progressed and their personnel changed, the Byrds experimented with psychedelic music, and in 1968 they integrated Nashville sounds that made them among the first to produce "country rock." Among other contributors to the folk rock sound in the mid- to late 1960s were the Turtles, the Lovin' Spoonful, Simon and Garfunkel, Sonny and Cher, the Mamas and the Papas, Buffalo Springfield, and, from Scotland, Donovan.

If rock and roll originally developed in the 1950s around the teen culture, a decade later a maturing rock sound was integral to an emerging counterculture. Experimentation with illegal drugs, especially hallucinogens like LSD, was part of the effort to find ways of viewing and living in the world other than that of the existing establishment. Although psychedelic music, also called "acid rock," was not always drug related, it generally tried to imitate hallucinogenic trips or create an atmosphere conducive to those experiences. As might be expected, a variety of individuals and organizations concerned about the impact of illegal drug use fought this trend, mainly by having songs pulled from radio airplay, and musicians sometimes used cryptic lyrics to confound those efforts.

Psychedelic music was daringly innovative, if not always successful. Its characteristic improvisation drew on jazz styles, but also incorporated blues,

country, and other sounds. Lyrically acid rock often dealt with social and political issues from an adult perspective, sometimes at the cost of teenage record
buyers. Early examples of this style came in spring 1966 with the Yardbirds'
"Shapes of Things" and the Byrds' "Eight Miles High."

With a history of bohemian activity and as a focal point of the new American counterculture, San Francisco became the center of the psychedelic sound.
The city's Haight-Ashbury district served as home for youthful cultural rebels,
dubbed "hippies" by the media. The Bay area also hosted a number of "acid
tests," which provided homemade LSD, light shows, and music by local bands.
The longest lasting of these bands was the Grateful Dead, which achieved its
only Top 40 hit in 1987 but built a reputation with long improvisational songs
in concert and on albums. Jefferson Airplane had more commercial success
than other area psychedelic bands, including the 1967 drug-soaked top-ten hit
"White Rabbit." Several other area groups had enthusiastic followings, but this
rarely translated into major recording success. San Francisco bands were unusually suspicious of national record labels, and many of the companies hoped
to make some fast profits by riding the latest musical trend. Bay area bands,
with their fondness for lengthy improvisation and resistance to radio-friendly
singles, found greater success on albums than on 45s.

This psychedelic wave fit comfortably with a couple of important changes
that affected the American music industry. Rock was entering its second
decade, and adult artists and fans increasingly favored more mature lyrics and
longer compositions. Albums, sometimes built around particular themes,
proved a better format for this audience, and in 1967 LPs outsold 45s for the
first time. That same year San Francisco's KMPX led a trend toward album-
oriented FM radio broadcasts. FCC rulings in the mid-1960s required different programming for AM and FM stations in the same market. While AM
stations continued their rotation of Top 40 hits, FM experimented and contributed to the LP's status as the best measure of musical quality.

The search for alternatives that marked the counterculture and its music
could be both exhilarating and terrifying. The quest was not without casualties. Although liberating in many ways, the counterculture's excesses claimed
the lives or dreams of more than a few. One writer concludes, "Some did discover an inner peace; others wandered so far from life that they could not find
their way home again."[39]

While psychedelic music generally resisted commercial control and corporate understanding, the Monkees represented blatant commercialism. Columbia Pictures created the Monkees to star as a rock group in a television comedy series designed to capitalize on the success of the Beatles and their film *A Hard Day's Night*. Selected for their personality and looks rather than their musical ability—although Mike Nesmith in particular was a talented musician and songwriter—the Monkees became major recording stars in 1966. The TV show presented the band members as talented musicians, but their recording company did not allow them to play instruments on record. Creative tensions led Nesmith to reveal the company's deception, and the group demanded an expanded role. More success followed, until NBC canceled the show in 1968 and Peter Tork left the group, which continued briefly as a trio. Despite criticism over being a "manufactured" group, the Monkees produced nearly a dozen Top 40 hits.

YOU SAY YOU WANT A REVOLUTION?

Before the fusion of folk and rock music in the mid-1960s, author Reebee Garofalo asserts, "the energy of rock 'n' roll had always been identified with rebellion but never with a cause."[40] That fusion, however, made popular music "an important site for cultural conflict and dialogue about prevailing values."[41] Initially folk musicians challenged traditional respectability or censorship. For instance, Bob Dylan withdrew from the *Ed Sullivan Show* when told he could not sing "Talking John Birch Society Blues," and several leading folk acts boycotted ABC's *Hootenanny* over blacklisting practices. When rock songwriters turned their attention to subjects other than romance, they addressed the major social and political issues of the day. Usually advocating liberal causes, they wrote passionately in favor of civil rights. Some artists insisted on racially integrated audiences before agreeing to play concerts in the South.

Although rock remains linked with dissent, the connection between music and politics is more complex. Musicians in the 1960s lacked consensus on antiwar activism or the desirability of dissenting lyrics. Brian Wilson of the Beach Boys, a steadfastly nonpolitical group, claimed, "You can always write about social issues but who gives a damn."[42] John Lennon challenged the notion that protest music was simply a fad. During a 1964 interview, when asked if the

Beatles planned on recording any antiwar songs, Lennon responded, "All our songs are antiwar."[43]

Historians similarly disagree over the impact of antiwar and protest music on society. Ray Pratt claims that "never before in our history has the dissension over a war been so overtly dealt with in popular song."[44] Terry Anderson believes that the later half of the 1960s produced "more protest songs on the top hundred charts than at any time in the history of rock."[45] Kenneth Bindas and Craig Houston disagree, arguing, "The attention given to the Vietnam War by the rock 'n' roll industry was minimal." Even they agree, however, that rock "became the first popular music to be antiwar."[46]

The recording industry was politically cautious and followed rather than led public opinion. Bindas and Houston correctly assert, "Most rock audiences were apolitical."[47] Nevertheless, artists themselves created an unprecedented if limited connection between popular music, especially folk and rock, and antiwar sentiment. Songs often placed the war within a larger dissenting context, such as generational conflict, civil rights, and suspicion of the government. Bob Dylan's early songs sharply condemning the American war machine did not appear on singles charts, but their biting words made enough of an impression from album play that they remain some of the most quoted song lyrics of the era. Dylan's "Masters of War," Pete Seeger's "Waist Deep in the Big Muddy," Phil Ochs's "I Ain't Marchin' Anymore," and Country Joe and the Fish's "Feel Like I'm Fixin' to Die Rag" are among many well-known folk songs that never reached *Billboard*'s top one hundred.

Political statements by rock singers followed. Standing at the center of the youth counterculture, rock offered an antiestablishment attitude—a rebelliousness that one rock musician typified when he called it "the last medium not totally controlled by business interests."[48] Antiwar rock grew slowly because of a small antiwar base of record buyers, conservative business practices, and fear of government reprisals against radio stations. Politicized songs increased in number with general antiwar sentiment, with lyrics typically evoking skepticism of government motives or an inability to change policy. "The social change came first," observed Gentle Soul's Pamela Polland, "and the music reflected that. But the music 'announced' the changes to wider audiences— it heralded the changes, and in so doing, it educated a broader public."[49] In the struggle between commerce and self-expression, musicians were gaining the upper hand.

Most forms of popular culture enjoyed great success throughout the 1960s. Television gained financial prosperity and a central place in the daily lives of many people. It also faced challenges from the highest levels to satisfy public as well as commercial interests. Both entertainment and documentary programming briefly provided more social relevance, but that declined as the decade progressed. This was offset to a degree as network news coverage increased in both time and scope. The promise of more significant change appeared in the beginnings of publicly supported noncommercial television and occasional cultural battles over programming.

Spectator sports, aided by television coverage, experienced tremendous growth. Established team owners fought against both new competing leagues and more active players' unions. The economics of major league sports was being transformed. In the face of growing civil rights activism, race relations underwent drastic improvement as well. Racial minorities achieved access, though still not equal access, to nearly all professional and university competition. The Cold War and vastly increased TV coverage made international sporting events more available and important as a measure of national pride.

Rock and roll music reached a new prominence within the music industry. It became the nation's dominant musical style as it moved well beyond its earlier regional and outsider origins. An influx of stylistic influences created new hybrids of sound. None were more surprising or sweeping than the British invasion beginning in 1964. Rock was the music of generational and cultural rebellion.

The movie industry struggled during much of this period. Creative and financial energy came from America's interactions with the international film community. Foreign and domestic influences combined to bring dramatic changes to motion pictures, breaking down long-standing production codes. The major studios continued their shift of emphasis from production and exhibition to financing and distribution, which opened the door to growing numbers of independent filmmakers. The industry moved even closer to its increasingly younger audience and television to find greater stability.

NOTES

1. Paul Monaco, *The Sixties, 1960–1969*, vol. 8 of *History of the American Cinema*, ed. Charles Harpole (New York: Scribner, 2001), 56.

2. Monaco, *The Sixties*, 68.

3. "Hollywood: The Shock of Freedom in Films," *Time*, December 8, 1967, 67.

4. "Television: The Season," *Time*, March 31, 1961, 36.

5. John Frankenheimer, quoted in John Bartlow Martin, "Television USA: Wasteland or Wonderland?" *Saturday Evening Post*, October 21, 1961, 23.

6. Daniel Melnick, quoted in Jack Weiner, "Disillusion Between the Lines," *Television Magazine*, June 1961, 92.

7. Newton Minow, quoted in Lester Thonssen, ed., *Representative American Speeches: 1961–1962* (New York: H. W. Wilson, 1962), 68.

8. Newton Minow, quoted in Mary Ann Watson, *Defining Visions: Television and the American Experience since 1945* (Fort Worth, TX: Harcourt Brace, 1998), 87.

9. Watson, *Defining Visions*, 87.

10. Mary Ann Watson, *The Expanding Vista: American Television in the Kennedy Years* (New York: Oxford University Press, 1990), 144.

11. Erik Barnouw, *Tube of Plenty: The Evolution of American Television*, 2nd rev. ed. (New York: Oxford University Press, 1990), 327.

12. Russell Baker, *The Good Times* (New York: William Morrow, 1989), 326.

13. Harry Castleman and Walter J. Podrazik, *Watching TV: Four Decades of American Television* (New York: McGraw-Hill, 1982), 170.

14. Barnouw, *Tube of Plenty*, 347.

15. Herbert G. Lawson Jr., "Drs. Kildare, Casey Get Guidance from Medical Association," *Wall Street Journal*, December 27, 1962, 1.

16. Watson, *Defining Visions*, 146.

17. Margaret Mead, quoted in Watson, *Defining Visions*, 59.

18. Betty Friedan, "The Monster in the Kitchen," in *TV Guide: The First 25 Years*, ed. Jay S. Harris (New York: Simon and Schuster, 1978), 98.

19. Barnouw, *Tube of Plenty*, 378.

20. Fred W. Friendly, *Due to Circumstances beyond Our Control* (New York: Random House, 1967), 213.

21. Walter Cronkite, *Who, What, When, Where, Why: Report from Vietnam by Walter Cronkite*. Originally broadcast February 27, 1968, over the CBS Television Network,

reprinted in Robert J. McMahon, ed., *Major Problems in the History of the Vietnam War*, 2nd ed. (Lexington, MA: DC Heath, 1995), 528–29.

22. Barnouw, *Tube of Plenty*, 396–99.

23. Barnouw, *Tube of Plenty*, 415.

24. Daniel Walker, *Rights in Conflict: Convention Week in Chicago, August 15–29, 1968* (New York: Dutton, 1968), vii; David Farber, *The Age of Great Dreams: America in the 1960s* (New York: Hill and Wang, 1994), 223.

25. National Commission on the Causes and Prevention of Violence, quoted in Watson, *Defining Visions*, 88–89.

26. Benjamin G. Rader, *American Sports: From the Age of Folk Games to the Age of Television*, 4th ed. (Upper Saddle River, NJ: Prentice Hall, 1999), 232.

27. Roone Arledge, quoted in Rader, *American Sports*, 235.

28. Lawrence M. Baskir and William A. Strauss, *Chance and Circumstance: The Draft, the War and the Vietnam Generation* (New York: Vintage, 1978), 48–49.

29. Myra MacPherson, *Long Time Passing: Vietnam and the Haunted Generation* (New York: New American Library, 1984), 169.

30. Dave Meggyesy, *Out of Their League* (Berkeley, CA: Ramparts, 1970), 147.

31. Chip Oliver, quoted in Howard Zinn, *Postwar America: 1945–1971* (Indianapolis: Bobbs-Merrill, 1973), 234.

32. Jim Bouton, *Ball Four* (New York: World, 1970), 84.

33. Bouton, *Ball Four*, 385.

34. Sandy Koufax, quoted in Randy Roberts, *Winning Is the Only Thing: Sports in America since 1945* (Baltimore: Johns Hopkins University Press, 1989), 136.

35. *Sports Illustrated*, October 15, 1979, 24.

36. Editors of Rolling Stone, *Rolling Stone: The Decades of Rock and Roll* (San Francisco: Chronicle Books, 2001), 105.

37. Timothy W. Ryback, *Rock around the Bloc: A History of Rock Music in Eastern Europe and the Soviet Union* (New York: Oxford University Press, 1990), 5.

38. John Lennon quoted in Philip Norman, *Shout: The Beatles in Their Generation* (New York: Fireside, 1981), 265–66; Linda Martin and Kerry Segrave, *Anti-Rock: The Opposition to Rock 'n' Roll* (Hamden, CT: Archon Books, 1988), 180.

39. Herbert I. London, *Closing the Circle: A Cultural History of the Rock Revolution* (Chicago: Nelson-Hall, 1984), 110.

40. Reebee Garofalo, *Rockin' Out: Popular Music in the USA*, 2nd ed. (Upper Saddle River, NJ: Prentice Hall, 2002), 176.

41. George Lipsitz, "Youth Culture, Rock 'n' Roll, and Social Crises," in *The Sixties: From Memory to History*, ed. David Farber (Chapel Hill: University of North Carolina Press, 1994), 208.

42. Brian Wilson, quoted in Glenn C. Altschuler, *All Shook Up: How Rock 'n' Roll Changed America* (New York: Oxford University Press, 2003), 175.

43. John Lennon, quoted in Jonathan Eisen, ed., *The Age of Rock: Sounds of the American Cultural Revolution* (New York: Random House, 1969), 6.

44. Ray Pratt, "'There Must Be Some Way Outta Here': The Vietnam War in American Popular Music," in *The Vietnam War: Its History, Literature and Music*, ed. Kenton J. Clymer (El Paso: Texas Western Press, 1998), 172.

45. Terry H. Anderson, "American Popular Music and the War in Vietnam," *Peace and Change* 11, no. 2 (1986): 58.

46. Kenneth J. Bindas and Craig Houston, "'Takin' Care of Business': Rock Music, Vietnam and the Protest Myth," *Historian* 52, no. 1 (1989): 1, 6.

47. Bindas and Houston, "'Takin' Care,'" 19.

48. "Don't Laugh, but the Next Step Could Be Pop as a Political Power," *Melody Maker*, October 26, 1968, 13.

49. Pamela Polland, quoted in Richie Unterberger, *Eight Miles High: Folk-Rock's Flight from Haight-Ashbury to Woodstock* (San Francisco: Backbeat Books, 2003), 300.

Booming Business: 1969 to 1975

The end of the 1960s marked several significant political events in American life. The 1968 Tet Offensive stimulated a reevaluation of American policy in Vietnam that ended military escalation and began the long process of withdrawal. The election of Richard Nixon to the presidency inaugurated a period of bitterly confrontational rhetoric between administration conservatives and liberal and countercultural elements in society. The murders of Martin Luther King Jr. and Robert Kennedy combined with urban race riots to dramatically erode public support for additional civil rights legislation. The postwar consensus in foreign policy was shattered, the liberal political agenda stalled, and generational and racial divisions raged. Society seemed to be splintering in a hundred different directions.

Culture in the United States mirrored politics in many respects. The definition of acceptable standards shifted in several forms of popular culture. The varieties of rock music multiplied so rapidly that rock encompassed sounds with little in common. Players' unions fundamentally changed the economics of professional sports. Breakthrough shows appeared on television that smashed previous barriers on language and political issues. Motion pictures, long struggling with declining attendance, abandoned their decades-old content standards and looked to the youth market for revival.

These changes occurred as control of entertainment industries was expanding beyond previous bases. Large conglomerates swallowed most of the major movie studios, and independent filmmakers increased their influence in the business. As rock splintered, superstars acquired more creative control, and a new musical subculture resisted mainstream commercial forces. Women entered the sports world in impressive numbers and with great enthusiasm, opening up opportunities denied most females for generations. Cable television challenged the networks' domination of broadcasting. The definition and control of popular culture slipped out of the grasp of its previously narrow base.

BLOCKBUSTERS

As the United States entered a late 1960s economic recession, largely caused by the Vietnam War, the American film industry endured a major recession primarily of its own making. The Hollywood studios suffered massive losses from 1969 to 1971. Blinded by the extraordinary success of Twentieth Century-Fox's *The Sound of Music* (1965), which grossed a record $135 million, the major studios spent the next few years producing films, especially expensive musicals, they hoped would become blockbusters. Fox alone lost nearly twenty-five million dollars on *Doctor Dolittle* (1967) and *Star* (1968). The addition of new film producers/distributors in the late 1960s contributed to an excessive number of films and the rising cost of creative personnel. Distributors' percentage of film grosses decreased as theaters took advantage of intensified competition. The majors lost five hundred million dollars from 1969 to 1972, and this recession wiped out 40 percent of Hollywood filmmakers' jobs.

For a time starting in the late 1960s, the studios increasingly relied on films directed toward young viewers to improve their fortunes. Nearly half of moviegoers were between the ages of sixteen and twenty-four. The success of youth-oriented films such as *Bonnie and Clyde* and *The Graduate*, and the unexpected popularity of *Easy Rider* in 1969, a low-budget movie that earned nearly twenty million dollars, led producers to try and capture the same audience with a series of films with youthful appeal. *Easy Rider* is a story about two alienated, drug-dealing motorcyclists who face social hostility and end up murdered by backward southerners. It was one of the first movies tied to a sound track of powerful late-1960s rock music. As often happens, filmmakers rarely found the magic of the original. Several films emphasized the counterculture, frequently linking it to illegal drug use, and featured common themes of generational rebelliousness and cutting-edge trendiness. Many used a rock music sound track and ad campaigns that echoed the alienation explicit in *Easy Rider*'s publicity tag line: "A man went looking for America, and couldn't find it anywhere." Among the best of this undistinguished genre are *M*A*S*H*, *Catch-22*, and *Five Easy Pieces*, plus two concert documentaries, *Woodstock* and *Gimme Shelter*, all from 1970. Only the 1971 independent film *Billy Jack* duplicated the low-budget, big-profit success of *Easy Rider*. Some of these films appealed to broader audiences, but each targeted teenage preferences. The drive for the youth market did not prevent economic recession in the film industry, though it did help spark a creative renaissance in the late 1960s and early 1970s.

Anxious to escape their financial problems, studios experimented with giving greater creative freedom to directors who seemed able to tap the youth market. Although driven by monetary concerns, the result was a flourishing of American auteurs in what was called the "New Hollywood." Auteurism, an idea originally introduced by French filmmaker Francois Truffaut, argued that a film should reflect the distinctive singular style of its director rather than a collective consensus of the studio or production team. This willingness to give some directors greater independence produced enough early success in the late 1960s to create a growing acceptance of auteurism as an appropriate method of filmmaking. It also contributed to the public's greater recognition and appreciation of the director as a creative force. Steven Spielberg called this era a time when "young people were allowed to come rushing in" with "an avalanche of brave new ideas."[1] Film historian David Cook claims this shift "brought with it a few years of real artistic freedom and resulted in some of the most original American films since the late forties."[2]

Several outstanding veteran directors created breakthrough films, including Arthur Penn (*Bonnie and Clyde*), Stanley Kubrick (*2001: A Space Odyssey*), Sam Peckinpah (*The Wild Bunch*), and Robert Altman (*M*A*S*H*). A younger group of directors without a previous record of success also produced notable pictures. Among these were Mike Nichols (*The Graduate*), Peter Bogdanovich (*The Last Picture Show*), William Friedkin (*The French Connection*), Bob Rafelson (*Five Easy Pieces*), and Alan Pakula (*Klute*). Many of the young directors of the 1970s learned their craft in university film schools, such as UCLA and USC in Los Angeles and New York University, rather than through apprenticeships or television. This new collection included Francis Ford Coppola (*The Godfather*), George Lucas (*American Graffiti*), Steven Spielberg

(*Jaws*), and Martin Scorsese (*Mean Streets*). As the average cost of producing a movie rose to $9.4 million by 1980 and marketing expenses climbed, however, studios and financiers grew less likely to turn over creative control to directors.

The lineup of major studios had changed since the postwar consent decrees. MGM, Paramount, Warner Brothers, Twentieth Century-Fox, and RKO all suffered from the sale of their theaters, and RKO left the industry completely. Universal, Columbia, and United Artists moved into the ranks of the majors. The loss of vertical control brought the decline of the studio system, as films were produced on an individual basis and corporate income became less stable. What the studios retained, however—their land, film libraries, and production facilities—made them tantalizing targets for corporate buyouts. By 1970 conglomerates bought Universal, Paramount, Warner Brothers, and United Artists, and MGM became the property of a wealthy individual, leaving only Twentieth Century-Fox and Disney with their original ownership. During the 1970s they divided the market share as follows: Paramount 15 percent, Warner Brothers 14.5 percent, Fox 13.9 percent, Universal 13.4 percent, MGM/United Artists 12.3 percent, Columbia 10.2 percent, and Disney 6.4 percent.[3]

The transfer of the major studios to conglomerate control followed similar paths. Financial troubles hit the studios in the late 1950s, followed by disastrous efforts to reverse their losses. Universal ended up in the hands of the Music Corporation of America (MCA). Purchased by Decca in 1951, Universal made several telefilms in the 1950s but ran a deficit in 1958. MCA, then a talent agency, bought Decca and Universal in 1962, but the courts forced MCA to sell its agent component. Despite inconsistent performance in the 1960s, Universal enjoyed greater popularity in the 1970s. Hits like *Airport* and *American Graffiti* carried it, and it owned distribution rights for *The Sting* and *Jaws*. In 1975 Universal led Hollywood with the most profitable year in industry history.

Paramount's final blow was the 1964 failure of *The Fall of the Roman Empire*. Gulf and Western bought the studio in 1966, and Paramount acquired Desilu Productions in 1967. The studio prospered in the 1970s, moving increasingly into distribution, reducing its film production, and using agent-packaged deals to make movies.

United Artists (UA) owned no studios or theaters but made its money on distributing in the 1950s and 1960s. Transamerica bought the company in

1967, but UA retained its creative autonomy. After absorbing losses in the early 1970s, UA contracted with MGM to become its sole distributor for ten years. A number of hits made United Artists very profitable for the rest of the decade. Failing to regain UA's autonomy from Transamerica in 1977, five key UA executives broke off and formed Orion Pictures Company in 1978. Kirk Kerkorian bought UA in 1981 and merged it as MGM/United Artists Entertainment Company. Cable television mogul Ted Turner bought the company in 1986, stripped the film library, and resold it to Kerkorian.

Metro-Goldwyn-Mayer operated in the red for the first time in 1957, rebounded with *Ben-Hur*, but lost money again in the early 1960s. Occasional hits like *Doctor Zhivago* and *2001: A Space Odyssey* only prolonged its decline, and Kirk Kerkorian gained control of MGM stock in 1969. To reduce the studio's debt he and president James Aubrey sold MGM properties, MGM Records, and old costumes and props and cut the number of employees by 80 percent. Critic Vincent Canby declared, "The Kerkorian-Aubrey management of MGM was the realization of everyone's worst fears of what would happen to Hollywood when the money-men take over."[4] Until its merger with United Artists in 1981, MGM operated throughout the 1970s as a relatively minor movie producer. Reducing the number of films and keeping budgets small were Aubrey's methods of staying solvent. He blamed the studio's problems on "this introduction of social issues into films." David Cook notes, "Aubrey epitomized the cost-cutting, anti-intellectual mentality that ruled the studios after the recession."[5]

Warner Brothers experienced its first deficit in thirty years in 1958 and hit bottom in 1964. The studio merged with Seven Arts to form Warner Brothers–Seven Arts in 1967 but changed back to Warner Brothers after its 1969 acquisition by Kinney National Services. Former agent Ted Ashley became Warner's CEO, and his budget consciousness led to a successful decade in the 1970s. Warner Communications linked film, music, and publishing to provide mutual aid to each product.

A few major studios avoided the trend of corporate absorption until later. Columbia Pictures created a Screen Gems division for producing television shows. Despite the diversification, Columbia suffered losses in 1958. It managed to slide by until the mid-1960s, when a few hits helped it recover, and in 1968 Columbia merged with Screen Gems to create Columbia Pictures Inc. Its distribution of *Easy Rider* "woke the industry abruptly to the fact that both the demographics and the tastes of its audience had changed."[6] By 1973, however, Columbia was nearly bankrupt. New management cut budgets and produced moderate hits before scoring big with *Close Encounters of the Third Kind* (1977). Coca-Cola bought Columbia in 1982.

Twentieth Century-Fox lost money in 1960, and *Cleopatra* dragged it down further three years later. Darryl Zanuck's return as president improved conditions until the end of the decade, but fights between Zanuck and his son, the company's production head, led to their ouster in the early 1970s. To cut the studio's debt, new management sold much of Fox's land, cut overhead, and closed the New York City office. By 1974 the studio was turning a profit based on small pictures and a few hits. *Star Wars* in 1977 marked Fox's high point in the 1970s. Sherry Lansing became Fox's studio production head in 1980, Hollywood's first female in that position. Oil magnate Marvin Davis bought Fox in 1981 but sold it to Rupert Murdoch in 1984.

Disney benefited from having its own distribution company, Buena Vista, starting in 1953. Rising animation costs led it increasingly to live films. Walt Disney's death in 1966 stimulated debate over the company's direction, and by the mid-1970s much of Disney's income came from older film rereleases. Conservative business practices and a refusal to address changing public tastes led to temporary, though profitable, stagnation. Disney became a major studio by building a diversified entertainment strategy.

Below the level of "major," other companies made their mark in film distribution in the 1970s. American International Pictures (AIP) became a leading youth exploitation studio. Consistent profits allowed it to establish a national distribution system. Several prominent actors and directors developed their craft working for AIP. In the 1970s AIP produced several martial arts films and black-oriented films that resulted in a new term, "blaxploitation." Ultimately, however, AIP fell prey to the lure of bigger-budget films and in 1979 suffered its first deficit year. After AIP merged with Filmways as Filmways/AIP, Orion bought the company in 1982. In its early years, however, AIP had pioneered the niche marketing and saturation booking later emulated by the major studios.

A few other small companies left their mark. Embassy Pictures formed in 1956 and profited from editing foreign films like *Godzilla* and *Hercules* for American audiences. Its success with *The Graduate* led to its purchase by the Avco conglomerate, and it became Avco Embassy. Allied Artists Pictures provided an outlet for talented young directors, and New World Pictures, founded by Roger and Gene Corman in 1970, was the largest independent production-distribution company in the United States a decade later.

Two so-called instant majors appeared in 1967 when television networks began feature film production to supply their own prime-time needs. These two, National General Corporation–CBS and Cinerama Releasing Corporation–ABC, also distributed films to theaters. Despite some good films, financial losses closed the CBS operation down after 1971. Cinerama Releasing Corporation also mixed hits with overall losses and closed in 1978. They had, however, enjoyed 10 percent of the market in 1970.

Reliance on young audiences and auteur directors—the latter for a very brief period—were not the only attempts to make the motion picture industry profitable again. Under industry pressure, the Nixon administration provided federal income and investment tax credits that eased studio financial burdens through the mid-1970s. The majors also responded by producing fewer films—from an average of 160 in the late 1960s to 80 by the mid-1970s.

No longer able to count on a consistent national audience, or to reliably predict audience tastes, Hollywood filmmakers looked for a new production formula in the early 1970s. What they came up with was the blockbuster. Experience—and the blockbuster mentality—indicated that most films lost money and persuaded the studios that films producing major profits occurred only occasionally. A small number of blockbusters sustained the industry through the 1950s and 1960s. Big-budget pictures were more likely, though not certain, to capture the public's attention, so the majors concentrated on developing projects that would sell to a public that had more choices than ever competing for their entertainment dollars. Going to the movies was no longer a habit, and people had to be drawn to the theaters. Movies were increasingly part of a larger marketing package rather than an isolated product. Linking film production with marketing meant producing films with maximum sales potential rather than primarily artistic considerations. Studios tried to enhance their chances for success by enlisting established stars and tying the film to as many products as possible. This meant primarily a successful book or play, and later a movie sound track album, but extended to include posters, toys, clothing, video games, and fast food, among other things, to maximize profitability.

Saturation booking replaced the traditional gradual release pattern of first run, second run, and sub-run theaters. With the older method films opened in a limited number of theaters, and studios heavily marketed only the ones that proved popular. The saturation strategy used massive prerelease publicity and nationwide opening in hundreds of theaters. The studios felt this created anticipation and avoided the loss of potential viewers through negative word of mouth or poor reviews. It also placed a premium on high ticket sales in a movie's opening weeks. Although exploitation films had used saturation booking for years, major studio feature releases adopted this method on a regular basis only in the 1970s.

Two early 1970s blockbusters from Paramount convinced the studios they were on the right track. For *Love Story* (1970) the studio had playwright Erich Segal write a novel based on his script, which was published prior to the film's release and became a best-seller. The novel generated broad public awareness and anticipation for the film. The movie sound track also sold well. Similarly, Paramount bought the rights to *The Godfather* (1972) well before the novel's completion by author Mario Puzo. The book's success paved the way for the film, which became the top-grossing motion picture ever produced to that time.

The Godfather sparked Hollywood's revival. Francis Ford Coppola directed the film, which won the best actor Oscar for Marlon Brando and earned three other cast members nominations for best supporting actor. The action takes place in New York City during the 1940s, focusing on Don Vito Corleone and his crime family. They were driven to working outside the system because of exclusion from that system. Eventually the old ways are threatened by new crimes (drugs), and the younger son, Michael, replaces his father. Universal opened *The Godfather* in about four hundred theaters, demanding millions in advance money plus an unprecedented 90 percent of the theater revenue for the movie's first three months. "The money up front, the favorable splits, the massive release," claims Peter Biskind, "resulted in a dramatic, not to say revolutionary, transformation of Paramount's cash flow."[7]

The blockbuster strategy brought a degree of financial stability to the film industry. Movie theater attendance had dropped to under sixteen million in 1971, but income from ticket sales nearly tripled during the 1970s. Three 1973 releases brought in over fifty-five million dollars each in film rentals: *The Exorcist*, *The Sting*, and the low-budget surprise *American Graffiti*. The majors

Marlon Brando in The Godfather *(AP/Wide World Photos)*

took 90 percent of the box office revenues during the decade, although they handled only one-third of the films distributed. Studio management, however, was much less secure. Studio heads were now employees, not the owner/moguls of the studio system's golden age.

The real benchmark in movie marketing came in 1975 with *Jaws*, directed by Steven Spielberg. *Jaws* combined extensive national prerelease publicity, saturation booking, strong links to other media, and related commercial products. The film was based on a popular novel that gave it name recognition, received publicity for months before its release, and enjoyed a generous TV ad campaign just before and during its opening in over four hundred U.S. theaters. The merchandising of hundreds of products helped the film make nearly $130 million, making it history's new top-grossing movie. As often happened, neither the studio nor the actors had predicted the movie's success. Costar Richard Dreyfuss expected the "turkey of the year."[8] In the wake of *Jaws*'s success, saturation bookings and extensive product tie-ins became standard practice for Hollywood's biggest films. In the future blockbusters would open in over two thousand theaters, bolstered by massive television ad campaigns. With so much more money tied up in a film's release, studios wanted a fast return. Movies with a disappointing opening faced a short run. According to Biskind, "*Jaws* changed the business forever."[9]

Independent producers filled the production gap left by the major studios. In the wake of *Jaws*'s unprecedented success, Hollywood's anticipation that each new film was a potential blockbuster meant "every film the majors produced was launched as if it were the second coming of Christ."[10] Although the major studios originated fewer film projects than before, they remained the primary film distributors and key financing sources. Paramount, for example, produced only twenty-eight of the sixty-seven films it distributed from 1973 to 1975.

In addition to using the blockbuster strategy, the film industry further protected itself through its involvement in television. Hollywood produced 70 percent of television's programming in the 1960s. The major studios also reaped profits from TV broadcasts of their feature films. The number of movies shown during TV prime time reached over 160 in 1970, with the studios receiving eight hundred thousand dollars per film. Televised movies became so popular that networks began producing their own films. By the 1970s movies constituted one-quarter of prime-time programming. By mid-decade made-for-TV movies outnumbered feature films broadcast on television. "Thus," notes David Cook,

> while feature-film production remained Hollywood's most salient and cultur-
> ally prominent role in the 1970s, its main function within the American media
> industry became that of TV *producer* and film *distributor*, shifting its posture
> dramatically from the classical era but completing a transition that had been
> ongoing since the consent decree.[11]

Producers also relied more heavily on reproducing past successes, either as sequels or as part of a popular genre. The percentage of sequels and reissued films—often used to generate more revenue for the sequels—quadrupled from the mid-1960s to the mid-1970s, accounting for nearly 18 percent of the total.

As the business side of the motion picture industry changed, the movies' content continued to evolve. The deceit and corruption of government revealed by the Vietnam War and the Watergate scandal produced increased public cynicism and suspicion. These attitudes found their way onto movie screens in the 1970s. Several films dealt with paranoid political conspiracies. *Executive Action* (1973) blamed President Kennedy's death on right-wing business interests. In *The Parallax View* (1974), a business enterprise assassinates political leaders who threaten its interests, while *The Candidate* (1972) portrays politics as a media-driven contest whose goal is election rather than implementing real change. The Central Intelligence Agency received attention from conspiracy theorists as well, in *Three Days of the Condor* (1975) and *The Killer Elite* (1975).

The political upheaval of the 1960s and early 1970s influenced various movie genres. Spaghetti westerns and especially Sam Peckinpah's *The Wild Bunch* (1969) set the standard for nontraditional portrayals of the Old West. Westerns such as *A Man Called Horse* (1970), *Little Big Man* (1970), and *Ulzana's Raid* (1972) condemned U.S. actions as aggressive and even genocidal, while establishing American Indians as heroic defenders of their society. The parallels with U.S. involvement in Vietnam were inescapable, and placing these views in a western film allowed freer expression than dealing directly with Southeast Asia. John Wayne westerns still appealed to some audiences, but "the heroic utopian mythography of the American West became impossible to sustain" after the twin tragedies of the war in Vietnam and President Nixon's shameful resignation.[12] The mythical West faded in a series of popular movies: *The Life and Time of Judge Roy Bean* (1972), *Jeremiah Johnson* (1972), and *Pat Garrett and Billy the Kid* (1973).

Perhaps more surprising was the success of other motion picture styles. Horror films, often cheaply produced in the past and relegated to niche markets, moved into the mainstream by the early 1970s. *Rosemary's Baby* (1968) was the first of several horror movies with religious themes, such as *The Exorcist* (1973) and *The Omen* (1976). George Romero's *Night of the Living Dead* (1968) was a low-budget model as well. Under the new rating system, graphic violence became an almost inevitable accompaniment to such films.

The Exorcist was most responsible for transferring shocking horror scenes to mainstream films. A film of teenage demonic possession, it was nominated for an Oscar as best picture and included language and scenes rarely before depicted on film for general audiences. The sensational aspects of the movie drew wide debate and, not surprisingly, provoked a series of films dealing with the occult.

Another formerly B-level genre was science fiction. *2001: A Space Odyssey* and *Planet of the Apes*, both from 1968, offered the first sign of the arrival of science fiction as potential blockbuster material. A series of disaster movies achieved great success as well. *Airport* (1970), *The Poseidon Adventure* (1972),

The Towering Inferno (1974), and *Earthquake* (1974) shared a collection of well-known stars addressing a natural or man-made catastrophe.

More pervasive than any of these styles was the proliferation of overt sensuality. Films became more sexually explicit. *Bob and Carol and Ted and Alice* (1969) dealt with mate swapping, *Carnal Knowledge* (1971) explored sexual anxieties, and *Last Tango in Paris* (1973) looked at extreme erotic fantasy. Russ Meyer was a leading figure in bringing blatant sex into public theaters. Sexual themes were joined at first by partial nudity and simulated intercourse and ultimately by full nudity and actual sex acts. Though hard-core films had been available previously in adult movie houses and from avant-garde figures like Andy Warhol, they entered the mainstream in 1973 with *The Devil in Miss Jones* and *Deep Throat*, both ranking among the year's top-dozen box office hits. Numerous local prosecutors challenged these and similar films on obscenity statutes, which undoubtedly kept them from ranking even higher. Filmmakers were participating in a larger shift in publicly accepted morality but not necessarily leading it. Clothing styles became both more attention getting and more revealing, language grew coarser, political arguments spilled into the streets, sexuality was more blatantly expressed and exploited. Many Americans disapproved of these trends, but they would not be rolled back.

Hollywood's most honored and influential films from the late 1960s to the mid-1970s represent a variety of different styles and subjects. Sam Peckinpah's *The Wild Bunch* (1969) depicts a small band of outlaws out of place on the dying western frontier. The climactic gun battle is among the most graphically violent in screen history. The only X-rated film to win the Academy Award for best picture was *Midnight Cowboy* (1969). In this movie directed by John Schlesinger, two drifters bond as they survive the bleak side of life in New York City. *Patton* (1970) was another winner of the best picture Oscar. It stars George C. Scott in a biography of the famous and controversial World War II general George Patton. William Friedkin directed *The French Connection* in 1971. This realistic police drama features "Popeye" Doyle as a policeman who straddles the line between legal and illegal actions as he pursues criminals and makes a major drug seizure. *American Graffiti* was George Lucas's 1973 look at the youthful innocence of the early 1960s. Set in small-town California, the movie follows four main high school characters for an entire day as they cruise in their cars, listen to rock and roll, search for romance, and contemplate their future.

Matching the success of *The Godfather* was *The Godfather, Part II* (1974). It elaborates on the themes introduced in *The Godfather*, covering three generations of the Corleone family. *Godfather II*, however, focuses on Michael Corleone's rule as head of the family's criminal organization and contrasts his father's rise to power with Michael's decline. *Chinatown* (1974) is a film noir crime drama set in Los Angeles during the 1930s. Roman Polanski directed stars Jack Nicholson and Faye Dunaway. The movie features numerous plot twists involving land and water schemes and dark family secrets. *One Flew over the Cuckoo's Nest* (1975) stars Jack Nicholson. Set in a mental hospital, the film is an allegory about rebellion against conformity and repression. McMurphy, the lead character, resists arbitrary bureaucratic rules, but his insistence on basic rights and individualism ultimately brings retribution in the form of a lobotomy. Director Robert Altman called *Nashville* (1975) his "metaphor for America."[13] Altman saw a fusion of entertainment and politics that worked against the public good, and his film reflects the era's social turmoil. This satire uses Nashville's country music scene to portray both popular culture and political campaigns as manipulative performances. In addition to this view of social shallowness, *Nashville* depicts a society that thoughtlessly accepts these deplorable circumstances.

The era of rebel directors was fading by the mid-1970s. The unsettled studio system allowed several directors the creative independence to act as auteurs in the late 1960s. Their efforts to reach the key youth market and the new MPAA rating system permitted them to bring a greater range of subjects to the screen. Some directors, however, took themselves too seriously. "The magazines told them they were geniuses," observed writer Mardik Martin, "They thought they were God."[14] Those whose work proved inconsistent soon lost their divine status. As the studios recovered economically during the blockbuster era, the business conglomerates that owned most of the major studios once again exerted their control. Executives nearly always ranked business decisions ahead of creative art. In some cases the auteur and his young audience moved away from films of rebellion without noticing how they were corporatized, "their films as branded merchandise to be consumed along with T-shirts, action figures, Happy Meals, and, by the end of the decade, miniaturized and badly framed versions of the films themselves called 'videos.'"[15] A director's connection to youth culture no longer ensured success. Although 90 percent of theater audiences were between twelve and thirty-nine, "this was no longer a counterculture audience. It was a *Porky's* audience."[16]

The rising expense of making movies drastically altered how they were produced. During the 1970s the average costs involved in making a picture rose from $1.9 million (1972) to $8.9 million (1979). With escalating costs, the majors produced fewer films, releasing about 150 films per year at the beginning of the decade but only 100 by the end. Since many film producers believed that the most popular stars were critical to selling a movie, the demand for these elite actors increased, which sent their incomes soaring. Under these circumstances agents substantially increased their influence within the industry, and management agencies played critical roles in getting films to the public. With studios focusing more on financing and distributing, agents took a greater role in developing movie projects. They often combined actors, writers, directors, and a script before selling the entire package to a studio for distribution. The most popular actors and their agents became the most influential decision makers in getting a new film produced. Creative value often suffered when agents pursued their own or their clients' financial interests above other concerns. The trend was set, however, and former agents ran six of the seven major studios by 1977.

The movie viewing experience continued to change as well. As more Americans moved to the suburbs, multiscreen theaters became increasingly common from the 1960s onward. Many of the newer theaters in the 1970s were part of shopping malls. The first double-screen theater opened in 1963, and by the mid-1970s some theaters offered eight screens. The number of screens grew, but the number of seats dropped, both in total capacity and per auditorium. Baby boomers provided larger audiences in the 1970s. Many of the new theaters were built without concern for style, offering small, plain rectangles and sometimes distorted projection images. Thin walls allowed sounds from adjoining movies to intrude. Dolby stereo sound systems, introduced in 1975, provided one of the few viewing improvements of the period for moviegoers. By 1979 twelve hundred U.S. theaters had Dolby sound. Eventually theaters returned to designs that offered the viewer more amenities.

Film exhibitors struggled through the industry's recession. Traditionally the distributors received 30 percent of the box office gross. While movie production was high and competition for bookings increased in the late 1960s, theaters were able to book films below that level. By the end of the 1970s, however, with a shortage of good films available, exhibitors paid an average of 45 percent. As the majors cut their film distribution, they sometimes successfully demanded 90 percent for blockbuster movies. Feeling they had little choice, exhibitors suffered. As the major studios increased their share of film rentals—the ticket money paid by theaters to distributors—exhibitors relied increasingly on concession sales for profit. Concessions accounted for 13.5 percent of theater revenue in 1972 but rose to 20 percent by 1982. This represented almost all of the profit for most theaters. Multiple screens also saved expenses for theaters. Saturation booking added to higher income, defraying the cost of national ad campaigns and, with the erosion of second-run theaters, keeping ticket prices higher. In 1978 the four largest theater chains were General Cinema Corporation, United Artists Theater Circuit, American Multi-Cinema, and Plitt Theaters.

Independent filmmakers benefited briefly from the industry recession of the late 1960s. They captured nearly 30 percent of the market share in 1971. With the exception of MGM, however, all the majors recovered in the early 1970s. They also seized much of the exploitation market once dominated by independents. By 1979 the independents' share of the market dropped to only 10 percent.

The movies experienced both financial crisis and creative renewal as the 1960s turned into the 1970s. Television enjoyed a more stable economic situation, but it too experienced a new phase of critical success.

RELEVANCE AND RATINGS
American society in the late 1960s was racked by social tensions and confrontations. Increasingly the war in Vietnam took center stage as the most divisive issue, but other concerns, such as civil rights for racial and ethnic minorities, remained and were joined by emerging struggles like the women's movement. As America's postwar social conflict peaked in 1968 and 1969, television faced equally challenging circumstances. The casting off or ignoring of traditions took place during a search for relevance, a demand that all stimuli somehow connect with contemporary life. For television viewers this meant a greater variety and number of racial and ethnic TV personalities, in entertainment, news, and commercials. The youth culture also inspired new styles in clothing and appearance.

Television programming underwent dramatic changes. Not a single top-ten show from the 1968–1969 season remained there five years later. Most notable was the appearance of producer Norman Lear's *All in the Family* on CBS in January 1971. This socially conscious comedy built around the character of Archie Bunker, a white working-class bigot, introduced previously taboo subjects and language. CBS considered *All in the Family* so risky that it ran a warning before the inaugural program. The show, however, was quickly accepted and became the most popular program on TV.

Lear created additional shows based on characters that first appeared on *All in the Family*. Other programs followed the process, resulting in hits like *Maude, The Jeffersons, Good Times, Rhoda,* and others. Unlike earlier programs, these spin-offs often made reference to or were visited by characters in related shows. Many of the programs produced during this period appeared on videotape rather than on film, with the actors taped live in front of studio audiences. In the wake of such changes, several long-running shows and performers dropped from sight, viewed by network executives or television audiences as too closely linked to an earlier era, and therefore irrelevant.

The more diverse TV population included a black junk dealer (*Sanford and Son*), an interracial marriage (on *The Jeffersons*), a Jewish neighbor (on *The Mary Tyler Moore Show*), and public housing occupants (*Good Times*). *Chico and the Man* (1974) featured a Chicano character played by Freddie Prinze, while the police comedy *Barney Miller* (1975) was built around an ensemble cast of Americans of Polish, African, Jewish, Japanese, German, and English descent. The most popular variety program in the early 1970s, *The Flip Wilson Show*, starred Wilson, an African American comedian.

The Mary Tyler Moore Show (1970) offered a rare starring role for a single career woman whose life wasn't built around the home or the pursuit of a mate. The lead character, Mary Richards, wasn't just killing time until marriage but lived independently and contentedly. Other TV characters reflected the changing status, choices, and opportunities of American women in the 1970s. Maude Findlay was a loud, outspoken liberal married to her fourth husband after three divorces. The character was a spin-off from *All in the Family* and became the focus of a separate show—*Maude*—in 1972. When Maude became pregnant at age forty-seven, she chose to have an abortion, a shocking topic and decision for television, even in 1972. The Supreme Court's *Roe v. Wade* decision legalizing abortion nationwide did not come until January

1973. Maude later went through menopause and had plastic surgery. Norman Lear, the creator of *Maude*, also developed *One Day at a Time* (1975). This comedy centered around a divorced mother who struggled successfully to provide for her two daughters. Other female characters appeared who competed equally with males in various occupations.

This new wave of topical comedies became television's primary outlet for examining socially relevant issues. Among the most important was M*A*S*H, which debuted in 1972 and was based on the hit film about a military surgical hospital. This series had a contemporary message despite being set during the Korean War. "We wanted to say that war was futile," said writer Larry Gelbart.[17] The show's ensemble cast—led by Alan Alda as "Hawkeye" Pierce—and excellent writers developed a hit that was equal parts comedy and drama. Its final episode in February 1983 was the most watched American TV broadcast in history.

Some of the most notable moments in television in the late 1960s and early 1970s came from news stories rather than entertainment. Television offered Americans close-up views of some the era's most fantastic events. Having watched for years the nation's developing space program, in 1969 viewers saw the first man walk on the moon. Regardless of national debates over the value and wisdom of the enterprise, the space missions provided gripping drama. They were among a growing number of events, however, that were shaped, at least in part, by how they would appear on television.

Richard Nixon, perhaps more than any other president, utilized television as a political tool. Through a long-accepted practice, TV networks have given presidents free airtime at their request. By using—some would say abusing— this medium through carefully selected appearances under their own managed conditions, occupants of the White House enjoy a tremendous political advantage over other branches of government and their political opponents. Nixon's misleading policy statements regarding the Vietnam War and his public talks, like the "Silent Majority" speech of November 3, 1969, skillfully attracted support and bought him time—four more years as it turned out—to try to achieve what other presidents had not.

Convinced that the press opposed them, the Nixon administration attacked the newspapers and networks in a series of rancorous and divisive speeches. Emerging as the champion of the political Right, Vice President Spiro Agnew created a major stir in 1969 with his attack on the media, criticizing national news organizations as liberally biased. At one point Agnew proclaimed: "Perhaps the place to start looking for a credibility gap is not in the offices of government in Washington but in the studios of the networks in New York."[18] The charges, however politically motivated, launched a brief period of self-analysis and hesitation among members of the press, both electronic and print. The long-term impact was minimal, and by the early 1970s dissenting views occasionally appeared on either network or public television. Nixon's historic visits to China and the Soviet Union in 1972 were similarly planned in great detail to achieve the fullest possible advantage from television coverage.

Nixon ultimately paid the price for his abuses. When the Senate Watergate hearings began in March 1973, the investigative committee opened its hearings to television, providing live looks at one of the nation's biggest political scandals. Public television, barely hanging on under conservative demands for decentralization and starved for funding by Nixon's vetoes, covered the Watergate hearings live and won significantly higher numbers of viewers. Ironically it was the Watergate hearings that firmly established public TV's reputation. As Robert MacNeil concludes, "For the first time in its brief history, it seemed the entire nation knew what public television was."[19] The networks rotated live coverage to limit their advertising losses, but the Watergate hearings often drew more viewers than their top daytime programs. The contest between president and legislature often played on television, between Nixon's speeches designed to divert attention or gain support and congressional investigations culminating in a vote for articles of impeachment. Nixon finally resigned on August 8, 1974.

Cable joined educational television in making major advances during the 1970s. The number of cable systems multiplied, reaching over a thousand in 1964. They initially offered only shows aired by existing stations but had the potential to develop original programming. Numerous small systems began to consolidate, with some companies reaching tens of thousands of subscribers. As broadcasters increasingly invested in cable and, in 1970, the number of subscribers reached 4.5 million, FCC restrictions loosened, and deregulation continued in the mid-1970s. The real revolution in cable TV came from satellite transmission. From Telstar's launch in 1962, transmission via satellite improved, allowing systems to broadcast over a much larger area. Home Box Office (HBO), begun in late 1972 as the first profitable pay cable channel, became the first service to broadcast by satellite, in 1975. The 1975 boxing match between Joe Frazier and Muhammad Ali proved the appeal of pay TV. Now HBO was available to many more cable companies, and its number of subscribers soared to nearly twelve million. Ted Turner made his WTBS station from Atlanta available on satellite to cable systems in 1975. This "superstation" was soon joined by Chicago's WGN and others, allowing cable TV to provide a choice to viewers that threatened network monopoly.

The portrayal of aggressive behavior on TV continued to be a concern in a time of growing social conflict. The concurrent rise of television's popularity and violent crime led many people to conclude that the two were connected. In 1969 Congress funded a study by the surgeon general on the effects of televised violence on the TV audience. His report, released in 1972, concluded that a significant connection existed between viewing violent behavior on TV and antisocial behavior. By the mid-1970s youthful offenders in particular were committing crimes copied from television episodes, leading to at least one lawsuit against a network for precipitating a crime. Grassroots organizations such as the National Citizens Committee for Broadcasting fought against the rising tide of TV violence, in this case by rating programs according to the number of violent acts and identifying the sponsors that supported them. The Parent-Teacher Association (PTA) held public inquiries around the country in 1976 on the same subject. As Erik Barnouw commented, "Television changes people's hairstyles, clothing, and the words they use—almost everything. I can't imagine that this constant display of violence would not affect them in some way, especially when it's shown as a way of solving problems. We are actually merchandising violence."[20]

While the debate over violence continued, concerns expanded to include the growing amount and graphic depiction of sexual activity on television. The two issues erupted again in the mid-1970s. Richard Wiley, chair of the FCC, and Senator John Pastore, chair of the Senate Subcommittee on Communications, were among those urging TV executives to address the issue or face possible government regulations. New CBS president Arthur Taylor pushed what became known as the "family hour" plan, later adopted by the National Association of Broadcasters Code Authority. The networks agreed not to air programs "inappropriate for viewing by a general family audience" between the hours of 7:00 and 9:00 p.m. eastern time. The networks shifted some shows into later time slots, but there was no real reduction of sex and violence in the programming offered. The effectiveness of this effort in shielding younger viewers from inappropriate content was questionable. Late-night programming grew coarser because of the greater use of recent motion pictures, which often addressed controversial or sensitive themes, used rough street language, or showed more graphic scenes of a sexual or violent nature than typically offered to television viewers. Ironically the growing coarseness of evening programming coexisted with the new emphasis on family viewing.

Surprisingly two separate court cases challenged the family hour, one filed by the Writers Guild of America and the other by Norman Lear. They argued that the networks had implemented the family hour under government threat in violation of the First Amendment. Witnesses for the Writers Guild testified to editorial intrusions over episode themes that seemed unsuitable for family-hour viewing. "I think we're doing a tremendous disservice to the American people," testified *Barney Miller* writer-producer Danny Arnold, "to kids, if we keep telling them that life is *The Brady Bunch*."[21] District Court Judge Warren Ferguson ruled on November 4, 1976, that the family hour, operated through the National Association of Broadcasters and under FCC pressure, did in fact violate First Amendment protections. If networks chose to impose such a policy individually they could, but none did. Although a court of appeals vacated the decision in 1979, the family-hour issue had been long forgotten by then.

Debates about program content often took place in public, but other changes took place behind the scenes. During the 1970s programmers and product advertisers more frequently utilized demographic information to target their products. Data provided by the A. C. Nielsen Company indicated who viewed what shows, breaking the audience down by factors such as age, geography, income, sex, and education. Sponsors knew from other sources the demographics of people who bought their products and increasingly matched their advertising dollars to shows that attracted viewers in their desired demographic. Programs that could generate the appropriate target audience reaped higher advertising rates. Because of this trend, shows watched by relatively low-spending groups, such as older citizens, were less profitable, which motivated networks to air programs directed at younger, higher-spending viewers. Even relatively high-rated shows, such as *Gunsmoke* and *Red Skelton*, were canceled because their viewers tended to come from the relatively unprofitable elderly rural population. Writers and others involved in the creative process found the pressure to write to specific demographic audiences intrusive. Ironically, as advertisers manipulated programming, televised cigarette commercials, TV's single biggest source of ad revenue, were banned in 1971 under congressional pressure.

Television from 1969 to 1975 provided entertainment that came much closer to reflecting the nation's diversity than previous TV fare. At the same time, the focus on younger viewers led to the elimination of series most popular with an older and rural audience. News coverage brought the high of a moon landing and the low of a collapsing presidency. With all of television's accomplishments, however, its content remained a public battleground.

PRIME-TIME SPORTS

The booming popularity of spectator sports continued during the 1970s. The number of professional franchises increased, television ratings grew, and access to athletic competition became more democratic than ever before. Some of sports' most memorable teams and personalities played in this era. It was also a time, however, when economics claimed a role almost as visible and important as athletic performance.

Popularity did not always translate into profits. Financial difficulties led to significant changes in franchise ownership in the 1970s. In 1975 only half of baseball's teams made money, fewer than 20 percent of basketball franchises were profitable, more than a third of hockey teams lost money, and almost one-third of NFL teams operated at a loss. Despite this performance, franchise values rose rapidly, and the number of sports franchises grew, motivated by several factors, including television influence, tax laws, and the geographically shifting economy. The rising costs meant that only corporations or incredibly rich individuals whose income came from other sources could afford to buy a team. New owners, either individual or corporate, used sports teams as tax write-offs more than profit-generating enterprises. Federal tax benefits meant that investors could reap financial dividends even if their team was a competitive failure but only for the duration of their product's depreciation. At that time they had to sell the franchise, usually for a generous profit regardless of competitive performance. Some owners deliberately sacrificed their team's future for a try at instant success. With short-term business interests rather than long-term team or league interests their main concern, athletic competition often suffered. As Randy Roberts notes, "Instead of the stability coming from an interested owner committed for a lifetime to the team, professional sports management in the 1970s and 1980s was characterized by instability and change."[22]

Much of this change came from the competition of new professional leagues. In 1967 Los Angeles businessman Gary Davidson founded the American Basketball Association (ABA), which lasted for nine years despite the instability of several franchises. The raiding of NBA rosters and escalating salaries led the NBA to absorb four of the ABA's remaining teams in 1976. Davidson also formed the World Football League (WFL), in 1974. Although it folded during its second season, it did lure a number of NFL stars away from their previous clubs. Both the ABA and the WFL failed to attract adequate television packages to ensure their profitability. A third Davidson creation was the World Hockey Association (WHA), beginning play in 1972. Despite signing perhaps the biggest star in the National Hockey League, Bobby Hull, the WHA survived but did not flourish. Eventually the NHL, having expanded from six teams to twelve only in 1966, absorbed four WHA franchises in 1979. Later challenges followed, but the established leagues prevailed against all competition.

One of the key issues for ownership was the dramatic escalation of player salaries. The increased strength of players' unions, the use of player agents to negotiate contracts, and support from court rulings helped bring this about. Marvin Miller became head of the Major League Baseball Players' Association in 1966, and the association signed the sport's first basic agreement in 1968, establishing among other things a higher minimum salary and a grievance system. In 1969 St. Louis outfielder Curt Flood, upset over being traded to Philadelphia at the end of the 1969 season, challenged baseball's reserve clause, suing baseball on the grounds that it unconstitutionally restricted his freedom to make contracts. A 1922 Supreme Court case had exempted Major League Baseball from congressional antitrust laws. This permitted baseball's use of the reserve clause, which tied a player to his team by contract and prevented him from moving to another team except through a trade. Although Flood lost his case before the Supreme Court in June 1972, a player strike that April won additional pension and health benefits. Under a new 1973 basic agreement, the "Flood Rule" gave players with ten years' experience and at least five years with the same team the right to block trades.

Another challenge to the reserve clause came in the mid-1970s. A 1974 arbitration hearing ruled that Oakland Athletics' owner Charles Finley had violated the contract of pitcher Jim "Catfish" Hunter, and declared Hunter a free agent. His ability to negotiate with several teams earned Hunter a five-year contract worth $3.75 million, a huge leap beyond his previous one-hundred-thousand-dollar salary. Players were stunned to see the potential impact of free agency.

Miller pushed ahead even further. He persuaded two pitchers, Andy Messersmith and Dave McNally, to play the 1975 season without a signed contract to test whether or not the reserve clause expired after one year; standard contracts allowed teams to renew unsigned contracts for one year. An arbitration panel upheld the one-year limit and declared both pitchers were free to negotiate with other teams. With the Supreme Court's decision not to challenge this ruling, the reserve clause was void. The owners locked players out of spring training facilities before the 1976 season until they could sign a new basic agreement with the players. The season opened late as negotiations continued, finally concluding in July with a new basic agreement. The players dropped their demand for complete free agency and granted owners the right to use contracts binding them to a team for six years, enabling them to pursue free agency thereafter. The average salary climbed to one hundred thousand dollars by 1981.

As professional athletes won a larger share of league revenues, women athletes became increasingly prominent in the 1960s. The vast majority of American professional athletes were men, and those who were women generally earned far less money. Nevertheless women began to make significant gains at the turn of the decade. Tennis was one of the first sports to see a breakthrough for women, and among the leading pioneers of this era was Billie Jean King. King was the decade's leading female tennis player and, as the 1970s opened, publicly challenged the standard practice of paying women tennis players a fraction of the money awarded male players. In 1971 King became the first female athlete to earn over one hundred thousand dollars in a year. She helped form a separate professional tour, the Women's Tennis Association, in 1973 to improve the status of female players. Enhanced by a sponsor and TV contract, the tour offered almost one million dollars in prize money by the mid-1970s. In 1974 King also founded the World Team Tennis League, which had men and women playing on the same teams. In a nationally televised match that was more symbolic than artistic, King won a celebrated victory over fifty-five-year-old Bobby Riggs, who had defeated the number two–rated women's tennis player, Margaret Court, earlier in 1973.

Women's athletics received a major legal boost in the early 1970s. The passage of Title IX of the 1972 Education Act prohibited sexual discrimination in

Billie Jean King (Library of Congress)

any educational programs receiving federal money. This opened the way for funding to flow into women's scholastic and intercollegiate sports, and varsity sports for girls and women sprouted all over the country. The number of high school girls playing in varsity competition rose nearly 600 percent during the 1970s, to almost two million. The number of college women in varsity sports doubled. Title IX proved controversial in part because no one knew exactly how to interpret its provisions. Critics feared an erosion of funding for men's sports, and the Department of Education looked for a way to implement the law. By the end of the 1970s the department required "equal opportunity for participation" and "equitable funding," though exactly how to achieve those goals remains a heated topic of debate to the present day. Prior to the passage of Title IX, scholastic sports for girls appeared sporadically at best, and at worst did not exist at all.

Prevailing public sentiment until the 1960s discouraged girls from engaging in athletic competition. Rationales ranged from the belief that athletic training would produce heavily muscled bodies that destroyed girls' femininity to worries that it would create extreme sexual desire or homosexuality. Since many believed that females lacked the physical traits to be competitive athletes, girls rarely received encouragement to pursue sports. The government's stance, implied through Title IX, helped spread a more accepting attitude toward female athletic competition. Billie Jean King maintained her dominance of tennis into the early 1970s, and when questioned about her passionate commitment to the game, she once replied, "They say, 'Why aren't you at home?' I say, 'Why don't you go ask Rod Laver why he isn't at home?'"[23] By the end of the 1970s girls were able to select from a growing list of school sports and, with an atmosphere of encouragement, became increasingly proficient in their skills. With the increased participation, girls' sports received greater attention from scientific investigations that challenged or disputed many of the established negative myths about the impact of athletics on girls.

For college women, the creation in 1971 of the Association of Intercollegiate Athletics for Women (AIAW) was an important move. The AIAW provided national direction to college women's sports. The organization initially banned athletic scholarships, but a 1973 court case forced a policy change two years later. By the end of the decade college women received athletic scholarships. With this infusion of money, women's intercollegiate sports began to reap both the benefits and the problems of men's programs. National championships for women began under the AIAW's forerunner in 1969.

The place of sports in society remained contested in the early 1970s. Athletes used to strict discipline and socially insulated by their endeavors were often antagonistic toward liberal campus demonstrators. Michigan State gridder Phil Hoag remembered, "There was no question that anytime you could punch one, you punched them."[24] Increasingly, however, athletes broke away from that conformity. Basketball All-American Bill Walton was arrested protesting the Vietnam War. Former football player Gary Shaw wrote of demeaning treatment at the University of Texas in *Meat on the Hoof*. Others questioned the pursuit of victory at all costs that occasionally spilled over in shocking display. At the end of a February 1972 basketball game, players and fans of the losing University of Minnesota team savagely attacked Ohio State players in what was called "an ugly, cowardly display of violence."[25]

Sport offered a very public arena to observe America's racial changes in the Vietnam era. Sports team members generally constituted a conservative element on most college campuses, but they sometimes moved faster than legal or political constituents. During the 1960s and early 1970s black athletes occasionally joined public dissent. Black football players at the University of Wyoming wanted to protest Mormon racial views by wearing black armbands during their game with Brigham Young University but were dropped from the team instead. At Syracuse University black football players quit spring practice when the head coach refused to hire a black assistant. Although these actions were part of a much larger period of discontent, both on and off college campuses, they were less effective than other avenues of change. As Benjamin Rader observes, "The token reforms, the rapid decline in general student and black unrest in the early 1970s, the built-in turnover of student athletes, and the changed cultural climate brought a quick end to the black athletic revolt."[26]

Black athletes did, however, continue to excel athletically in much greater proportion than their population size in society. This success certainly had an impact on the lives of young blacks looking for career and financial rewards, skewing them toward the long-shot odds of a professional career. The domination of many elite sports by African Americans in the late 1960s elicited a public debate over the influence of race in sports. The general argument revolved around whether the results were genetic or cultural.

If most obvious signs of racial discrimination were gone by the late 1960s, certain forms remained. In team sports some coaches used "stacking"—channeling black players toward certain positions—to reserve positions regarded as requiring leadership or quick thinking for whites. In 1976 half of baseball's major league outfielders and first basemen were black, but only 4 percent of pitchers or catchers. In football blacks rarely played quarterback but generally dominated running back, receiver, and defensive backfield positions. Many basketball coaches wanted a white player at point guard. This practice gradually eroded over time.

The racial segregation of universities in the Deep South further eroded during the early 1970s. Southern Methodist University brought in the Southwest Conference's first black football player in 1971. By the 1971–1972 academic year every school in the Southeastern Conference had at least one black athlete. With these barriers finally removed the change was dramatic. By the end of the 1970s African Americans made up over 25 percent of SEC football players and nearly two-thirds of SEC basketball players.

Beyond their social implications, sporting events remained extremely popular as a form of entertainment. One measure of their continued popularity was the success of prime-time football on television. Roone Arledge was responsible for the move. In cooperation with the NFL, he inaugurated *Monday Night Football* in 1970, a program still running over thirty years later. It became the leading sports program on TV, ranking as high as number fifteen in the Nielsen ratings during the 1977–1978 season. The move to prime time represented a risk since the networks expected a much larger audience in that slot than pro football attracted during Sunday afternoons. Arledge again targeted casual fans, enticing them with more cameras, replays, and analysis than ever. He tried to make even ordinary games vibrate with playoff excitement. The heart of the broadcasts, however, was the three-man crew he used as announcers. Keith Jackson—replaced after the first year by Frank Gifford—handled play-by-play, former pro quarterback Don Meredith provided game insights and homespun humor, and Howard Cosell, a controversial veteran of many *Wide World of Sports* telecasts, offered analysis. Cosell was among the first to place his sports reporting within the larger context of American society, bringing journalistic criticism to the games, something rare amid the fawning and hyperbole that often came from league-approved announcers. Although he was often perceptive, Cosell's abrasive self-importance attracted a good deal of audience criticism, and even occasional death threats. His verbal sparring with Meredith in the broadcast booth provided the type of entertainment Arledge had hoped for. By the 1970s pro football's live attendance averaged over 90 percent capacity, and televised audiences rose from an average of eleven million in 1967 to twenty million in 1977.

The American Football League pulled major upsets over the NFL in Super Bowls III and IV. Behind quarterback Joe Namath's guarantee, the New York Jets stunned the Baltimore Colts in 1969, and the following year the Kansas City Chiefs defeated the Minnesota Vikings. After the leagues completed their merger, the Miami Dolphins won consecutive titles in 1973 and 1974, with the 1973 squad going undefeated. That same year running back O. J. Simpson became the first player to rush for over two thousand yards in a single season.

College football continued to rank just behind pro football in national popularity. From 1968 to 1975 Nebraska and Oklahoma each won two national titles. Other schools most often near the top of the polls included Ohio State, Notre Dame, and Penn State in the East and Texas and USC in the West. Among the many outstanding players, Ohio State's Archie Griffin became the only two-time winner of the Heisman Trophy. Despite its appeal, college football became increasingly expensive, and relatively few university programs were self-supporting. During the 1960s and early 1970s, forty-two schools eliminated their football teams. Benjamin Rader reports, "Throughout the era of televised sports, nearly 90 percent of college athletic programs operated at a deficit."[27]

The game many consider the greatest in college history came on Thanksgiving Day in 1971. Number one Nebraska and number two Oklahoma had completely dominated their opponents all season, and the game's buildup was intense. Both had explosive offensive teams, and Nebraska had the nation's top defense. After trailing at halftime, Nebraska came back to win 35–31 and finished the year as national champion.

Like football teams, college basketball teams competed for national rankings, but they also had postseason national championship tournaments that grew in size over time. During the 1960s and 1970s, UCLA put together one of the most remarkable championship runs in history, winning ten out of twelve national titles from 1964 to 1975, including seven in a row. Coach John Wooden and star players like Lew Alcindor (later Kareem Abdul-Jabbar) and Bill Walton set the standard for modern sports dynasties. During one stretch UCLA won eighty-eight straight games. David Thompson and North Carolina State grabbed the 1974 championship. Other All-Americans included prolific scorers Pete Maravich of Louisiana State University, who averaged over forty-four points per game for his career, Purdue's Rick Mount, and Niagara's Calvin Murphy. In women's college basketball, tiny Immaculata College swept the AIAW's first three national titles from 1972 to 1974.

Professional basketball's New York Knicks became the NBA's glamour franchise for a time, taking two championships in the early 1970s. The Los Angeles Lakers set a record during the 1971–1972 season by winning thirty-three games in a row and took that year's league title. Among individual players achieving consistent all-pro recognition were Abdul-Jabbar, Jerry West, Walt Frazier, John Havlicek, and Billy Cunningham.

Baseball continued to enjoy one of its most dynamic eras. Both leagues expanded, with the Kansas City Royals and Seattle Pilots joining the American League and the Montreal Expos and San Diego Padres added to the National League. The Pilots moved to Milwaukee in 1970, becoming the Brewers, and the Washington Senators became the Texas Rangers in 1972. Among individual performances, Nolan Ryan set a new record in 1973, striking out 383 batters in a single season. The following year Hank Aaron broke Babe Ruth's career home run mark of 714, and Lou Brock stole 118 bases, another single-season record. Another barrier fell in 1975 when Frank Robinson became the manager of the Cleveland Indians, the first African American to lead a Major League Baseball team. Baseball had two superior teams during the era. Cincinnati's "Big Red Machine" featured Johnny Bench, Pete Rose, and Joe Morgan and won the World Series in 1975 and 1976. The 1975 Reds won 108 games and, in one of the most dramatic World Series ever, defeated Boston in the ninth inning of the seventh game. The Oakland Athletics took three consecutive titles in the early 1970s with stars Vida Blue, Jim Hunter, and Reggie Jackson. The most amazing World Series championship, however, came from the 1969 New York Mets, a 1962 expansion team that had never before finished with a winning record.

In the NHL, Montreal captured the Stanley Cup three times between 1969 and 1975, with Boston and Philadelphia each winning twice. Bobby Orr and Phil Esposito of Boston and Philadelphia's Bobby Clarke swept all the regular season MVP awards.

Boxing provided one of sport's most dramatic moments in the early 1970s. In March 1971 heavyweight champion Joe Frazier fought Muhammad Ali. Ali's title had been taken by boxing commissions over his refusal to accept military induction, but both fighters were undefeated. The match generated great anticipation, as much for its cultural symbolism as its athleticism. In a classic boxer versus puncher confrontation, Ali's jabs ravaged Frazier's face, but Frazier's harder punches put Ali on the canvas in the fifteenth round, and the champion won a close decision. They met twice more with Ali winning both matches, including the September 1975 "thrilla in Manila."

Horse racing experienced an equally thrilling event. After going twenty-five years without a Triple Crown winner, thoroughbred racing fans found a superhorse. Secretariat claimed the 1973 Kentucky Derby and the Preakness in record times, then captured the Belmont by a stunning thirty-one lengths in one of the most memorable performances in the sport's history. Forego made his own claim to fame, starting a run of three consecutive horse-of-the-year awards in 1974.

Olympic competition again took place under challenging conditions. The 1972 summer games in Munich, Germany, were tragically interrupted when Palestinian terrorists took eleven Israeli Olympians hostage, eventually killing them all. The murders tarnished some otherwise exhilarating events. Mark Spitz swam brilliantly in taking seven gold medals. Soviet gymnast Olga Korbut won two gold medals and helped stimulate young American girls to take up the sport. In a heated controversy, the Americans lost their first Olympic basketball game, falling in the gold medal game to the Soviet Union. American women won three gold medals at that year's winter games in Sapporo, Japan, one in alpine skiing and two in speed skating.

Various sports adjusted their rules to become more appealing and telegenic. Baseball tried to increase offensive production in 1969 through modifications such as lowering the pitching mound from fifteen inches to twelve and reducing the size of the strike zone. Four years later the American League instituted the designated hitter to bat in the place of typically weak-hitting pitchers. Perhaps more than any other sport, football accommodated the needs of commercial television. By the middle of the 1970s the NFL added fourteen timeouts to its televised games for commercials, adding roughly a half hour to their length. Always searching for programming, television created artificial events such as *The Superstars* competitions, begun in 1973, pitting star athletes from various sports in contests outside their own specialties. Spin-offs of this idea, known by critics as "trashsports," proliferated in the wake of good audience ratings.

Though some changes came on the fields of play, professional sport in particular was primarily affected by changing economic concerns. Athletes moved closer to equal partnership with owners in sharing the profits generated by their play. For the first time women received significant government support for their athletic endeavors. For fans, the games continued to get bigger and better.

FRAGMENTS AND ROOTS

Rock and roll had never been a single sound, but entering the 1970s the music branched into so many different directions that it was hard to locate its center. Quiet introspective soloists, country twangs, deafening metal bands, and classically trained musicians all claimed the generic rock label. The music also acquired greater cultural, and occasionally political, significance, standing as it did at the center of the counterculture. The mass festivals, especially Woodstock, are among the era's most memorable icons. Ultimately, however, the growing complexity of the music and the huge scale of concerts stimulated a new wave of simple compositions played at a frantic pace in intimate locations. It seemed like the evolution of revolution.

By the late 1960s rock bands had proven their ability to attract crowds far larger than those held by more traditional indoor venues. This appeal led to a trend of large outdoor festivals, usually stretched out over two or three days, featuring several prominent acts and a countercultural atmosphere. Based on earlier musical festivals of folk music or jazz, the first major rock gathering was the Monterey International Pop Festival on June 16 to 18, 1967, the "summer of love" in the San Francisco Bay area. Music festivals did not always turn out as planned. Some cities tried to prohibit mass concerts, and promoters might promise acts they could not deliver, provide inadequate sites and services, or focus only on making a profit. Monterey, however, was an artistic success despite the presence of many concertgoers who refused to buy tickets or arrived stoned or drunk. Thirty thousand showed up Friday, sixty thousand on Sunday. Several San Francisco area bands were joined by other nationally known artists, including Simon and Garfunkel, the Animals, the Byrds, Otis Redding, the Who, the Mamas and the Papas, and Jimi Hendrix.

After Monterey, rock festivals spread across the country. The Woodstock Music and Art Fair best symbolizes the counterculture of the late 1960s. Twenty-four-year-old John Roberts organized the event for August 15 to 17, 1969. The promoters filmed the event, hoping to emerge with a commercially successful movie. Ticket revenue failed to meet expectations, as the ticket system broke down under the unexpected crush of people streaming to Max Yasgur's farm near Bethel, New York. The promoters planned for fifty thousand people, but nearly a half million showed up, and the outnumbered authorities generally ignored drug and nudity laws. The crowd overwhelmed the sanitation facilities, while food and water nearly ran out. Traffic jams meant supplies, food, and performers had to be brought in by helicopter. Drugs were plentiful, but medical aid was limited. Torrential rain and mud made things worse, but people pulled together out of common need. An atmosphere of protest against the Vietnam War existed, but it remained largely submerged. Woodstock primarily represented personal rather than political rebellion. What they came for was the music. Over two dozen bands played, including many of rock's biggest acts: Jimi Hendrix; Janis Joplin; Joan Baez; the Who; the Grateful Dead; the Jefferson Airplane; Creedence Clearwater Revival; Crosby, Stills and Nash; Sly and the Family Stone; Joe Cocker; and Santana. The experience had a galvanizing

effect on the counterculture. As Janis Joplin noted, "We used to think of our-
selves as little clumps of weirdos. But now we're a whole new minority
group."[28] Although the concert lost $1.3 million, the movie and sound track
made millions. Much of the press and public praised a vision of a new generation with countercultural values, hailed as "Woodstock Nation." That image
suffered a severe blow within months.

The Rolling Stones offered a free concert in December 1969, but a late change
of site caused numerous problems. Hastily assembled at the Altamont Speedway
near San Francisco, the concert deteriorated into widespread drug abuse and violence. The Rolling Stones hired the Hell's Angels motorcycle gang to handle security for the three hundred thousand who attended. When people pressed
close to the stage, the Angels beat them back. Bands interrupted their playing to
pacify the crowd but without success. The Angels injured several people and
knocked out Jefferson Airplane member Marty Balin when he interceded to
stop another beating. During the Rolling Stones' evening performance, the
Hell's Angels killed a man. Mass festivals would continue, but the earlier promise of universal togetherness faded. "The violence at Altamont," writes Reebee
Garofalo, "served notice of the counterculture's impending demise."[29]

Rock concerts could, however, assist in alleviating global suffering. The
Concert for Bangladesh served as the model for several others that followed.
Civil war and devastating floods during 1971 created a major disaster in what
would become the new Asian nation of Bangladesh. Motivated by Ravi
Shankar, George Harrison organized two benefit concerts at New York's Madison Square Garden on August 1, 1971. In addition to Harrison and Shankar,
performers included Eric Clapton, Bob Dylan, Ringo Starr, Billy Preston, Leon
Russell, and Badfinger. The concerts, along with album and film revenue, generated nearly eleven million dollars for relief, although most of that was delayed nearly a decade by an Internal Revenue Service audit.

Rock and roll's main connection to social causes, however, continued to be
the Vietnam War. Several notable artists played at a Concert for Peace at New
York's Shea Stadium on August 6, 1970. Antiwar rock reached its commercial
peak in 1970 and 1971, when fifteen songs hit the top one hundred. Songs opposing war continued through the mid-1970s, but their criticism was usually
vague or generic. Musical antiwar statements appeared in a wide variety of
styles—from Creedence Clearwater Revival's "Fortunate Son" and Crosby,
Stills, Nash and Young's electric "Ohio" to John Lennon's anthemic "Give

Peace a Chance," Edwin Starr's soul hit "War," and progressive rockers Emerson, Lake, and Palmer's "Lucky Man."

More common was a generalized dissatisfaction with the dominant culture. For some artists the fight began with the music industry itself, which sought to shape and sell their sound for profit. While musicians certainly hoped to make money from their craft, they were also creating something with great intrinsic value they were unwilling to alter for commercial reasons. The contradictions between commercialism and rock ideology were on blatant display in record advertisements that made such absurd pronouncements as "The Revolutionaries Are on Columbia" and "The Man Can't Bust Our Music."[30] If business interests usually prevailed, performers whose success made them powerful enough or who were especially tenacious gained unprecedented artistic freedom. For those operating from the counterculture, the message often reflected the sentiments of the Jefferson Airplane: "We are all outlaws in the eyes of America."[31]

In the end rock and roll's most significant impact was primarily personal. Even that, however, had larger implications. "For some, revolution was an act of self-development," remarks Garofalo, "not the overthrow of one political system by another."[32] Rock's origins are, and rock continues to be, closely connected to the youth culture. Its challenge to the middle class, especially in its early years, was largely in style, since its lyrics generally reinforced prevailing values. Even then, as Herbert London argues, "rock music is the medium used to convey social change."[33] As the Vietnam generation aged, it continued to support maturing styles of rock and roll. By the late 1960s rock adopted the language of the counterculture, and its lyrics could be as unsettling to listeners' ears as its screaming guitars. New York Times journalist Richard Goldstein perceived that "to do away with revolution in rock, one would have to ban the music itself."[34] Even Motown, with Barry Gordy's reluctance to record anything remotely controversial, released songs with social and political relevance by the end of the decade.

As the war divided the American public, rock and roll splintered into numerous directions. Radio stations throughout much of the 1960s had played a fairly uniform list of songs, exposing hit records to a massive national audience. By the mid-1970s rock music dominated the airwaves, but the music industry increasingly marketed to a variety of demographic groups. More rock stations played specific sounds: current Top 40, older classics, soul music, progressive, hard rock. It was no longer possible for a single station to play all the rock people wanted to hear. The experience of a pervasive shared sound was dissipating. *Rolling Stone* magazine identified the transition at the beginning of the 1970s: "There was no unifying presence in rock, no sense that its audience was party to something subversive or threatening, and no artist whose latest record had to be heard by every fan and musician." It was the decade when rock "became diffuse, scattered and unfocused, fragmenting into little genres whose fans paid less and less attention to the other little genres. In the Seventies, rock had a hundred different focal points. . . . Instead of a center, rock had a batch of radio formats."[35]

Rock music in the late 1960s and early 1970s diverged into several different streams. Some performers sought to return to the music's roots, while others moved in entirely new directions. The folk music revival of the late 1950s, which contributed to the folk-rock sound of the Byrds and Bob Dylan, also stimulated a more obvious country influence on rock by the later 1960s. This was part of the latest wave of stripping away recent layers of innovation and getting back to rock and roll's original inspirations. Mainstream groups had occasionally released songs with a heavy country flavor, such as the Beatles' "Act Naturally" and Buffalo Springfield's "Kind Woman," but those were rare exceptions. A number of former folk singers led the way, including Dylan and former Byrd member Gram Parsons. The style's characteristic sound usually included close vocal harmony, with acoustic and pedal steel guitars. Parsons was involved in, and largely responsible for, some of the earliest and best examples of country rock, most notably the Byrds' *Sweetheart of the Rodeo* (1968) and the Flying Burrito Brothers' *The Gilded Palace of Sin* (1969). Dylan's 1968 album, *John Wesley Harding*, and *Nashville Skyline* the following year also launched the sound. These artists and others frequently used Nashville studio musicians in their recordings. Country rock proved to be a phase for most of these artists, who then moved on to other styles. It also never achieved widespread commercial success, with notable exceptions in the 1970s by the Eagles, Linda Ronstadt, and a few others. It did, however, filter into the work of artists such as The Band, Creedence Clearwater Revival, the Grateful Dead, Neil Young, and even the Rolling Stones. Groups like Poco and Pure Prairie League successfully carried country rock through the 1970s and into the 1980s.

Beginning around 1970, predominantly white southern bands emerged with a blues-based sound dominated by hard-rocking guitars. Most of these southern bands followed the lead of the Allman Brothers, which featured two lead guitars and extended improvisational jams and drew on the region's other styles of soul and country. The music's characteristics of lengthy jams and either country- or blues-style vocals made it more suitable for albums than for Top 40 radio. The Allmans' real popularity came from live concerts. Unfortunately, two of its members, including lead guitarist Duane Allman, died in accidents by 1972, although the group continued to tour and record afterward. A second leading southern band, Lynyrd Skynyrd, suffered similar losses when a 1977 plane crash took the lives of three band members, including lead singer and writer Ronnie Van Zant. Most of these bands shared not only a sound but a reputation for wild living and regional pride in the South. The latter quality is best epitomized by Lynyrd Skynyrd's defense of "Sweet Home Alabama" against the blistering indictment of Neil Young's "Southern Man." The Marshall Tucker Band, Molly Hatchet, and .38 Special enjoyed runs of success in the 1970s and 1980s. With the Allman Brothers and the Marshall Tucker Band under contract, Capricorn Records briefly became the nation's largest independent label.

Another group of musicians achieved popularity at about the same time but at the other end of the musical spectrum. Years of social activism had achieved only mixed success in fighting war and racial discrimination, and audiences welcomed the personal reflections offered by folk-influenced singers in the early 1970s. Solo performers accompanied by an acoustic guitar or piano sang introspective ballads usually written by themselves. These singer/songwriters, although not discarding social causes, dealt primarily with personal issues and frequently reflected loneliness and alienation. Their earnest communication of their own thoughts, sometimes labeled "confessional" singing, appealed to audiences seeking "authenticity."

Probably the best-known singer/songwriter of this type, and the one who enjoyed the longest-lasting success, is James Taylor, whose 1970 hit "Fire and Rain" and album *Sweet Baby James* made him a star. The album featured several songs written during recovery from heroin addiction and dealt pointedly with the losses and revelations of that experience. Carly Simon, married to Taylor from 1972 to 1983, had several hits in the 1970s, headed by 1972's "You're So Vain," written about a former romantic encounter. She and Taylor also recorded a couple of hit duets. Canadian Joni Mitchell was a successful songwriter for others before reaching the charts herself in 1970. She recorded four Top 40 hits in the first half of the decade and peaked with 1974's *Court and Spark* album. Carole King had enjoyed a very successful songwriting career before divorcing her husband and songwriting partner, Gerry Goffin, and moving to Los Angeles. With some encouragement from James Taylor and others, she returned to recording. Her 1971 album *Tapestry* was critically acclaimed and remains one of the biggest-selling records in rock history, staying at number one for fifteen weeks. Paul Simon uncoupled from Art Garfunkel and produced a series of critically and commercially successful albums, as well as a half dozen top-ten singles. Jim Croce mixed pensive love songs and humorous stories. He enjoyed two number one hits before dying at age thirty in a 1973 plane crash. London native Cat Stevens had eleven Top 40 songs, the last in 1977, but abandoned professional music shortly thereafter when he converted to Islam.

Progressive rock was a musically demanding and lyrically serious style and represented the antithesis of rockabilly's unrestrained, get-up-and-dance enthusiasm. Progressive rockers combined elements of classical music with rock and relied more on electronic synthesizers and keyboards than most other styles. Unsurprisingly, given the classical musical training of many progressive rockers, they emphasized technical proficiency, often showcased in lengthy instrumental solos. Lyrical themes were often rooted in myth, fantasy, and psychedelia. Progressive bands represented the latest step in the growing seriousness of rock music, which came out of the folk and psychedelic movements.

Progressive rock was primarily a British phenomenon. The first significant appearance of the new sound came from the Moody Blues' 1967 album, *Days of Future Passed*. This record includes an orchestra and a mellotron—a keyboard instrument that uses tape to reproduce the sounds of various instruments and voices—to combine rock and classical music with mystical lyrics. Pink Floyd broke out in 1973 with *Dark Side of the Moon*, which stayed on the American album charts longer than any other rock album, over fourteen years. They led several other British psychedelic bands in experimenting with jazz and classical music in the late 1960s, including the Nice, Procol Harum (whose "A Whiter Shade of Pale" was based on a Bach composition), and Jethro Tull. Until the 1970s, however, only the Moody Blues achieved international star status. The early work of King Crimson, led by guitarist Robert Fripp, shared the melodic sound of these transitional bands before setting a standard that gave more importance to complexity and skill than other pop music. At their best progressive bands brought more sophistication to rock than any other style; at their worst they brought more ostentation.

By the early 1970s progressive rock had matured, with the most popular bands including the trio of Emerson, Lake and Palmer; Yes; Genesis; Pink Floyd; and Jethro Tull. Emerson, Lake and Palmer's 1970 debut album featured loud organs and synthesizers and lengthy compositions, sometimes borrowed from classical composers. After adding keyboardist Rick Wakeman, Yes released *Fragile* in 1972, with synthesizers and other keyboards backing fantasy lyrics and three songs of at least eight minutes in length. An abbreviated version of "Roundabout" broke into the American top-twenty singles chart. Jethro Tull's *Aqualung* (1971) offered serious looks at spirituality in folk-based songs that incorporated synthesizers, mellotron, and Ian Anderson's trademark flute. *Selling England by the Pound*, Genesis's 1973 release, contains some of rock's most sophisticated lyrics. Like their psychedelic predecessors, progressive rock's lengthy compositions worked better on albums, but shortened versions of songs occasionally moved up the singles charts via radio airplay. In the early 1970s these bands were as popular as the pop- and blues-based rockers.

American bands were more likely to integrate certain aspects of classical music than to duplicate British efforts, but Kansas, Asia, and the Electric Light Orchestra were among those that achieved commercial success with this style. Progressive rock declined after the mid-1970s, as bands evolved toward styles with broader appeal, reached the limits of their creativity or went beyond the audience's endurance, broke up, or fell prey to the next wave of rock and roll's ongoing evolution.

Among blues-based rockers in the very late 1960s, some played a faster, louder, guitar-driven style that came to be known as "heavy metal." Its ominous, distorted electric guitar sound is rooted in Link Wray's 1958 hit "Rumble" and was expanded by some of the British invasion bands. The term itself came from a line in Steppenwolf's 1968 hit "Born to Be Wild" that referred to "heavy metal thunder." That thunderous sound was evident on the first albums from heavy metal's most influential band, Led Zeppelin. Beginning with their 1969 debut, Led Zeppelin's first ten albums all reached the *Billboard* charts' top ten, six of them reaching number one. They defined heavy metal for those that followed. The music featured high piercing vocals, flashy guitar solos, and aggressive drumming, while Led Zeppelin's lyrics played on myths and folklore.

Singer Robert Plant's voice sounded "like a primeval wail," and lead guitarist Jimmy Page exhibited the speed and proficiency that defined heavy metal's best players. All of this hit the audience with such volume that "you feel your eardrums being pushed inward like sails full of wind."[36] Their signature song, "Stairway to Heaven," is an eight-minute masterpiece about a mythic quest that builds from a simple acoustic opening to soaring electric intensity. Black Sabbath and Deep Purple were other early purveyors of this style.

Heavy metal received extensive criticism from established music reviewers and made only rare appearances on the singles charts. The bands made their mark through touring and album sales. Their song lyrics earned charges of male chauvinism, and the audiences of these all-male bands were predominantly young white working-class men. Opponents also criticized the groups for links to mysticism and the satanic. These attacks seemingly made little difference, as some of the metal bands used their outlaw image as a marketing tool. Shows became more dramatic and filled with explosions and flashes. Alice Cooper led the way in shocking stage performances, and Kiss followed with full makeup and costumes. After heavy metal enjoyed a wave of success in the early 1970s, its popularity waned until a resurgence in the 1980s.

For those concerned about finding a musical center, rock critic Jon Landau offered his assessment in May 1974. "I saw rock and roll's future," Landau prophesied, "and its name is Bruce Springsteen."[37] Springsteen hit the cover of both *Time* and *Newsweek* in the same week in October 1975. With his rough-textured voice, Springsteen and the E Street Band projected a blue-collar image and played exhaustive marathon concerts. He would enjoy a long and successful career, largely built on his ability to link the best of different rock and roll eras. One writer calls him "the single artist who brought together all the exuberance of '50s rock and the thoughtfulness of '60s rock, molded into a '70s style."[38]

Rock music had become increasingly complex throughout the 1960s and early 1970s, with jazz and classical influences requiring greater instrumental virtuosity and folk adding more sophisticated lyrics. The enormous popularity of the top bands enabled them to sell out large stadiums holding tens of thousands of people. These trends, however, created a growing gap between performer and audience; neither the music nor the artist was as accessible to the listeners. A new wave of rockers returned to the basics, using a guitar, three chords, and a few words about mundane subjects to generate some excitement. Their music became punk rock.

The simple, aggressive, and amateurish sound of 1960s American garage bands anticipated the music of the punk movement. Garage bands played for fun and local celebrity, and the lucky few managed to generate a hit record. Primitive groups like the Velvet Underground and Iggy Pop and the Stooges served as creative influences for punk. The Velvets wrote songs about the darker side of life, while Iggy Pop sang disjointed compositions and indulged in self-mutilation on stage. Few clubs would book them, and their records received little promotion or sales.

The punk sound and attitude emerged in the mid-1970s from New York City, centered on the Manhattan club CBGB. The band Television, led by Tom Verlaine, blazed the trail for the punk sound, but Patti Smith was the first CBGB artist to make an impact beyond the local scene. Originally a writer and poet, Smith began performing musically, and her 1976 recording, *Horses*, was punk's first significant album. Perhaps the most influential of the early punk bands, the Ramones, started at CBGB in 1974. They played original songs that were fast, short, and uncomplicated, both lyrically and instrumentally. The Ramones signed with Sire Records, releasing their first album in 1976, but their recordings made little impact in the United States. They achieved more popularity in Britain after touring there. Two other groups that kept the punk attitude but developed a more polished sound were Blondie and the Talking Heads, both of which achieved greater commercial success in the later 1970s. Generally speaking, punk music challenged the major record labels and influenced the sound of mainstream rock but never approached the commercial success of progressive rock.

Punk was a reaction to mainstream rock. As nonconformists, punks often wore short hair and torn clothes rather than adopt the glittery outfits or polished dance steps of some of the era's biggest acts. The punk style also contained a political element, although to what degree is a question of some debate. Simon Frith calls punk "a radical rejection of record company habits" and considers "punk's musical simplicity . . . a political statement. The ideology of the garage band is an attack on the star system."[39] Garofalo is less impressed with punk as a political movement, claiming that punk's "myth was always more powerful than its reality."[40]

Punk had a greater impact in Great Britain, where a faltering economy and class antagonism turned it into a larger movement with some political overtones. The Sex Pistols led the way in 1975, bringing their own jolt of defiant energy to rock and roll. One writer describes their act: "The music was abrasive, the look repulsive, the concerts wild."[41] The Sex Pistols' first hit was 1976's "Anarchy in the U.K." The song reached the British top twenty despite a TV interview that included obscene language and resulted in a national scandal. Airplay virtually disappeared, and nearly all of the band's concert tour was canceled. Their 1977 follow-up, "God Save the Queen," topped the British charts despite being banned from airplay by the BBC. The band fell apart during a January 1978 tour of the United States. The Clash was stronger musically and developed a mainstream audience while retaining its political edge. Their major label debut in 1977 was called "the first major Punk statement," and they first hit the American charts in the 1980s.[42]

Punk's second surge was called "new wave." Artists were more proficient, less inclined to shock, and had a more commercial sound. The most successful, in addition to previously mentioned Blondie, the Talking Heads, and the Clash, were Elvis Costello, the Police, and the Pretenders, most of whom enjoyed great success into the 1980s. New wave bands sometimes added reggae and R&B influences missing from punk. Other groups followed, but by the end of the 1970s the original punk sound had nearly run its course. It would, however, reemerge in the late 1980s in the guise of alternative music.

Chaotic social conditions in the late 1960s could not help but influence cultural enterprises. For some industries this meant expanding opportunities both artistically and financially. Rock and roll music encompassed increasingly diverse styles that were marketed by yet another wave of independent record labels. Motion pictures enjoyed a period of directorial creativity even as the once tightly held Hollywood studios became part of huge conglomerates and were joined by newly influential independent producers. In sports, opportunities for women expanded and barriers to racial minorities fell, while the growing number of professional franchises spread decision making to a larger group of owners than ever before. Artistic boundaries on television stretched to new limits at the same time the networks maintained their dominance in the face of government attack.

In some cases this expansion was only temporary. Auteurism suffered as commercial interests prevailed in the movies, and the music industry giants absorbed many of the smaller rebels. In the ongoing cycles of expanding and contracting control over cultural endeavors, however, this phase permitted ex-

perimentation and opportunity. As the reason behind the Vietnam generation's label finally came to an end in 1975, the role of popular culture stood
transformed from what it had been thirty years earlier. Film and music had
helped push sexuality into public discussion. Sport was a strong contributor
to racial integration. Nearly all cultural forms advanced the notion of a distinctive youth generation, and all became increasingly interconnected. Popular culture, more than ever before, offered the public a view of itself that was
close to its true diversity. If the future appeared slightly unsettled, it held the
promise of still greater achievements.

NOTES

1. Steven Spielberg, quoted in Peter Biskind, *Easy Riders, Raging Bulls: How the
Sex-Drugs-and-Rock-'n'-Roll Generation Saved Hollywood* (New York: Simon and
Schuster, 1998), 14–15.

2. David A. Cook, *Lost Illusions: American Cinema in the Shadow of Watergate and
Vietnam, 1970–1979*, vol. 9 of *History of the American Cinema*, ed. Charles Harpole
(New York: Scribner, 2000), 69.

3. Justin Wyatt, *High Concept: Movies and Marketing in Hollywood* (Austin:
University of Texas Press, 1994), 85, 71. MGM and United Artists did not merge
until 1981. For a slightly different time period, Wyatt separates their market share as
United Artists 11.5 percent and MGM 5.8 percent.

4. Vincent Canby, quoted in Cook, *Lost Illusions*, 303.

5. James Aubrey Jr., quoted in "Making the Movies Into a Business," *Business Week*,
June 23, 1973, 117; Cook, *Lost Illusions*, 304.

6. Cook, *Lost Illusions*, 315.

7. Biskind, *Easy Riders*, 163.

8. Richard Dreyfuss, quoted in Biskind, *Easy Riders*, 266.

9. Biskind, *Easy Riders*, 278.

10. Cook, *Lost Illusions*, 19.

11. Cook, *Lost Illusions*, 22.

12. Cook, *Lost Illusions*, 182.

13. Robert Altman, quoted in Jack C. Ellis, *A History of Film*, 2nd ed. (Englewood Cliffs, NJ: Prentice Hall, 1985), 400.

14. Mardik Martin, quoted in Biskind, *Easy Riders*, 415.

15. Cook, *Lost Illusions*, 157.

16. Biskind, *Easy Riders*, 433.

17. Larry Gelbart, quoted in Todd Gitlin, *Inside Prime Time* (New York: Pantheon, 1983), 217.

18. Spiro Agnew, quoted in Erik Barnouw, *Tube of Plenty: The Evolution of American Television*, 2nd rev. ed. (New York: Oxford University Press, 1990), 444.

19. Robert MacNeil, *The Right Place at the Right Time* (Boston: Little, Brown, 1982), 288.

20. Erik Barnouw, quoted in Mary Ann Watson, *Defining Visions: Television and the American Experience since 1945* (Fort Worth, TX: Harcourt Brace, 1998), 94.

21. Danny Arnold, quoted in Geoffrey Cowan, *See No Evil* (New York: Simon and Schuster, 1979), 178.

22. Randy Roberts, *Winning Is the Only Thing: Sports in America since 1945* (Baltimore: Johns Hopkins University Press, 1989), 145–46.

23. Billie Jean King, quoted in Robert Lipsyte, *SportsWorld* (New York: Quadrangle, 1975), 223

24. Phil Hoag, quoted in David W. Zang, *Sports Wars: Athletes in the Age of Aquarius* (Fayetteville: University of Arkansas Press, 2001), 79.

25. William F. Reed, "An Ugly Affair in Minneapolis," *Sports Illustrated*, February 7, 1972, 18.

26. Benjamin G. Rader, *American Sports: From the Age of Folk Games to the Age of Television*, 4th ed. (Upper Saddle River, NJ: Prentice Hall, 1999), 303.

27. Rader, *American Sports*, 274.

28. Janis Joplin, quoted in "A Whole New Minority Group," *Newsweek*, September 1, 1969, 20.

29. Reebee Garofalo, *Rockin' Out: Popular Music in the USA*, 2nd ed. (Upper Saddle River, NJ: Prentice Hall, 2002), 198.

30. Simon Frith, *Sound Effects: Youth, Leisure, and the Politics of Rock 'n' Roll* (New York: Pantheon, 1981), 170.

31. Jefferson Airplane, "We Can Be Together," *Volunteers* (RCA Victor 4238, 1969).

32. Garofalo, *Rockin' Out*, 192.

33. Herbert I. London, *Closing the Circle: A Cultural History of the Rock Revolution* (Chicago: Nelson-Hall, 1984), 8.

34. Richard Goldstein, "Why Do the Kids Dig Rock," *New York Times*, November 24, 1968, H1.

35. Steve Pond, "The Seventies," *Rolling Stone*, September 20, 1990, 53.

36. Stephen Davis, *Hammer of the Gods: The Led Zeppelin Saga* (New York: Ballantine, 1985), 51, 151.

37. Jon Landau, quoted in James Miller, *Flowers in the Dustbin: The Rise of Rock and Roll, 1947–1977* (New York: Fireside, 1999), 320.

38. Vladimir Bogdanov, Chris Woodstra, and Stephen Thomas Erlewine, eds., *All Music Guide: The Definitive Guide to Popular Music*, 4th ed. (San Francisco: Backbeat Books, 2001), 384.

39. Simon Frith, "Beyond the Dole Queue: The Politics of Punk," *Village Voice*, October 24, 1977, 78.

40. Garofalo, *Rockin' Out*, 253.

41. Miller, *Flowers*, 328.

42. Jon Savage, *England's Dreaming: Anarchy, Sex Pistols, Punk Rock and Beyond* (New York: St. Martin's, 1991), 330.

5

The End of the Tunnel

By the end of the 1970s the Vietnam generation was well into adulthood, acquiring an expanding share of the nation's responsibilities and benefits. If only symbolically, the transition to a new decade marked the beginning of a new era. The launching of ESPN and the Cable News Network (CNN) in 1979 and 1980 would eventually allow these and other cable channels to challenge the networks for both highly desirable programming and prestige. John Lennon's murder on December 8, 1980, stunned rock fans the world over. For some his death signified the end of countercultural dreams. The U.S. Summer Olympic boycott in 1980 and the lengthy baseball strike of 1981 showed conclusively how far political and economic issues had become entwined with sports. When Marvin Davis bought Twentieth Century-Fox in 1981, the last of the five original major film studios lost its independent status. Once the nation's supreme cultural symbol, the movies had become another conglomerate product—though a highly visible one.

Receding from memory in the face of these events was the recently concluded war. From 1955 to 1975 the Vietnam War was a major intrusion on American life. For some people either conducting or opposing the war became the very center of their lives. This was especially true after 1965. For many others it was possible to avoid much of the war's impact but nearly impossible to escape its presence. Anyone with a television encountered Vietnam in network news coverage. Radios and phonographs provided occasional

musical statements about war and other social issues. Sports fans could easily
miss the war's impact on their favorite team, but athletes, too, sometimes challenged the very tenets of American sporting life. Only in motion pictures was
this trend reversed. Moviegoers saw little of the war until its conclusion and
then saw it played out again in their local theaters.

HOLLYWOOD'S VIETNAM

Filmmakers treated the Vietnam War much differently than they had World
War II. During the Second World War Hollywood worked cooperatively with
the U.S. government, allocating almost 25 percent of its wartime feature films
to war-related themes. When combined with newsreels, the film industry's
output provided an ongoing portrayal of events that strongly supported the
national effort and government policy.

Vietnam inspired little of this conduct. The lack of a clear beginning to the
conflict and the presence of growing dissent made any major Hollywood production a financial gamble. Prior to the commitment of American combat
troops, however, the conflict in Southeast Asia did appear occasionally on
movie screens. Films like *China Gate* (1957) and *The Quiet American* (1958)
viewed the political and military situation there through the lens of the Cold
War. *China Gate*, starring Gene Barry and Angie Dickinson, deals with the
French-Indochina War, portraying French forces and an American explosives
expert as defenders of liberty against barbaric communists. *The Quiet American*, based on Graham Greene's novel, features American Alden Pyle, played
by Audie Murphy, supporting the French war effort by encouraging a nation-
alist alternative to the communists. Michael Redgrave plays a British journalist who better understands the complexity of Vietnamese society. Ultimately
Pyle is murdered by communists.

Perhaps the most analytical early film was *The Ugly American* (1963), starring Marlon Brando. Brando plays Harrison Carter MacWhite, the new U.S.
ambassador to the fictitious country of Sarkhan, substituting for Vietnam. As
Sarkhanese communists stir up opposition to an American-supported Freedom Road project, MacWhite meets with an old friend, rebel leader Deong,
who views the Sarkhanese government as an American puppet. Their encounter convinces MacWhite that Deong is a communist, although Deong is
walking a dangerous line in trying to gain communist support without losing
control of his following. As a military insurgency escalates, MacWhite finally

recognizes the complexity of Sarkhanese politics and that Deong is the target of a communist assassination attempt. Deong is killed after agreeing to form a coalition government with the existing head of state, and MacWhite calls on the U.S. fleet to save the situation. The ambassador's final televised plea to the American public is switched off, symbolizing the nation's apathy. These early films share common assumptions: that communism is monolithic and unciv- ilized, that Americans are politically naive about Asia but motivated by hu- manitarian concern, that neutrality is not a viable alternative to revolution, and that resistance to communist aggression is a necessary response.

The war years produced only a single major combat film, *The Green Berets*. John Wayne stars as Colonel Mike Kirby in this hawkish interpretation of the war. David Janssen portrays liberal newspaper reporter George Beckwith, whose skepticism about the war disappears when he accepts the colonel's invi- tation to join him in Vietnam. The film portrays principled but unappreciated Americans fighting ruthless communist invaders, compares South Vietnam to revolutionary America, and accepts as fact a Soviet drive for global domina- tion. Beckwith's character represents conservatives' belief that a liberal media undermined the nation's will to win. Financially the film was a moderate suc- cess, but critics generally despised it. Coming as it did after the Tet Offensive, the film's political viewpoint no longer seemed credible.

After *The Green Berets* nearly a decade passed before the war stood at the center of another major Hollywood film. In the meantime the war served as background for several movies depicting Vietnam veterans, usually suffering from psychological or physical problems inflicted by their tour of duty. *Taxi Driver*'s (1976) Travis Bickle is a paranoid insomniac who attempts a political assassination. In 1977's *Heroes*, Henry Winkler plays a veteran troubled by flashbacks and post-traumatic stress syndrome. A psychotic former POW plans a terrorist bombing of the Super Bowl in *Black Sunday* (1976). In these and numerous lower-budget movies the war plays only a secondary role, serv- ing mainly as an explanation for the actions of war veterans who have diffi- culty adjusting to nonmilitary life.

By the late 1970s, with the war finally over and a public consensus that the war was a mistake—although there was not consensus on why it was a mistake—major studios were ready to address the war directly. The break- through year was 1978, when *The Boys in Company C*, *Go Tell the Spartans*, *Coming Home*, and *The Deer Hunter* all debuted. The latter two were major award winners. *Coming Home* dealt with the struggle of individuals to come to grips with the war's impact on their lives. Jon Voight plays a bitter and antagonistic veteran whose legs are paralyzed. Jane Fonda is the inhibited wife of Bruce Dern, an officer who went to Vietnam hoping to become a hero but who instead became greatly disillusioned. Fonda, a VA hospital volunteer, meets Voight during his treatment there, and ultimately both are transformed by their love affair. Fonda becomes confident and independent, while Voight evolves into a well-adjusted activist. Dern, however, is dangerously withdrawn upon his return to the United States. In the film's most compelling moment, two scenes are intercut: while Voight addresses a high school assembly with an emotional plea to consider the consequences of military service, Dern leaves his dress uniform on the beach and swims into the ocean to commit suicide.

The *Deer Hunter*, along with *Coming Home*, persuaded filmmakers that the highly divisive war could now be addressed directly to attentive audiences. The Academy Award winner as best picture, *The Deer Hunter* revolves around a tightly knit group of friends in a patriotic ethnic Pennsylvania steel town. Three men, Michael, Nick, and Steven (played by Robert De Niro, Christopher Walken, and John Savage), are captured while serving in Vietnam and forced by their captors into playing Russian roulette. Although they escape, Nick becomes deranged and Steven suffers crippling wounds. The men are unable to fully reintegrate into society upon their return home, and the final scene following Nick's funeral reveals a confused and broken community. Controversy grew out of the Russian roulette scene—which liberal critics claimed was inaccurate and racist—and the cast's postfuneral singing of "God Bless America," derided as an unrealistic adherence to the nation's militaristic myths. Many viewers, however, were less certain of the film's political viewpoint.

Francis Ford Coppola directed 1979's *Apocalypse Now*, a surreal story about Captain Willard, sent by military intelligence to assassinate the renegade Colonel Kurtz, who is leading an army of Asian tribesmen inside Cambodia. The story line is less important than the images that evoke a sense of the war's insanity. In one example an American commander attacks a village because its beach provides good surfing. *Coming Home*, *The Deer Hunter*, and *Apocalypse Now* all serve more as metaphors for the war than as realistic portrayals of events.

The "stab-in-the back" thesis often appeared to varying degrees in films during the early and mid-1980s. This conservative conspiracy theory held that American military forces had been effective and heroic but were undermined by hostile or weak-minded influences at home: the media, the antiwar movement, politicians, and others. This viewpoint peaked with 1985's *Rambo*, starring Sylvester Stallone as the title character, first portrayed in the film *First Blood* (1982). Former Green Beret John Rambo accepts a mission for the CIA, a phony mission as it turns out, to search for U.S. POWs inside postwar Vietnam. When he actually finds American prisoners and attempts a rescue, the CIA leaves him to be captured. Rambo ultimately escapes and leads his comrades to safety, killing hundreds of Vietnamese and Soviet troops in the effort. The movie was a huge financial success and made a significant political impact in the conservative Reagan years, supporting conspiracy theorists' views that American soldiers had been denied victory by devious politicians and that Americans remained behind in Southeast Asia against their will. Other movies with this perspective include *Uncommon Valor* (1983) and *Missing in Action* (1984).

As this nonhistorical wave of movies began to fade, other writers and directors created a series of films that provided some of the most realistic portrayals of the war yet seen. The 1984 movie *The Killing Fields* followed journalist Sydney Schanberg and Cambodian Dith Pran during the Khmer Rouge's genocide in that country. *Platoon* (1986), directed and written by Vietnam veteran Oliver Stone, was often cited as the most realistic of all the Hollywood productions. Charlie Sheen plays the film's narrator, Chris Taylor, while the story pits Sergeants Barnes and Elias against each other in a struggle over the "moral" way to wage war. Stone's writing not only encompasses the heat of combat and the oppressive conditions Americans faced in Vietnam but also examines military atrocities, racism, command failure, and other tensions within the armed forces. *Platoon* won Academy Awards for best picture and best director. *Full Metal Jacket* (1987) follows marine recruits through boot camp and then to Vietnam, where they endure the Tet Offensive. *Casualties of War* (1989) depicts an American squad that kidnaps, rapes, and murders a Vietnamese girl. Only one squad member challenges this brutal behavior, as the film questions the war's impact on Americans and American society. Based on veteran Ron Kovic's autobiography, Oliver Stone's *Born on the Fourth of July* (1989) traces Kovic's evolution from a naive marine enlistee, who is paralyzed during his second tour of duty in Vietnam, to an ardent antiwar activist. Among the most recent Vietnam-centered movies is *We Were Soldiers* (2002), a combat story based on Lieutenant Colonel Harold Moore's account of the war's first major battle, in the Ia Drang Valley.

The motion picture industry's depiction of the Vietnam War covers a wide range of territory, both artistically and ideologically. While many of the films were eminently forgettable, some attained Hollywood's highest honors. Despite the creative achievements of the finest works, movie producers embraced the issue cautiously until it proved to be profitable. The emphasis on commercialism, however, was not limited to a particular time or theme.

BEYOND *STAR WARS*

Still caught in recession, the major studios reduced the number of films they produced after 1972. By keeping supply down they hoped the rising demand would allow them to squeeze more money from theaters, including 90 percent of the gross for blockbusters. Universal, for example, released only eleven movies in 1976. Each major picture, however, carried the weight of the studio's hopes. Out of 119 major films in 1977, thirteen generated half of the studios' total income. The major studios served essentially as financiers and distributors, while the creative process relied increasingly on independent production teams.

The growing expense of moviemaking prodded the industry into increased concern with marketing. By 1979 the average cost of making a movie was ten million dollars, with an additional six million dollars spent on promotion. One way of generating extra revenue was product placement, which started in the late 1970s. This practice basically wove commercials into films by putting particular brands of cars, drinks, clothes, or other consumer items on the screen in exchange for money. When taken to extremes, some manufacturers created entire movies that served as commercials for their products.

A film's sound track was another important way of maximizing its revenue. The recording industry grew from one billion dollars in record and tape sales in 1967 to two billion dollars in 1973 to four billion dollars in 1978, surpassing the film industry's income. With the more widespread use of Dolby noise reduction and stereo sound, several movies emphasized modern music. Few of these films, however, were moneymakers. Among the youth-oriented exceptions were *Saturday Night Fever* (1977), which exploited and sustained the disco music craze, and *Grease* (1978), both starring John Travolta. These two pictures released their sound track music before their films to generate interest, as songs climbed the charts prior to the movies' appearance. Both were enormously successful films, and combined they sold nearly sixty million sound track albums.

Moviemaking beyond the mid-1970s continued to utilize the blockbuster strategy. *Star Wars* (1977) broke the record set by *Jaws* to become Hollywood's biggest moneymaker, with $193 million in film rental income. George Lucas wrote and directed the film, a science fiction story that matched a small rebel alliance against an evil galactic empire. It combined futuristic technology and intergalactic space travel with medieval chivalry. Among the outmanned rebels was young Luke Skywalker, who relied on the mysterious power of "the Force" in battling the empire's military leader, Darth Vader. By licensing related products that reaped huge benefits, *Star Wars* established new standards for movie possibilities. *Star Wars* became the motion pictures' first real franchise, earning even more in merchandise sales than the film, an estimated one billion dollars by the end of the 1970s. One screenwriter called it "a virtual money-printing machine."[1] Its cutting-edge computerized special effects and status as the first movie released with four-track Dolby stereo sound made it an unprecedented viewing experience. The degree of success enjoyed by *Star Wars* exceeded everyone's expectations, and Lucas planned eight additional movies to complete the story.

From 1975 to 1979, blockbusters and the limited number of feature films pulled Hollywood out of the industry's 1969–1974 recession. Efforts to create new blockbusters, however, were inconsistent. As film executive Andrew Fogelson commented on the public's reception, "Sometimes when we think we've done everything right, when we've met our own list of criteria for what a blockbuster is, they tell us we're not even close."[2] Saturation booking—opening a film at nearly two thousand theaters, by the 1980s—and heavy TV advertising remained the staples of trying to create a hit but were not guarantees. Two films produced by United Artists at the end of the decade, *Apocalypse Now* (1979) and *Heaven's Gate* (1980), represented the excess of trying to create blockbuster films. The films were wildly over budget in their production, and their lack of financial success caused United Artists's sale to MGM.

Science fiction spectaculars became the popular new blockbuster genre. Three of the biggest were *Close Encounters of the Third Kind* (1977), *Invasion of the Body Snatchers* (1978), and *Alien* (1979). Several more followed into the 1980s. When films like *Star Wars* and *Star Trek* (1979) turned into franchise series, they brought in huge merchandising deals that were so profitable that some movies became product enhancers, rather than the products enhancing the films. Even movies with minimal expectations and relatively low budgets like *Rocky* (1976) and *Smokey and the Bandit* (1977) brought surprisingly large profits and turned into franchises.

Another popular film genre in the late 1970s was the previously marginalized horror movie. Boosted by the success of mainstream occult hits like *The Exorcist*, other horror pictures entered the mainstream. Several of them produced numerous sequels. Brian De Palma's *Carrie* (1976) and *Dressed to Kill* (1980), Wes Craven's *Last House on the Left* (1972), John Carpenter's *Halloween* (1978), and Sean Cunningham's *Friday the 13th* (1980) are among the most successful in this style. Working on low-budget horror movies gave these directors a way into filmmaking, giving them access to the major studios as Hollywood discovered the popularity of exploitative horror.

Halloween led slasher movies into middle-class suburban theaters. Most followed a predictable formula: a psychotic man pursues sexually active young women and kills them in graphic depictions of violence. Many used hand-held cameras to provide the stalker's perspective, helping the audience to identify with the killer. Starting in the late 1970s, slasher movies appeared almost as if off an assembly line. Horror films had shifted their focus from monsters to psycho-slashers, a style David Cook calls "the most extreme expression of misogyny in the history of American cinema."[3] Slasher movies' ability to attract generous financing grew out of earlier successes. In 1981 horror movies accounted for one-third of the year's top moneymakers.

Young people provided significant support for many of these movies. By the late 1970s, 57 percent of the movie audience was between twelve and twenty-four years old. To tap this audience, regardless of whether a film emphasized adventure, violence, or sexuality, filmmakers often gave their pictures an adolescent appeal. The age of moviegoers helped account for the huge surprise success of films such as *National Lampoon's Animal House* (1978).

Several top adult-oriented films continued to reflect the countercultural suspicion of powerful institutions intensified by the war and the Nixon administration. *All the President's Men* (1976) tells the Watergate story based on accounts by two *Washington Post* reporters. *Network* (1976) features an all-star cast and an Oscar-winning script written by Paddy Chayefsky. This is a dark satire of television journalism, where quality receives less emphasis than entertainment and ratings. When a mentally unstable news anchor challenges the system, network executives manipulate his outrage for higher ratings. *The China Syndrome* (1979) links the nuclear power industry to weak government oversight and media collusion.

Other outstanding films fell outside of these categories. Woody Allen wrote, directed, and costarred with Diane Keaton in *Annie Hall* (1977). This humorous story follows two insecure adults as they deal with the experience of falling in and out of love. It defeated *Star Wars* for that year's best picture Oscar. Another best picture winner was 1979's *Kramer vs. Kramer.* Dustin Hoffman and Meryl Streep both won acting awards for this movie about a painful divorce and child custody battle. Martin Scorsese directed *Raging Bull* (1980), a dramatic story about the tragic life of boxer Jake La Motta. Robert De Niro earned an Academy Award for his work in the title role.

After years of financial trouble, Hollywood settled on the blockbuster method to generate profits. Although successful, this approach to filmmaking left little room for the small, intimate, artistic film that occasionally found a sizable audience. It was also difficult to predict, leaving producers hoping for the spectacular rather than the disaster.

CABLE AND COMMERCE

The dramatic expansion of cable TV turned individual homes into private theaters. The number of cable systems grew from twenty-five hundred at the end of the 1960s to sixty-six hundred in 1985, and the number of subscribers rose from about fifteen million at the end of the 1970s to fifty-three million by the end of the 1980s. With the addition of successful satellite-based cable networks such as ESPN (1979), USA (1980), and CNN (1980), cable provided sports, music, news, movies, and other programming around the clock.

The networks had broadcast movies for several years, and Hollywood produced many films specifically for TV broadcast. During the 1979–1980 TV season, for example, 60 percent of movies appearing on the television networks were made for TV. Feature films that ran on television, however, were often edited to fit TV time frames and allow commercial ads, which disturbed viewers hoping to see motion pictures in their original form. The two biggest complaints of people viewing movies on TV were commercial interruptions and a long wait for the appearance of feature films. Cable television promised to solve both those problems by broadcasting unedited and uninterrupted movies. Home Box Office (HBO) moved to satellite distribution in 1975 and was a key in developing cable TV. It had twelve million subscribers by 1983. Rivals appeared within a few years, including Showtime, the Movie Channel, and Cinemax. Viewers paid a monthly fee to see the movies without the annoying distractions of network TV. Later, as cable stations expanded and became more important in developing and broadcasting television programming, many of them reverted to showing edited movies with commercial interruptions.

Commercialism threatened to overwhelm American culture by the 1970s. Television had been closely linked with the consumer society since its inception, but over time the distinction between commerce and entertainment became noticeably blurred. Advertising in the 1960s increasingly emphasized disposable products and linked consumer items with desirable traits. Products were often portrayed not just as fulfilling a particular function but as contributing, or creating, a personal image. More people abandoned the value of conservation, so prevalent during the Depression and World War II, for the new need to consume.

Television in particular helped grow new consumers by targeting advertising toward children. Saturday mornings had become, by the early 1960s, almost exclusively devoted to children's shows. With children particularly susceptible to advertising techniques, the emphasis on selling foods with high sugar content encouraged kids to develop eating habits with both short- and long-term problems. Fried foods high in fat received heavy plugs on television commercials as well. Toy manufacturers spent heavily to sponsor children's programming. Some children's advocate groups and other critics of this trend favored a complete ban on TV advertising directed toward children. The networks, however, agreed only to reduce the amount of time devoted to ads during children's shows. During the antiregulatory Reagan administration in the 1980s, even those limited gains disappeared. In fact, some children's shows were designed entirely as marketing tools for specific products.

Advertising helped television prosper but not without costs. In 1977 advertising brought $3.6 billion to the networks, and program sales to foreign countries brought an additional $180 million. For the first time, however, at least one poll showed a decline of public "esteem" for television. The networks faced growing challenges from new technology and cable systems. Even public television, despite some impressive programming achievements, became more commercial, as fund-raising and corporate sponsorship became necessary for its survival.

Commercialism increasingly infected other forms of popular culture. Sporting contests and their venues carried the burden of corporate names. Everything, it seemed, was for sale. Sports contests on TV became wall-to-wall commercial plugs, from the announcers interspersing game action with ads to corporate logos fastened to playing surfaces or uniforms. Most disturbing was the inherent contradiction in using countercultural symbols to sell the products of mainstream culture. Rock and roll artists linked themselves to corporate sponsors for tours or had, either deliberately or unknowingly, their music associated with commercial products. The rebelliousness of classic rock and roll was aggressively harnessed by Madison Avenue to sell a string of products that could not be more tied to "the system." Advertising encouraged Americans to partake of almost everything to excess in the drive to consume. According to Mary Ann Watson, "The role of TV advertising was to stimulate wants far beyond a baseline of security and comfort. . . . What advertising sold most effectively was the notion that living with limits was unnecessary."[4]

Even America's political candidates became commodities to sell to the public. As noted scholar Erik Barnouw observes of the post-Watergate political scene: "Politics had become sales pitches. . . . Alone among major democracies, the United States had incorporated election campaigns into its merchandising procedures."[5] Singer Jackson Browne makes a similar statement in his song "Lives in the Balance":

> They sell us the President the same way
> They sell us our clothes and our cars
> They sell us everything from youth to religion
> The same time they sell us our wars.[6]

The heavy reliance on expensive TV advertising made fund-raising more critical, and election finance reforms made political action committees (PAC), which raise money to contribute to campaigns, more important power brokers. Ronald Reagan, a movie actor with over fifty roles and a television spokesman for General Electric, was the perfect president for the new era.

As complicit as television was in all this, however, there were other forces at work. In a highly commercialized culture, even minor challenges can have major implications. Despite commercial television's preference for the status quo, it was often disruptive. Out of its need to attract young viewers, television presented sympathetic treatment of dissenting culture, which some scholars see as "a force for change and upheaval," with the networks contributing to "fundamentally changing the American social and cultural landscape."[7] That same drive to reach young audiences led other cultural forms to emphasize at different times themes of anxiety, discontent, and rebellion.

One recurring anxiety for viewers was violent program content. Television violence was one of the industry's dependable issues, bound to produce a major reaction every decade. The wives of over fifty members of Congress spoke out as part of a "crusade against TV violence" in 1977, and a conservative Christian organization called the "Moral Majority" threatened to boycott sponsors of violent programming. Republican presidential candidate Ronald Reagan became the standard-bearer for this constituency.

Again, public pressure appeared to have an impact. Some programs reduced the amount of violent content, while others were replaced by comedies or other styles that deemphasized aggressive action. By the end of the 1977–1978 television season, the National Citizens Committee for Broadcasting had ended its scrutiny of network programming, persuaded that its goal had been met.

Once again, however, victory was short-lived. The growing availability by the 1980s of cable television, not subject to restrictions placed on broadcasting that used public airwaves, included uncut feature films and original programs that pushed up against and sometimes broke through the boundaries of acceptable TV fare. The Reagan administration, despite its criticism of some TV content, was not inclined to impose government regulation on the industry. A 1982 report identified a definite link between TV action and public behavior, but that had no noticeable impact on the trend of rising screen violence.

By the time the 1970s passed their midpoint the barriers to televised sexuality were also crumbling. *Charlie's Angels* (1976) starred three beautiful women as undercover police detectives, but the focus was less on interesting stories than on formfitting clothes and skimpy bathing suits and lingerie. The more blatant on-screen sexuality went hand in hand with the reduction in violence prompted by grassroots criticism. In 1977, two situation comedies, *Three's Company* and *Soap*, headed what some critics called the "T & A Season." With the expansion of cable television, networks escalated the sexual content of their programs, both comedies and dramas.

Homosexuality was almost nonexistent on television throughout this entire period. On rare occasions stereotypical characters appeared but nearly always in a comedic context, and never in a clearly stated manner. A 1972 TV movie, *That Certain Summer*, was perhaps the first TV show to deal with a gay relationship in a receptive manner. The breakthrough year was 1977, when more than a half dozen situation comedies introduced homosexual characters, as did a number of TV movies. In most cases heterosexuals eventually accepted the gay characters. The depiction of homosexuality on television, however, reflected ongoing debates in the larger society about the proper boundaries of human sexual behavior. Even well beyond the 1970s actors playing gay characters stirred controversy.

Television's most watched shows in the second half of the 1970s were comedies. *Happy Days* (1974–1984), its spin-off *Laverne and Shirley* (1976–1983), *Welcome Back, Kotter* (1975–1979), and *Three's Company* (1977–1984) built stories around ridiculous situations. *M*A*S*H* (1972–1983) and *Barney Miller* (1975–1982) were among shows providing more realism and introspection. The MTM Company succeeded with both comedy and drama in the late 1970s, producing *Lou Grant* (1977–1982), *The White Shadow* (1978–1981), *WKRP in Cincinnati* (1978–1982), and *Taxi* (1978–1983). All of these were popular, but while absurdity usually received higher ratings, realism took the Emmy Awards.

One of television's truly memorable events was the broadcast of the miniseries *Roots*, aired on eight consecutive nights in January 1977. Over 130 million people watched the twelve-hour production, which followed one African American family's 150-year journey from enslavement to freedom and did so from a black perspective. Few experiences of the time did more to encourage interracial understanding.

The viewing habits of Americans changed, however, as more choices became available in the cable era. While *The Cosby Show* (1984–1992), which featured an African American family parented by a doctor and an attorney, became the top program in the 1980s, black and white audiences diverged in the 1990s. Kate Meyers sees *Cosby* as a transitional program, noting, "Before the demographically divvied, zillion-channel cable universe arrived, *Cosby*

All in the Family *(Chester Maydole/MPTV.net)*

was the last show everyone watched."⁸ Whites tended to watch shows featuring white characters, and blacks tented to watch shows featuring black characters. With its offerings so much more diverse than before, television ironically found it difficult to retain its gift as a unifier.

BORN TO RUN

The development of punk music in the 1970s had reminded fans of the raw energy and crude outlook that characterized much early rock and roll. At the opposite pole from punk was disco music. Disco was polished, sensuous, technologically complex, and heavily produced and emphasized challenging dance steps. The style emerged from urban dance clubs that often featured light shows and typically used recorded rather than live music to save money. The more polished soul music known as the "Philadelphia sound" became one of the most preferred styles. Most early dance records received little airplay but sold through their exposure in the clubs. An occasional record rose up the pop charts, but most record companies did not see much commercial appeal in dance music and failed to promote it aggressively. Several songs broke through, however, in 1976, and artists like Donna Summer, KC and the Sunshine Band, and the Village People became stars. The Bee Gees finally pushed disco music into the mainstream with the huge success of the 1977 film *Saturday Night Fever* and its sound track album. As disco artists enjoyed a brief period of commercial success, their influence even extended to some of rock's biggest acts. The rapid, repetitive beat seemed to be everywhere, but it soon became annoying and produced a hostile backlash. Disco faded from popularity as quickly as it had risen.

The U.S. music industry experienced a recession starting in 1979. Income from recorded music dropped to $3.7 billion from $4.1 billion the previous year. Sales remained unstable, dipping to a low of $3.6 billion in 1982. Record companies reduced their workforces, limited their output, and signed fewer artists. Between 1978 and 1984 the number of new releases was cut almost in half. The development of compact discs (CDs) in the late 1970s helped fuel a recovery. Their production costs were about the same as those of records and tapes, but their sound quality and durability made them highly desirable and permitted companies to charge higher prices. By the end of the 1980s CDs were outselling LPs.

One of the things that contributed to the industry's recovery was a growing trend adding a visual component to new songs. The widespread packaging of new musical releases with an accompanying video represented a serious alteration in the recording industry's marketing efforts. Video clips for songs appeared sporadically in the 1960s but spread first in Europe during the late 1970s as a way to get exposure beyond the limited number of radio stations. In the United States, television deregulation in the early 1980s brought a vast expansion of cable TV, and Warner Communications started its MTV channel on August 1, 1981. Its staple was broadcasting music videos provided by the record companies. Many of the early videos offered the artists in fairly standard concert settings, but over time videos became increasingly theatrical. Little-known bands with the right look could get on MTV when they might not find room on the radio. While radio stations played primarily older songs, MTV went overwhelmingly with recent releases. Other cable stations followed in showing music videos as part of their programming, such as the USA channel's *Night Flight*. According to one industry executive, "Video is doing what tours used to do, putting the artist in front of the audience."[9]

Despite its early success, MTV attracted a good deal of criticism. Because the station targeted a specific audience demographic, and because Britain was more aggressive and advanced in merging music and video, MTV's early rotation of music videos featured British and American groups that were overwhelmingly white. The impact of British artists on the American music charts led some to declare a "second British invasion." Critics frequently condemned MTV for ignoring black artists. Not until Michael Jackson's phenomenal best-selling album *Thriller* appeared in 1982 did the racial barrier begin to fall. The network also received criticism for the way many videos portrayed women, either as sexual objects or as victims of violence.

Rock's image fared much better when its performers mixed entertainment with compassion. A series of concerts and multistar performances connected rock to progressive social causes in the 1980s. In 1984 Bob Geldof of the Irish punk band Boomtown Rats responded to a TV documentary on famine in Africa by cowriting the song "Do They Know It's Christmas." He organized Britain and Ireland's biggest pop stars to record the song under the name Band Aid. Profits from its sales went to the famine's sufferers. Geldof's lack of prominence in America doomed his efforts to organize a similar project in the United States, but Michael Jackson took a leading role in an American response to the African famine. Jackson cowrote "We Are the World" with Lionel Richie and was one of an assembly of major U.S. stars who recorded as USA for Africa. Some attacked the song and effort as ethnocentric, presumptuous, or corporate driven, but it reached the top of the American charts in spring 1985, and its financial impact was impressive.

Concerned musicians followed these recordings with a massive concert staged in London and Philadelphia, with the two sites joined by a television broadcast. Bob Geldof organized over sixty artists for this sixteen-hour concert, Live Aid, on July 13, 1985. The motive was to benefit starving victims of Ethiopia's civil war. Nearly 162,000 attended live, and TV broadcast the event to an additional 1.6 billion people. Live Aid was both widely praised and criticized for superficial coverage and commercialization, but it raised sixty-seven million dollars.

Mainstream music in the 1980s featured songs that were danceable, sensuous, and video friendly. Michael Jackson was a versatile performer who sang funk, pop, and ballads equally well. He was also a gifted dancer whose signature "moonwalk" was among the steps that made his concerts a memorable visual experience. His brilliantly conceived videos of his 1982 album *Thriller* helped it become the biggest-selling album in history and revolutionized musical video production, turning it into an art form of its own. Video also played a key role in the popularity of Madonna. Her early hits were dance oriented, and she turned her talent for provocative self-promotion into superstardom. Prince mixed rock and funky soul music. His 1984 album, *Purple Rain*, sold over ten million copies, but his drive to experiment led to inconsistent success thereafter, mixed with flashes of brilliance. From Ireland came U2, whose political and religious themes stood out from most 1980s rock. One writer declared, "There rarely was a band that believed so deeply in rock's potential for revolution as U2."[10] Their career peaked with *The Joshua Tree* in 1987.

Dissatisfaction with mainstream commercial rock and roll generated a reaction in the 1980s built around a rougher sound and more pessimistic lyrics. Influenced by 1970s punk groups, these underground bands often added touches of heavy metal and scorned major label success and commercial appeal. Many developed local followings, recorded on small independent labels, and attracted broader attention from college radio stations that programmed alternative music to the chart-based songs of the major commercial stations.

Stevie Wonder (Walter P. Reuther Library, Wayne State University)

Tensions arose, however, when groups achieved greater popularity and the attention of more-established recording companies. Popular music scholar Reebee Garofalo notes this conflict as previously marginalized music finds possible entry into the mainstream: "The idea that music can only retain its integrity before it reaches a mass public leads to the tendency to lionize artists when they are least successful and to dismiss them precisely at the moment of their greatest impact."[11]

The first alternative band to achieve mainstream stardom was R.E.M. This Georgia quartet built a dedicated fan base throughout the 1980s by playing more folk-based and melodic songs than most punk-influenced groups. Strong airplay from the increasingly important college radio stations solidified their reputation. They charted a top-ten single in 1987 and released their first major label album with Warner Brothers in 1988.

The most distinctive alternative style came from the Seattle area. These so-called grunge bands recorded for the local Sub Pop label before their discovery by the national media. Most of them later joined companies that offered them greater exposure, creative opportunities, and financial independence. Soundgarden signed with a major label in 1988 (A&M), Alice in Chains went with Columbia, Pearl Jam to Epic, and Nirvana with DGC. Nivana's 1991 album, *Nevermind*, broke open the gates to Seattle alternative bands, reaching *Billboard*'s top position.

MONEY AND MIRACLES

Economic concerns continued to be among the most visible issues in professional sports in the post–Vietnam War years. Relations between ownership and players proved to be especially contentious in baseball, with the owners relatively inept at dealing with the union. Contract negotiations prior to the 1981 season broke down. The owners hoped to crush the union, apparently unable to find any other option to prevent one another from dramatically escalating salaries. They proposed a plan that would compensate teams losing a free agent with a player from the signing team's roster, end arbitration, and replace individual negotiations with a salary schedule. Their obvious intent was to limit player movement and keep salaries from rising, essentially canceling the benefits of free agency. Not surprisingly the players objected and went on strike from mid-June to early August, canceling over seven hundred games. The owners' resolve collapsed once they exhausted their strike insurance. A compromise settlement allowed owners a reduced compensation agreement, but minimum and average salaries soared during the 1980s.

When free agent signings stopped after the 1985 season, the suspicious players' union sued for restraint of trade. An arbitration ruling in September 1987 found the owners guilty of collusion and ordered payments totaling $280 million to the affected players. Through the union's enormously successful collective bargaining, the average Major League Baseball salary rose from $19,000 in 1966 to $46,000 in 1975 to $891,000 in 1991.

Players in the National Basketball Association won similar gains for free agency. Ultimately the league adopted a salary cap for each team in 1983, limiting the amount a team could devote to salaries. The NBA's free agency allowed teams to match the offers of other teams and keep their players. Football was least affected by this trend. Relatively few players changed teams during the 1970s, and salaries were below those of other major sports. The NFL had established a system of free agency in 1961, commonly called the "Rozelle Rule" after the league commissioner, which required teams signing a free agent to compensate the player's former team. Teams rarely pursued top players to avoid losing high draft choices or other talented players. The courts struck down the Rozelle Rule in 1975 as a restraint of trade, but the players accepted a modified compensation rule in their 1977 contract with the league, resulting in only a minimal increase in player movement. When efforts to improve their contract in 1982 failed, the players went on strike for nearly two months. Despite some modifications in free agency and compensation, football remained the lowest paying of the major sports. Another NFL strike in 1987 collapsed in failure, but league salaries averaged $250,000 in 1991. Hockey players lacked a collective bargaining contract until 1975.

Generally speaking, professional sports salaries rose dramatically during the late 1960s and 1970s. NBA players went from an average salary of $20,000 in 1967 to $170,000 in 1980. NFL player salaries rose from $25,000 to $79,000 in the same period, and Major League Baseball players improved from $19,000 to $144,000.

Professional team owners, faced with mounting labor costs and desires for greater profits, found new ways to enhance their income. They often used a city's desire for the prestige of a franchise and the belief that professional teams stimulated the local economy to win economic concessions—tax breaks and public financing of stadiums, for example—that often fed private gain at public expense. Owners sometimes used the threat of relocation to demand even newer and more profitable stadium deals. Many new stadiums were built in suburbs near major highways for easy access, avoiding the congestion and dilapidated conditions of many inner cities. Critics complained about misplaced priorities but rarely stopped newly proposed stadiums.

Television provided perhaps the most dependable revenue of all. In 1977 the three networks combined to pay $656 million to the NFL over four years, almost six million dollars per team for TV revenue alone. The cost of network broadcast rights to Major League Baseball exploded in 1983, increasing 400 percent in one year. In addition to league rights, each team could make deals with local stations, and the larger media markets, notably New York, took in much larger sums than smaller cities, ultimately creating a competitive imbalance based on ability to buy more talented players. Television was less impressed with pro basketball than the other major spectator sports, and the NBA's revenues from TV remained relatively small until the 1980s.

Television rights, especially for the United States, also provided large sums of money to Olympic organizers. With costs increasing, however, only government subsidies and commercial tie-ins could pay for everything. Responding to disappointing numbers of U.S. Olympic medals in recent games, Congress passed the Amateur Sports Act in 1978, giving the USOC more authority in coordinating the training and subsidizing of U.S. Olympic athletes. Other changes in the mid-1970s eliminated many of the remaining distinctions between amateur and professional athletes.

The 1976 Summer Olympic Games took place in Montreal, Canada, and were again plagued by political problems. This time several African nations boycotted because New Zealand's rugby team had toured sports pariah South Africa. Another foreign teenage gymnast, this time Romania's Nadia Comaneci, captured America's imagination as she took a total of five medals and earned seven perfect scores in her events. The American star was John Naber, whose five swimming medals included four gold. Innsbruck, Austria, once again hosted the Winter Olympics in 1976. Speed skater Sheila Young won three medals, including one gold. Peter Mueller also took gold in speed skating, and Dorothy Hamill collected the women's figure skating title.

Ironically the end of the decade brought far more attention to the winter games. The United States boycotted the 1980 Summer Olympics held in Moscow to protest the Soviet Union's invasion of Afghanistan. With Cold War tensions again peaking, the winter games in Lake Placid, New York, offered two breathtaking performances. Eric Heiden turned in an unsurpassed individual exhibition, winning all five speed skating events. In team competition the U.S. hockey players pulled off the "miracle on ice," an astounding upset of the Soviets in the semifinals on their way to winning the gold medal.

By the late 1970s networks were spending a disproportionate amount of money on sports. With the explosion of cable TV, sporting events and news were available to viewers almost constantly. Cable TV introduced two sports-oriented networks, USA Network in 1975 and the Entertainment and Sports Programming Network (ESPN) in 1979. Eventually ESPN competed successfully with the major networks for the rights to televise some of the nation's biggest sporting events. Televised sports were able to give viewers an event that live audiences could not receive. Many fans preferred watching events on TV to being there live. Critics, however, contended that TV added too much promotional hype, put too much emphasis on "highlights," and added far too many playoff games to league championships. By providing a constant flow of games, television made each less significant.

Professional football surpassed baseball as the nation's most popular spectator sport by the late 1970s. The NFL's annual championship, the Super Bowl, became America's most watched sporting event. As early as the middle of the 1960s, televised pro football games drew twice the number of viewers as baseball games. Football rule changes in the 1970s allowed offensive linemen to better protect the quarterback, and defensive backs were limited in the amount of contact they could make with receivers. This opened up the passing game remarkably, although offenses and defenses took turns in countering the best strategy of the other. Despite the league's efforts to maintain competitive parity, certain teams dominated this era. The Pittsburgh Steelers established a dynasty in professional football, taking four Super Bowls from 1975 to 1980. San Francisco collected four titles in the 1980s. Most sports expanded their playoff systems to create additional interest and revenue. The NFL increased the number of playoff teams from four to eight. In 1977 it also went to parity scheduling, which had weaker teams playing each other more frequently, helping them remain in playoff contention longer.

Baseball maintained its position as the summer game, even as changes occurred. The competitive balance of power shifted. In the American League, the New York Yankees won nine out of ten pennants and four World Series titles from 1955 to 1964. In the National League the Brooklyn/Los Angeles Dodgers took six out of twelve pennants and four World Series championships from 1955 to 1966. The St. Louis Cardinals and Milwaukee Braves were the only other teams to win more than one league title from 1955 to 1968. When the leagues split into divisions, competition was much more evenly divided. Between 1969 and 1980 the National League's most successful teams were the Cincinnati Reds (with four league and two World Series titles), Los Angeles Dodgers (three pennants), New York Mets (two pennants, one World Series), and Pittsburgh Pirates (two pennants, two World Series). The Baltimore Orioles (with four league wins and one World Series win), the Oakland Athletics (three pennants, three World Series), and New York Yankees (three pennants, two World Series) led the American League. Not until 1978, however, did baseball's major league attendance match its 1948–1952 mark, and minor league baseball suffered serious decline in the postwar years.

College basketball's annual NCAA championship tournament grew into one of the nation's most popular events. In the years following John Wooden's retirement after UCLA's 1975 title, a half dozen universities would claim multiple championships, led by Indiana, Kentucky, and Duke with three apiece. Indiana's 1976 championship team was the last to go undefeated. A record TV audience for college basketball watched Larry Bird and previously undefeated Indiana State fall in the 1979 finals to Earvin "Magic" Johnson's Michigan State squad.

Professional basketball eventually made a strong connection with the public. From 1960 to the late 1970s the NBA's attendance grew from two million to ten million. The 1970s brought greater competitive balance, with eight different teams winning titles in that decade. By the mid-1980s the NBA had become the fastest growing of the major sports, stimulated by the arrival of stars like Larry Bird, Magic Johnson, and Michael Jordan. The Boston Celtics and Los Angeles Lakers battled for team supremacy, combining for nine titles in the second half of the 1970s and the 1980s.

Superb performances came from other sports as well. In the post–Vietnam War years the NHL experienced successive dynasties by the Montreal Canadiens, New York Islanders, and the Edmonton Oilers. Edmonton's Wayne Gretzky took nine of the ten MVP awards in the 1980s. In thoroughbred racing, two more horses joined the ranks of Triple Crown winners: Seattle Slew took the crown in 1977, and in 1978 Affirmed held off Alydar in all three dramatic races.

Golf's brightest stars were Tom Watson, who won his first of eight majors in 1975, and Nancy Lopez, who earned the first of her four player-of-the-year titles in 1978. Chris Evert ranked number one in women's tennis for five years from 1975 to 1981. The top men's players often came from Australia, but American Jimmy Connors ranked first from 1974 to 1978.

Women's sports likewise underwent a dramatic transformation. The NCAA began sponsoring national championship tournaments for women in 1980, and within a few years the AIAW had folded. With an immediate need for qualified and experienced coaches, many men accepted positions coaching women's teams, sometimes reluctantly, and in the decade following the passage of Title IX the number of female head coaches in women's college sports fell from 85 percent to under 50 percent. A few women's college games had appeared on television by the end of the 1970s, but still women's sports had not begun to approach the paid attendance or popularity of men's sports.

Sport presented one of the most visible areas of change in American racial relations. Harry Edwards's complaint in 1969 that "black athletes do not become congressmen" or "cash in on . . . endorsements" was no longer valid just a few years later.[12] Former track star Ralph Metcalfe became the first, but not the last, prominent black athlete to serve in Congress, winning election in 1971. Advertising dollars also shifted progressively to African Americans as they acquired leading roles at the highest levels of sport. By the early 1990s blacks made up over three-fourths of NBA rosters, over two-thirds of NFL players, and 16 percent of Major League Baseball teams.

With improvements came difficulties. In the 1980s college sports faced growing problems related to rising costs of athletic programs, academic work of the athletes, and unethical conduct of university athletic departments. Questionable activities included recruiting players unprepared for college-level work, students getting college credit for courses not attended, players taking courses to maintain athletic eligibility rather than complete degrees, altering transcripts, making illegal payments to players, doing athletes' schoolwork for them, and pressuring faculty for undeserved grades. A 1988 NCAA study showed college athletes spent thirty hours each week on their sports and only twenty-six hours per week on academic work. Football programs became too expensive for many colleges.

Powerful interests usually blocked significant reform of the system. Efforts to enforce reasonable standards, such as the 1986 NCAA Proposition 48, requiring a minimum score on college admissions exams, met with loud oppo-sition. Since recruiting athletes is such an important part of success in college sports, it has long been an area for obvious cheating and abuse. The pressure to win at the highest level frequently translates into disproportionately high salaries, sometimes making men's basketball or football coaches the highest-paid employees in the university. Despite this emphasis on winning and gen-erating revenue, most athletic departments cannot support themselves and require funds from the university budget. Controlled by athletic directors and coaches from major sports conferences and universities, the NCAA has con-sistently served those interests at the expense of others, including smaller col-leges and athletes. Richard Davies notes that the NCAA has historically operated "to enhance the power and independence of athletic departments within their institutional setting."[13]

Sport at all levels dealt with a series of additional troubles, both old and new. Drug abuse became further entwined with athletics. Painkillers and per-formance enhancing drugs offered ways to compete more successfully. The use of anabolic steroids to increase muscular strength had been part of sport since the 1940s but increased over time. Fans and critics alike worried about their impact on the records and traditions of the games, as well as on the ath-letes themselves. Politically, many Americans saw success in the Olympic Games as a sign of national vigor and Cold War pride. When carried to ex-treme, however, this attitude sounded like jingoism. Commercial interests such as shoe and clothing manufacturers became increasingly influential, sponsoring athletic teams and programs and manipulating athletes. To one observer, modern life eroded one of sports' cherished claims. "In the end, American society did not come unglued in the '60s, but our sports were trans-formed," writes David Zang. "Right now, organized sport serves a plurality of gods. . . . It serves them because the conditions of the Vietnam era peeled away the façade of character-building."[14]

In the second half of the twentieth century, sport moved far away from ear-lier views of amateur athletics. Individuals who wanted to achieve the highest accolades became full-time athletes, and many were willing to do so because the financial rewards became much greater in many sports. The ability of an athlete to train for a few months prior to a world-class event and prevail dis-appeared during this era. Professional athletes flourished even beyond the tra-ditional mass spectator sports. International sport also became much more

prevalent. Many American athletes participated in international tours, especially in sports like track and field and tennis. Professional U.S. leagues either
placed franchises in Canada or played games in Japan, Mexico, England, and
elsewhere to stimulate foreign interest. Increasingly professional and college
teams brought foreign players into the United States.

A popular culture revolution took place in the United States from 1950 to
1980. One measure of this transformation is that popular culture is now recognized as an essential part of most people's lives. For the hours spent outside
of work or sleep, playing in or attending athletic events, watching television,
building an afternoon or evening around going to the movies, or listening to
live or recorded rock and roll takes up a major part of our leisure time. Once
thought of as a trivial though enjoyable addition to the important business of
life, popular culture is now accorded growing appreciation as a central part of
"real life." In recent years scholars have devoted increasing attention to studying various aspects of popular culture, offering their assessments in books, articles, and college courses.

   Popular culture became a more democratic enterprise during the Vietnam
era. Television grew from a limited curiosity controlled by three networks to a
pervasive force providing viewers with hundreds of options. Its impact has
been an ongoing source of debate since its inception, and will continue to be,
with Americans spending so much time focused on their TV screens. The motion picture industry lost its dominant position as the Hollywood studio monopolies gave way to new systems of producing, marketing, and exhibiting
films. Even as the studios struggled with economic problems in the 1960s and
1970s, the movies both reflected and challenged the nation's social values.
Rock and roll built its popularity around appeals to youthful record buyers
and remained the preferred music of the Vietnam generation as they matured.
Though its blurring of racial distinctions and its sexual overtones, political
statements, and generational rumblings initially troubled many, in the long
run rock prevailed. The corporate establishment turned to rock to sell its
products, and churches that once condemned it as "the devil's music" sang
their new hymns to a rock and roll beat. Sports in this era reached true prominence. Overcoming repeated assaults on its integrity in the wake of gambling,
academic dishonesty, drug scandals, and more, sport became a national obsession. Athletes are among the world's most recognizable individuals, and

elite athletes are among its best compensated. At their best sports remain games enjoyed by children and adults of all ages.

In addition to undergoing their own fundamental changes, these cultural forms all contributed to other social transformations. Among the most dramatic changes for women was the encouragement and opportunity to participate in athletic competition. Sports also served as a critical battleground as African Americans fought for equal rights and respect in the United States. Black musical traditions clearly contributed to breaking down racial barriers as racially mixed audiences enjoyed a common sound. Rock and roll was the music that usually accompanied generational anxiety and rebellion, both personal and public, individual and collective. The sexual revolution was most publicly displayed on film, while images of the Vietnam War burned into the nation's collective consciousness through television.

Nearly all popular culture moved toward youth. Audiences for films and music in particular became younger over time. To reach their consumers, cultural industries emphasized subjects and styles they hoped would appeal to that age group. While this targeting of successive waves of teenagers could energize the larger society, this trend also worked to the detriment of less desirable demographic groups.

Each segment of popular culture had earlier seen the others as a threat to be avoided or defeated. All saw their survival as best achieved through individual effort. By the end of the era they had become intimately connected. Hollywood, initially threatened by television's potential to draw away its audience, discovered that it could strengthen its studios by providing filmed programming for the networks. Sports also feared early television's potential for undermining attendance and revenue, but improved broadcast technology and high broadcast fees ultimately brought professional leagues and college sport powers enormous sums of money. Rock and roll scared all the other segments of popular culture. Its connection, both real and imagined, with juvenile crime, violence, and lewdness kept it from being embraced at first. The movies' played a role in this negative association through *Blackboard Jungle*, then defended rock and roll in a lengthy series of films designed to attract its young supporters. By the late 1960s rock sound tracks and movies were mutually supportive. Television and rock were never quite as comfortable with each other, but in the early 1970s late-night concert programs finally presented rock musicians on their own terms. Sport's often staid traditions and time-warp organ music kept rock and roll at a safe distance for a time. Recent trends toward loud, rhythmic music, suggestive clothing, and stage performances at sporting events make those earlier times seem almost incomprehensible.

In these times, Americans found themselves at the crossroads. The Vietnam War challenged America's consensus in foreign affairs. Civil rights activists demanded a reassessment of cherished political ideals. Women shook assumptions about domestic life, and the effects rippled throughout society. Environmentalists confronted corporate power and notions of materialism. At the same time the pillars of America's popular culture experienced similar dramatic shifts, being themselves fundamentally transformed and helping to transform people and institutions that they encountered. If they looked carefully, people could see it. The revolution was televised.

NOTES

1. Daniel Curran, *Guide to American Cinema, 1965–1995* (Westport, CT: Greenwood, 1998), 327.

2. Andrew Fogelson, quoted in William Bates, "Hollywood in the Era of the 'Super-Grosser,'" *New York Times*, December 24, 1978, sec. 2, 11.

3. David A. Cook, *Lost Illusions: American Cinema in the Shadow of Watergate and Vietnam, 1970–1979*, vol. 9 of *History of the American Cinema*, ed. Charles Harpole (New York: Scribner, 2000), 237.

4. Mary Ann Watson, *Defining Visions: Television and the American Experience since 1945* (Fort Worth, TX: Harcourt Brace, 1998), 179.

5. Erik Barnouw, *Tube of Plenty: The Evolution of American Television*, 2nd rev. ed. (New York: Oxford University Press, 1990), 483.

6. Jackson Browne, "Lives in the Balance," *Lives in the Balance* (Asylum Records 60457, 1986).

7. Aniko Bodroghkozy, *Groove Tube: Sixties Television and the Youth Rebellion* (Durham, NC: Duke University Press, 2001), 25, 249.

8. Kate Meyers, "Cosby's Last 'Show,'" *Entertainment Weekly*, May 3, 1996, 90.

9. Eric Gelman, "Rocking Video," *Newsweek*, April 18, 1983, 97.

10. Stephen Thomas Erlewine, "U2," at www.allmusic.com/cg/amg.dll (accessed May 29, 2004).

11. Reebee Garofalo, *Rockin' Out: Popular Music in the USA*, 2nd ed. (Upper Saddle River, NJ: Prentice Hall, 2002), 367.

12. Harry Edwards, *The Revolt of the Black Athlete* (New York: Free Press, 1969), xxvii.

13. Richard O. Davies, *America's Obsession: Sports and Society since 1945* (Fort Worth, TX: Harcourt Brace, 1994), 210.

14. David W. Zang, *Sports Wars: Athletes in the Age of Aquarius* (Fayetteville: University of Arkansas Press, 2001), 158.

Bibliographical Essay

Scholarly and popular writing on American popular culture has flourished in recent years. Among the best overviews of the cultural history of motion pictures during the Vietnam War era are Robert Sklar, *Movie-Made America: A Cultural History of American Movies*, rev. ed. (New York: Vintage, 1994); Ronald Davis, *Celluloid Mirrors: Hollywood and American Society since 1945* (Fort Worth, TX: Harcourt Brace, 1997); Leonard Quart and Albert Auster, *American Film and Society since 1945*, 2nd ed. (New York: Praeger, 1991); and Charles Champlin, *The Movies Grow Up, 1940–1980* (Chicago: Swallow/ Athens: Ohio University Press, 1981). Excellent surveys of television history include Erik Barnouw, *Tube of Plenty: The Evolution of American Television*, 2nd rev. ed. (New York: Oxford University Press, 1990); Mary Ann Watson, *Defining Visions: Television and the American Experience since 1945* (Fort Worth, TX: Harcourt Brace, 1998); Albert Abramson, *The History of Television, 1942 to 2000* (Jefferson, NC: McFarland, 2003); and Harry Castleman and Walter J. Podrazik, *Watching TV: Four Decades of American Television* (New York: McGraw-Hill, 1982). For sports history, consult Randy Roberts, *Winning Is the Only Thing: Sports in America since 1945* (Baltimore: Johns Hopkins University Press, 1989); Richard O. Davies, *America's Obsession: Sports and Society since 1945* (Fort Worth, TX: Harcourt Brace, 1994); Kathryn Jay, *More Than Just a Game: Sports in American Life since 1945* (New York: Columbia University Press, 2004); and for a broader context, Benjamin G. Rader,

American Sports: From the Age of Folk Games to the Age of Televised Sports, 4th ed. (Upper Saddle River, NJ: Prentice Hall, 1999).

Good introductions to rock and roll are Paul Friedlander, *Rock and Roll: A Social History* (Boulder, CO: Westview, 1996); James Miller, *Flowers in the Dustbin: The Rise of Rock and Roll, 1947–1977* (New York: Fireside, 1999); David Szatmary, *Rockin' in Time: A Social History of Rock and Roll*, 5th ed. (Upper Saddle River, NJ: Pearson Prentice Hall, 2004); and Reebee Garofalo, *Rockin' Out: Popular Music in the USA*, 2nd ed. (Upper Saddle River, NJ: Prentice Hall, 2002).

Among studies of the 1950s, William Boddy, *Fifties Television: The Industry and Its Critics* (Urbana: University of Illinois Press, 1990) provides an overview for television. Other works focus on themes. Frank Sturcken's *Live Television: The Golden Age of 1946–1958 in New York* (Jefferson, NC: McFarland, 1990) is self-explanatory, while Karal Ann Marling, *As Seen on TV: The Visual Culture of Everyday Life in the 1950s* (Cambridge, MA: Harvard University Press, 1994) looks at the interplay of television and the wider culture. Christopher Anderson, *Hollywood TV: The Studio System in the Fifties* (Austin: University of Texas Press, 1994) details the positive links between movies and television, while Thomas Doherty, *Teenagers and Teenpics: The Juvenilization of American Movies in the 1950s* (Boston: Unwin Hyman, 1988) chronicles the increasing reliance of the movies on younger audiences. Charlie Gillett, *The Sound of the City: The Rise of Rock and Roll*, rev. ed. (New York: Pantheon, 1983) goes beyond the 1950s but is especially good on the early development of rock and roll. Another good musical survey of the decade is Arnold Shaw, *The Rockin' '50s: The Decade That Transformed the Pop Music Scene* (New York: Hawthorne Books, 1974). Two books by John A. Jackson, *Big Beat Heat: Alan Freed and the Early Years of Rock and Roll* (New York: Schirmer Books, 1991) and *American Bandstand: Dick Clark and the Making of a Rock 'N' Roll Empire* (New York: Oxford University Press, 1997), deal with influential disc jockeys. For baseball before the 1960s, see John P. Rossi, *The National Game: Baseball and American Culture* (Chicago: Ivan Dee, 2000). On race and integration in baseball, see Robert Peterson, *Only the Ball Was White: A History of the Legendary Black Players and All-Black Professional Teams* (New York: Oxford University Press, 1970); Jules Tygiel, *Baseball's Great Experiment: Jackie Robinson and His Legacy*, expanded ed. (New York: Oxford University Press, 1997); and Mark Ribowsky, *A Complete History of the Negro Leagues, 1884–1955* (New York: Birch Lane, 1995).

The Cold War's impact on the movie industry can be found in Nora Sayre, *Running Time: Films of the Cold War* (New York: Dial, 1982); Peter Biskind, *Seeing Is Believing: How Hollywood Taught Us to Stop Worrying and Love the Fifties* (New York: Henry Holt, 2000, 1983); and Larry Ceplair and Steven Englund, *The Inquisition in Hollywood: Politics in the Film Community, 1930–1960* (Garden City, NY: Anchor/Doubleday, 1980). Thomas Doherty, *Cool Medium: Television, McCarthyism, and American Culture* (New York: Columbia University Press, 2003); J. Fred MacDonald, *Television and the Red Menace: The Video Road to Vietnam* (New York: Praeger, 1985); and Paul Buhle and Dave Wagner, *Hide in Plain Sight: The Hollywood Blacklistees in Film and Television, 1950–2002* (Palgrave Macmillan, 2003) look at anticommunism in television.

For the 1960s, Paul Monaco, *The Sixties, 1960–1969*, vol. 8 of *History of the American Cinema*, edited by Charles Harpole (New York: Charles Scribner's Sons, 2001) and Ethan Mordden, *Medium Cool: The Movies of the 1960s* (New York: Alfred A. Knopf, 1990) survey the decade in different ways. In television, Mary Ann Watson, *The Expanding Vista: American Television in the Kennedy Years* (New York: Oxford University Press, 1990) looks at the beginning of the 1960s, and Aniko Bodroghkozy, *Groove Tube: Sixties Television and the Youth Rebellion* (Durham, NC: Duke University Press, 2001) examines the impact of the counterculture. Nick Bromell, *Tomorrow Never Knows: Rock and Psychedelics in the 1960s* (Chicago: University of Chicago Press, 2000) does the same thing for music, and Robert Stephen Spitz, *Barefoot in Babylon: The Creation of the Woodstock Music Festival, 1969* (New York: Viking, 1979) tells the story of the youth culture's biggest event. Motown's history receives good coverage in Nelson George, *Where Did Our Love Go? The Rise and Fall of the Motown Sound* (New York: St. Martin's, 1985); Suzanne E. Smith, *Dancing in the Street: Motown and the Cultural Politics of Detroit* (Cambridge, MA: Harvard University Press, 1999); and Gerald Posner, *Motown: Music, Money, Sex, and Power* (New York: Random House, 2002). The impact of the counterculture on athletics is apparent in contemporary accounts by Harry Edwards, *The Revolt of the Black Athlete* (New York: Free Press, 1969), and Jack Scott, *The Athletic Revolution* (New York: Free Press, 1971). A historical approach is David W. Zang's *Sports Wars: Athletes in the Age of Aquarius* (Fayetteville: University of Arkansas Press, 2001). Terry H. Anderson's *The Movement and the Sixties: Protest in America from Greensboro to Wounded Knee* (New York: Oxford University Press, 1995) puts much of the decade's cultural history in a broader context.

For key transitions in the movies during the 1970s, David A. Cook, *Lost Illusions: American Cinema in the Shadow of Watergate and Vietnam, 1970–1979,* vol. 9 of *History of the American Cinema,* edited by Charles Harpole (New York: Charles Scribner's Sons, 2000) provides an excellent overview. Peter Biskind, *Easy Riders, Raging Bulls: How the Sex-Drugs-and-Rock-'n'-Roll Generation Saved Hollywood* (New York: Simon and Schuster, 1998) and Michael Pye and Lynda Myles, *The Movie Brats: How the Film Generation Took Over Hollywood* (New York: Holt, Rinehart and Winston, 1979) reveal the complex generational tensions in American film. For television, see Sally Bedell, *Up the Tube: Prime-Time TV and the Silverman Years* (New York: Viking, 1981).

James L. Baughman, *The Republic of Mass Culture: Journalism, Filmmaking, and Broadcasting in America since 1941,* 2nd ed. (Baltimore: Johns Hopkins University Press, 1997) examines television's impact on other media industries. TV's relationships with other aspects of popular culture also appear in Jack Banks, *Monopoly Television: MTV's Quest to Control the Music* (Boulder, CO: Westview, 1996); Benjamin G. Rader, *In Its Own Image: How Television Has Transformed Sports* (New York: Free Press, 1984); Marc Weingarten, *Station to Station: The Secret History of Rock and Roll on Television* (New York: Pocket Books, 2000); and Kerry Segrave, *Movies at Home: How Hollywood Came to Television* (Jefferson, NC: McFarland, 1999).

On the relationship between history and film, Robert Brent Toplin, *History by Hollywood: The Use and Abuse of the American Past* (Urbana: University of Illinois Press, 1996) is a good introduction. Albert Auster and Leonard Quart, *How the War Was Remembered: Hollywood and Vietnam* (New York: Praeger, 1988) and Jeremy M. Devine, *Vietnam at 24 Frames a Second* (Austin: University of Texas Press, 1999) look specifically at movies and the Vietnam War. Jack C. Ellis and Virginia Wright Wexman, *A History of Film,* 5th ed. (Boston: Allyn & Bacon, 2001) provides an international survey.

For debates over cultural values, see John Belton, *American Cinema/American Culture* (New York: McGraw-Hill, 1994); Gregory D. Black, *The Catholic Crusade against the Movies, 1940–1975* (Cambridge: Cambridge University Press, 1998); Michael Medved, *Hollywood vs. America: Popular Culture and the War on Traditional Values* (New York: HarperCollins, 1992); Geoffrey Cowan, *See No Evil: The Backstage Battle over Sex and Violence on Television* (New York: Simon and Schuster, 1979); and John E. O'Connor, ed., *American History/American Television* (New York: Ungar, 1983). Rock and roll's opponents are explained in Linda Martin and Kerry Segrave, *Anti-Rock: The Opposition to Rock 'n' Roll* (Hamden, CT: Archon Books, 1988) and Kerry Segrave, *Payola in the Music Industry: A History, 1880–1991* (Jefferson, NC: McFarland, 1994). Economic issues receive emphasis in Douglas Gomery, *Shared Pleasures: A History of Movie Presentation in the United States* (Madison: University of Wisconsin Press, 1992); Justin Wyatt, *High Concept: Movies and Marketing in Hollywood* (Austin: University of Texas Press, 1994); and Janet Wasko, *Hollywood in the Information Age: Beyond the Silver Screen* (Austin: University of Texas Press, 1994), all of which deal with the movies. Steve Chapple and Reebee Garofalo, *Rock 'N' Roll is Here to Pay: The History and Politics of the Music Industry* (Chicago: Nelson-Hall, 1977) and Fred Goodman, *The Mansion on the Hill: Dylan, Young, Geffen, Springsteen and the Head-On Collision of Rock and Commerce* (New York: Times Books, 1997) look at the tensions between the creation and selling of music. Leslie Savan, *The Sponsored Life: Ads, TV, and American Culture* (Philadelphia: Temple University Press, 1994) critiques commercial advertising, and Charles P. Korr, *The End of Baseball as We Knew It: The Players Union, 1960–81* (Urbana: University of Illinois Press, 2002) gives an example of the changing economy of sports.

The pervasive issue of race appears in Allison Graham, *Hollywood, Television, and Race during the Civil Rights Struggle* (Baltimore: Johns Hopkins University, 2001); Donald Bogle, *Primetime Blues: African Americans on Network Television* (New York: Farrar, Straus and Giroux, 2001); Melvin Patrick Ely, *The Adventures of Amos 'n' Andy: A Social History of an American Phenomenon* (New York: Free Press, 1991); Michael T. Bertrand, *Race, Rock, and Elvis* (Urbana: University of Illinois Press, 2000); Thomas Cripps, *Making Movies Black: The Hollywood Message Movie from World War II to the Civil Rights Era* (New York: Oxford University Press, 1993); Frank Fitzpatrick, *And the Walls Came Tumbling Down: Kentucky, Texas Western, and the Game That Changed American Sports* (New York: Simon and Schuster, 1999); Amy Bass, *Not the Triumph but the Struggle: The 1968 Olympics and the Making of the Black Athlete* (Minneapolis: University of Minnesota Press, 2002); and Douglas Hartmann, *Race, Culture, and the Revolt of the Black Athlete: The 1968 Olympic Protests and Their Aftermath* (University of Chicago Press, 2003).

For individual sports, consult Benjamin G. Rader, *Baseball: A History of America's Game*, 2nd ed. (Urbana: University of Illinois Press, 2002); John Sayle Watterson, *College Football: History, Spectacle, Controversy* (Baltimore:

Johns Hopkins University Press, 2000); and Jeffrey T. Sammons, *Beyond the Ring: The Role of Boxing in American Society* (Urbana: University of Illinois Press, 1988). The Olympic Games are covered in Allen Guttmann, *The Olympics: A History of the Modern Games*, 2nd ed. (Urbana: University of Illinois Press, 2002) and Richard Espy, *The Politics of the Olympic Games* (Berkeley: University of California Press, 1979). Both discuss the politics associated with the modern Olympic movement. Women in sports are discussed in Allen Guttmann, *Women's Sports: A History* (New York: Columbia University Press, 1991) and Mariah Burton Nelson, *Are We Winning Yet? How Women Are Changing Sports and Sports Are Changing Women* (New York: Random House, 1991). For differing views of college athletics, see Jack Falla, *NCAA: The Voice of College Sports* (Mission, KS: National Collegiate Athletic Association, 1981); Murray Sperber, *College Sports, Inc.: The Athletic Department vs. the University* (New York: Henry Holt, 1990); and Arthur A. Fleisher III, Brian L. Goff, and Robert D. Tollison, *The National Collegiate Athletic Association: A Study in Cartel Behavior* (Chicago: University of Chicago Press, 1992). Elliott J. Gorn and Warren Goldstein, *A Brief History of American Sports* (New York: Hill & Wang, 1993) looks at sports' impact on culture.

Todd Gitlin, *Inside Prime Time* (New York: Pantheon, 1983) is one of the best early accounts of the network television business. More recent works include J. Fred MacDonald, *One Nation under Television: The Rise and Decline of Network TV* (Chicago: Nelson-Hall, 1990) and Josh Ozersky, *Archie Bunker's America: TV in an Era of Change, 1968–1978* (Carbondale: Southern Illinois University Press, 2003). Steven D. Stark, *Glued to the Set: The 60 Television Shows and Events That Made Us Who We Are Today* (New York: Free Press, 1997) analyzes the mutual impact of television and American society. See also Ella Taylor, *Prime-Time Families: Television Culture in Postwar America* (Berkeley: University of California Press, 1989), which discusses TV portrayals of family life, and Robert Sklar, *Prime-Time America: Life On and Behind the Television Screen* (New York: Oxford University Press, 1993). Public television receives coverage in William Hoynes, *Public Television for Sale: Media, the Market, and the Public Sphere* (Boulder, CO: Westview, 1994); James Day, *The Vanishing Vision: The Inside Story of Public Television* (Berkeley: University of California Press, 1995); and Laurence Jarvik, *PBS: Behind the Screen* (Rocklin, CA: Forum, 1997).

Informative scholarly interpretations of rock and roll appear in Glenn Altschuler, *All Shook Up: How Rock 'N' Roll Changed America* (New York: Oxford University Press, 2003); Jim Curtis, *Rock Eras: Interpretations of Music and Society, 1954–1984* (Bowling Green, OH: Bowling Green State University Popular Press, 1987); and Simon Frith, *Sound Effects: Youth, Leisure, and the Politics of Rock 'n' Roll* (New York: Pantheon, 1981). Greil Marcus, *Mystery Train: Images of America in Rock 'N' Roll Music,* 4th rev. ed. (New York: Plume, 1997) is one of the best works by a music critic.

Biographies of rock artists abound. Good examples include Philip Norman, *Shout! The Beatles in Their Generation* (New York: Simon and Schuster, 1981); Stephen Davis, *Hammer of the Gods: The Led Zeppelin Saga* (New York: Ballantine, 1986); Robert Shelton, *No Direction Home: The Life and Music of Bob Dylan* (New York: Ballantine, 1986); Peter Guralnick, *Last Train to Memphis: The Rise of Elvis Presley* (Boston: Little, Brown, 1994); Alice Echols, *Scars of Sweet Paradise: The Life and Times of Janis Joplin* (New York: Owl Books, 1999); and Dave Marsh, *Bruce Springsteen: Two Hearts; The Definitive Biography, 1972–2003* (New York: Routledge, 2003).

For specific styles of rock and roll, see Gerri Hirshey, *Nowhere to Run: The Story of Soul Music* (New York: Crown, 1984); Nicholas Schaffner, *The British Invasion: From the First Wave to the New Wave* (New York: McGraw-Hill, 1982); and Richie Unterberger, *Eight Miles High: Folk-Rock's Flight from Haight-Ashbury to Woodstock* (San Francisco: Backbeat Books, 2003). Interesting studies of some of rock and roll's classic record labels are found in Colin Escott with Martin Hawkins, *Good Rockin' Tonight: Sun Records and the Birth of Rock 'N' Roll* (New York: St. Martin's, 1991) and Peter Guralnick, *Sweet Soul Music: Rhythm and Blues and the Southern Dream of Freedom* (New York: Harper and Row, 1986), which focuses on Stax Records.

Reference works can both entertain and inform. Among the best for rock and roll music are Joel Whitburn, *Joel Whitburn's Top Pop Albums, 1955–2001* (Menomonee Falls, WI: Record Research, 2001) and *Joel Whitburn's Top Pop Singles, 1955–1999* (Menomonee Falls, WI: Record Research, 2000); Luke Campton and Dafydd Rees, *Rock and Roll: Year by Year* (London: DK, 2003); and Patricia Romanowski and Holly George-Warren, eds., *The New Rolling Stone Encyclopedia of Rock and Roll,* rev. ed. (New York: Fireside, 1995). For the movies, see Daniel Curran, *Guide to American Cinema, 1965–1995* (Westport, CT: Greenwood, 1998); Thomas Whissen, *Guide to American Cinema, 1930–1965* (Westport, CT: Greenwood, 1998); Ephraim Katz, ed., *The Film Encyclopedia,* 4th ed. (New York: HarperResource, 2001); and Steven Jay Schneider,

1001 Movies You Must See before You Die (Hauppauge, NY: Barrons, 2004). For television, consult Horace Newcomb, ed., *Museum of Broadcast Communications Encyclopedia of Television*, 3 vols. (Chicago: Fitzroy Dearborn, 1997); Tim Brooks and Earle Marsh, *The Complete Directory to Prime Time Network and Cable TV Shows, 1946–Present*, 8th ed. (New York: Ballantine, 2003); and Alex McNeil, *Total Television: The Comprehensive Guide to Programming from 1948 to the Present*, 4th ed. (New York: Penguin, 1996). Works on multiple sports include Arnold Markoe, ed., *The Scribner Encyclopedia of American Lives: Sports Figures*, 2 vols. (New York: Scribner, 2002) and Thomas W. Brucato, *Major League Champions, 1871–2001* (Lanham, MD: Rowman & Littlefield, 2002). For specific sports see Will McDonough, ed., *The NFL Century: The Complete Story of the National Football League, 1920–2000* (New York: Smithmark, 1999); Jan Hubbard, ed., *The Official NBA Basketball Encyclopedia*, 3rd ed. (New York: Doubleday, 2000); and John Thorn, *Total Baseball: The Official Encyclopedia of Major League Baseball*, 7th ed. (Kingston, NY: Total Sports, 2001).

Index

217

Friendly, Fred, 14, 101
Fripp, Robert, 170
Frith, Simon, 173
Fulbright, J. William, 101
Full Metal Jacket (1987), 183
Funicello, Annette, 86
The Funk Brothers, 121
Fury, 40

Garfunkel, Art, 170
Garofalo, Reebee, 129, 166–67, 173, 197
Garrett, Mike, 112
Gaye, Marvin, 121
"Gee," 30
Gelbart, Larry, 9, 151
Geldof, Bob, 194–95
The Gene Autry Show, 41
General Cinema Corporation, 86, 149
General Electric Company, 189
General Electric Theatre, 38
General Teleradio, 40
Genesis, 171
Gentle Soul, 130
Get Smart, 95
Gibson, Althea, 23, 62
Gibson, Bob, 110
Gibson Guitar Company, 32
Gidget (1959), 57
Gifford, Frank, 60, 161
The Gilded Palace of Sin, 168
Gillette, Charlie, 69
Gillette Cavalcade of Sports, 21
Gillette Razor Company, 22
Gimme Shelter (1970), 137
The Girl Can't Help It (1956), 56
"Give Peace a Chance," 166
Go, Johnny, Go! (1959), 56
"Go Away Little Girl," 122

Go Tell the Spartans (1978), 181
"God Save the Queen," 174
Godard, Jean-Luc, 52
The Godfather (1972), 137, 142, 147
The Godfather, Part II (1974), 147
Godzilla (1954), 140
Goffin, Gerry, 119, 170
The Goldbergs, 16
Goldstein, Richard, 167
Goldwater, Barry, 94
golf, 19, 24, 82, 111, 202; and race, 23, 62, 115
Gomer Pyle, U.S.M.C., 98
Good Times, 150
"Good Vibrations," 120
Goodyear Television Playhouse, 38
Gordy, Berry, Jr., 120–21, 167
Gosden, Freeman, 15
Gould, Jack, 72
The Graduate (1967), 87, 136–37, 140
Graham, Billy, 12
The Grateful Dead, 128, 165, 168
Grease (1978), 185
"Great Balls of Fire," 67
"The Great Pretender," 68
Green Acres, 98
Green Bay Packers, 109
The Green Berets (1968), 181
Greene, Felix, 102
Greene, Graham, 180
Greenfield, Jeff, 70
Greenwich, Ellie, 119
Gretzky, Wayne, 201
Griffin, Archie, 161
Guess Who's Coming to Dinner (1967), 88
Gulf and Western, 138
Gunsmoke, 41, 91, 154
Guthrie, Woody, 125

About the Author

Mitchell K. Hall received his PhD from the University of Kentucky and is a professor of history at Central Michigan University. He is the president of the Peace History Society and a former editor of the journal *Peace and Change*. His previous publications include *Because of Their Faith: CALCAV and Religious Opposition to the Vietnam War* (1990) and *The Vietnam War* (2000). He teaches, among other courses, the history of the rock and roll era.